TEACHER TRAINING AND EDUCATIONAL RESEARCH

TEACHER TRAINING AND EDUCATIONAL RESEARCH

Edited by
S.R. Sharma

ANMOL PUBLICATIONS PVT. LTD.
NEW DELHI - 110 002 (INDIA)

ANMOL PUBLICATIONS PVT. LTD.
H.O.: 4374/4B, Ansari Road, Darya Ganj,
New Delhi-110 002 (India)
Ph.: 23278000, 23261597
B.O.: No. 1015, Ist Main Road, BSK IIIrd Stage
IIIrd Phase, IIIrd Block,
Bangalore - 560 085 (India)
Visit us at: www.anmolpublications.com

Teacher Training and Educational Research

Reprint, 2008

PRINTED IN INDIA

Printed at Mehra Offset Press, Delhi.

Preface

For the improvement of any educational programme, the component of teacher training is the most important. Researches in the field of Teacher education have been made much head away in the most of the developed countries of the world. The developing countries are also trying to update their educational systems. They have identified teacher training areas for research and development.

This book examines the problems of educational research in the field of teacher training and is highly useful for researchers of the developing world.

The editor is grateful to all those sources which have been used in this book.

Editor

Contents

1

Introduction

RESEARCH AND THE TEACHER

"We must here consider what the teacher may expect from research, and what, contrariwise, research requires of the teacher. According to Buckingham, research.

> will not only powerfully and rapidly develop the technique of teaching, but will also react to vitalise and dignify the work of the individual teacher. It is my firm belief that the emancipation and professionalising of the teachers' calling rests far more upon the originality, insight and expertness which the teacher evinces than upon any considerations having to do with salary, tenure or legal status. Society cannot be compelled to respect anybody or anything. The surest way to win respect is to be respectable. If, as has often been observed, there is no such general belief in the expertness of those engaged in other occupations, it is worth considering whether the public is right about it—whether the teacher really has, to the extent that the professional or craft worker has, a special competency peculiar to his calling. In my judgment, nothing would so effectively obtain for the teaching body the professional expertness and the reputation for having it as the open-eyed, open-minded scientific spirit of inquiry.

When the teacher's technique is based on research, teaching will no longer be regarded as one of the black arts, but will assume the status not of a dismal science, but of a progressive and enlightened procedure. The more highly skilled and better informed teacher will find new interest in his work and a new confidence in his own abilities.

As the office of the teacher is thereby dignified, there will be a corresponding decline in the role of the amateur in Education. Education is at present one of those unfortunate subjects on which, like Economics at an Election time, everyone is an authority. Research, we trust, will alter this. As Sir John Adams has said: "Gone is the old easy approach to the educational platform. Day by day it is requiring more courage to get up in an educational meeting and talk at large."

There is constant criticism of the teacher's work, or rather of the products of his work—much of it no doubt justified. But what one is inclined to challenge is the underlying assumption that the defects, that are indicated or admitted can be removed merely by intensified effort on the part of the teacher or of the pupil. Such intensification of effort will lead only to increased strain on the teacher and increased resentment on the part of the pupil. Research will doubtless reveal that the failure to get the expected results is due to inefficient and uneconomical methods, and will lead us to seek a change of procedure rather than a mere intensification of effort. Research should accordingly, by putting more scientific weapons at the disposal of the teacher, economise effort and increase efficiency; it is in fact likely to lead to what Ballard has termed "leisurely methods":

> In nearly all schools the early number work is now individual, and in many schools it is spontaneously undertaken by the children. They receive no formal lessons, and sometimes indeed are allowed to neglect number for days and weeks together. The teachers no longer strain and strive to impart new numerical ideas. And yet the average number of items correct at a given age is the same to-day as it was fifteen years ago. The leisurely methods of to-

day are just as effective as the strenuous methods of the past.

The same conclusion was reached as the result of tests on children's testimony; teachers formerly spent much time in the old object-lesson days on teaching young pupils the qualities of objects, but the use of terms denoting qualities appears spontaneously at a certain stage of development without the teacher's help. By the introduction of modern incentives pupils' handwriting can be kept up to the required standard without copybook exercises. The substitution of silent reading or reading for meaning for oral class reading (which did not succeed in teaching the pupil to comprehend printed matter, but merely to "keep the place"), will economise the teacher's time and temper. In many cases pupils are bored by being taught what they already know merely because it is in the syllabus of work. A diagnostic test applied before commencing a subject might reveal that much that would otherwise have been taught may be assumed; thus an investigation into "The Child's Knowledge of Number on Entering School" suggested that children who on entering school had quite an extensive acquaintance with cardinal numbers had little or no appreciation of the ordinal arrangement, whereas the school teaching concentrates on the cardinal arrangement and ordinarily neglects the ordinal. By research on such lines time will be saved for real education, and the pupils' energies released for such.

The teacher will also find that the testing devices employed in research in education will come to be utilised as teaching methods. The Montessori exercises are to a large extent psychology laboratory tests employed for training instead of testing. Thorndike's read-and-answer situation tests have, as already mentioned, been responsible for the great impetus recently given to silent reading or reading with intelligence. Freeman's analytic scale of handwriting can obviously be applied in the teaching of the subject. Certain mental tests, for example Stern's picture tests, could be made the topics for English composition. The tests which research has evolved will thus extend the teacher's repertoire and enrich the pupils education, because they are usually nearer to life than the formal content of the older instruction.

The teacher might also expect from the adoption of the checking devices necessitated by research work, some relief from the drudgery of correction. The new types of recording cards, filing arrangements, etc., will doubtless also become features of the new education as research methods come to be practised in the schools.

The teacher may also derive benefit from the objective testing of his own efforts; inspection instead of remaining a matter of arbitrary personal opinion may in time avail itself of the research procedure and adopt a scientific attitude.

If research will benefit the teacher it will also make certain demands on him. The claim to omniscience on the part of the teaching profession will have to be abandoned. There was a time when teachers took all knowledge for their province and proposed to teach all things to all men; now we leave omniscience to the daily press. Research will teach us humility, that there is much still to be discovered about the educative process. Teaching will through the adoption of the research attitude become even more than ever the great adventure.

Research will put an end to the a priori criticism and rejection of new methods. If one is not prepared to accept the results of a method based on scientific research, one must repeat the investigation and disclose the flaw in the procedure.

The teacher will be expected to display a willingness to further research by affording facilities for its prosecution in schools, and the greater the number of teachers who are initiated into the methods of research the more readily will this be achieved. The teacher will also have the opportunity of completing the task of the research worker by putting the latter's results to the test of practice. It will be his privilege to turn the thought of the researcher into a practical reality. Winch has issued a warning that "If teachers stand aside and do not help, they will only have themselves to thank if methods are imposed upon them from the results of experiments which they do not understand, which are not really applicable to their work and in which they have no share."

In his Research for Teachers Buckingham has said :

> I distinguish the modern teacher from the teacher of twenty-five or thirty years ago as a person who desires to have at his command the results of that surprising period of research which entered upon its present stage about the year 1910.

With the extension of the facilities for training in, and the wider dissemination of the results of, research, may it soon be possible to apply the term "modern," in Buckingham's sense, to all teachers !

2

Research

Research and knowledge

The initial and in-service education and training of teachers is one of those human activities to the proper performance of which many different disciplines and forms of understanding are centrally relevant. So many that it is impossible for any one programme of training to reflect more than a small proportion of what is known, or for any one person to claim mastery of more than a tiny part of the available knowledge.

There is obviously a sense in which a great variety of disciplines are in some way 'relevant' to almost any kind of human activity. Levi Strauss' analysis of the 'culinary triangle' and the status associations that follow from it are no doubt significant for the maketing policies of food manufacturers, although it can be suspected that most of them get along adequately without knowing about such matters. Teachers can often manage perfectly well without much knowledge of educational theory—indeed, if such knowledge has not been properly assimilated into a set of skills it is likely to hinder rather than help their performances (Polanyi, 1958, p. 49).

But in a complex, multi-faceted activity such as teacher education, with its many separate elements and the demands it makes for a wide range of specialized expertise, disciplines such as psychology, sociology, philosophy, anthropoloy, political science, history, linguistics—to name only some of the most obvious contenders—provide many ideas and information centrally relevant to the planning of programmes and procedures.

The imperfections of our existing programmes, to which professional, public and political criticism of recent years is adequate testimony, is due at least in part to the fact that we have so far failed to devote adequate resources of time and money and human ability to bringing available knowledge to bear upon what we are trying to do when we claim to educate and train teachers.

As a field of study and enquiry, teacher education has not attracted many first class scholars, fewer still original talents. As an area of applied research, it has failed to achieve priority in the research budgets of most European countries. It has not hitherto been recognized as a major stimulant of innovation and change in schools. It has not been regarded as a major factor to be reckoned with in evaluating the interaction of education and society along the vitally important dimension of equality.

For all these reasons, teacher education remains an activity characterized by implicit rather than explicit theory, and one to which research-based knowledge makes only a rather limited contribution. From time to time particular disciplines and interest break through the established framework of courses and practical work, jostling existing elements out of their accepted positions and requiring a reorientation of programmes in the direction of including more psychology, or more philosophy, or more about special education, or methods of teaching reading, or the needs of immigrants, or the new mathematics, to name but a few of the claimants for attention in recent decades.

New courses and subjects get written in, others atrophy or are excluded, mainly as a passive response to outside pressures rather than a considered judgment about what constitutes an optimum combination of courses and experience. Sometimes changes in course structure and approach are brought about by alterations in the institutional framework within which teacher education is carried on, as in the case of the integration of teacher education into the universities in some of the German Lander and the virtual disappearance of the single-purpose training college in England and Wales.

It is the argument of the chapters that follow that the improvement of teacher education is dependent upon its becoming a more self-conscious process, upon more attention being given to ways in which research-based knowledge from the different disciplines centrally relevant to the preparation and in-service education of teachers can be brought to bear on the design of programmes, the teaching of courses and the organization of practical work.

No claim is made that the following pages contain a comprehensive review of the research and ideas relevant to this task. Instead, it is hoped that what is said will encourage a more catholic and broadly-based approach to a definition of what research is relevant for the improvement of teacher education, and that governments and research agencies will be willing to give more attention to finding ways in which to use the fruits of existing and ongoing work from a variety of disciplinary fields to enhance the efforts of their colleges and universities.

Research and practice

To be aware of the existence (if not always of the content) of tens of thousands of research reports, monographs, theses, journal articles and books that contain facts, figures and findings relevant to the improvement of teacher education, at the same time as being in contact with the realities of what goes on in colleges and universities, and the dissatisfactions that students and teachers express about the quality and content of what they receive by way of professional preparation, gives the impression of an almost unbridgeable gap between possibility and practice. What makes the gap so wide? Would the outcomes of teacher education be improved by making more research-based information available to tutors and lecturers and professors who work in this field?

A familiar answer to this question is that absence of agreement on the objectives of education in general and of teacher education in particular, reflecting the fact that in pluralistic societies there are legitimate differences of view about what constitutes the desirable outcomes of the educational process, must invitably limit the extent to which the 'scientific' application of research will produce improvements in practice.

This is, of course, a real and important objection to any simple-minded view that improvement would follow a clearing of the channels of communication between researcher and practitioner. Yet if this limitation affects the scope of what can be done, it still leaves open the question of what areas of action and decision in teacher education are susceptible to improvement on the basis of better research-based information, and what kinds of research are needed to facilitate such improvement. It also leaves us with the task of identifying what other general characteristics of the research-practice nexus are relevant to an understanding of contemporary trends in teacher education.

There are two general points that need to be made in this context.

First, the mere existence of large quantities of information in the form of research reports and abstracts does nothing whatsoever to ensure that the findings concerned, however relevant they may be, are incorporated into practice. Among the many things needed are carefully thought out 'linkage structures' which order the results of research in relation to problems of practice in such a way as to facilitate a mutual cross-fertilization—a problem that has attracted its own quota of research effort (Havelock, 1973; Hoyle, 1972).

Second, there has to be recognition that our ability to improve the quality of teacher education (based upon research, systematic curriculum development, improvements in teaching technique, and improved organization within teacher education institutions) and our willingness to bear to costs of such improvement constitute separate questions. On the basis of what is now known about how individuals learn, on the strength of the techniques available to train individuals in instructional methods and in the monitoring and evaluating of their own performance and that of their pupils and students, it is perfectly clear that, given the necessary resources, marked improvements in learning are perfectly possible. Fundamentally, it is not a question of lack of knowledge, or the absence of technique, or a conflict of values.

The major conflicts focus around the willingness of individuals, institutions and societies to deploy their limited resources on the improvement of teaching rather than on the achievement of other objectives. Thus the political issues are not so much disagreements about the aims and objectives of education, but about the allocation of scarce resources between different kinds of activity, of which education is only one. Any university or college librarian knows that if every education student was really hard-working and dedicated to the improvement of his own practice and learning outcomes in the classrooms in which he worked, then it would be impossible to provide the necessary seats, books, and support services in the quantity and quality demanded. Few institutions and societies are in a position to meet the demands that performance fully in accordance with the rhetoric and aspirations of particular occupational groups would place upon them. Improvements in the quality of teacher education and of teaching in our schools are not dependent upon the outcomes of large quantities of newly-commissioned research, or waiting upon some conceptual or methodological breakthrough in understanding or technique. Teacher education and teaching could both be improved on the basis of knowledge currently available, given the political will to devote resources to this rather than other educational and non-educational activities. We already known far more than we can use. This is not an argument for some kind of moratorium on new work—there in much that still needs to be done—but it is to suggest that the limitations on improvement are structural, political and economic rather than conceptual.

Linkage structures

The links between educational research and the education of teachers are of three main kinds—research relevant to teacher education, research by those engaged in teacher education, and, finally, research on teacher education (Taylor, 1969b). It is with the first and the third of these that this book is concerned, although inevitably a good deal of the relevant work has in fact been undertaken by men and women employed in universities and colleges where teachers are educated and trained. It is not intended to repeat or update surveys of research on teacher education published during the past ten years, although this work will be drawn upon where it remains pertinent to the analysis and description of present-day problems.

The links between research on teacher education and what actually happens in the lecture and seminar rooms of colleges and departments, in classrooms where students practice and where, as qualified teachers, they carry on their trade are much less clear than they need be. This is due primarily to a single factor. There is an absence of intellectual and organizational structures, and linkage personnel, by means of which the results of large quantities of empirical research in psychology, sociology, anthropology, politics and other social sciences, and a great deal of the more speculative research and writing characteristics of the humanities and philosophy, can be presented in a form that lends new meanings to the experiences that the student and teacher obtain during the course of their practice.

The existence of research reports, unpublished theses and dissertations, journal articles, books and monographs, and other printed sources which report the outcomes of studies in these and other fields, by itself does nothing to ensure the improvement of teaching. This is not to suggest that those who produce these publications should assume such responsibility. If they did so, it is unlikely that they would ever complete their work and bring it to the point of publication.

Nor is it enough to devise means whereby the results of all this work can be categorized, classified and organized. Again, these are necessary processes, considerably facilitated by the existence of systems such as ERIC (Educational Resources Information Centre) in the United States, the UNESCO International Bureau of Education Thesaurus, the London Educational Thesaurus and, most recently, the EUDISED (European Documentation and Information System for Education) system. The introduction of computer retrieval systems adds a further dimension to the technological aids to the classification and organization of knowledge. But all this says nothing about the use to which all this knowledge will be put.

Nor, again, is it enough to produce surveys and reviews of the available literature, helpfully organized under such headings as 'Input Variables, Process Variables and Output Variables' (Taylor, 1969b; Lomax, 1972). Such surveys provide useful maps of the territory, but do nothing to guarantee that the teacher will want to start on any particular journey, or will be able to find his way to a desired destination. Thesauri, catalogues, surveys, abstracts and all the apparatus by means of which researchers and librarians seek to introduce order into the melee of research activity that goes on in most developed countries are necessary but not sufficient conditions for the improvement of teaching.

It is wholly unrealistic to expect that teachers carrying a full timetable and attempting to cope with the many demands on their energies and abilities that contemporary school conditions require can seek out, understand and assimilate into their practice the findings of even a minute proportion of the studies that have now been conducted which are in one way or another relevant to the improvement of teaching. Equally, those engaged in the education of teachers, whether as lecturers and tutors in colleges and departments of education, as inspectors and advisers, and as administrators at local, regional or national level, are usually not in a position to draw upon more than a tiny fraction of the work that has potential significance for planning and executing their tasks.

It is evident from the recent, as well as the earlier, history of teacher education that the impact of research is greatest when it is organized and mediated through a more or less dogmatic pedagogical system such as that of Herbart (Taylor, 1975b) or the performance-based/competency-based teacher education movement in the United States, or systems individualized instruction such as the 'Keller Plan' (Keller and Sherman, 1974).

In fact, only a fairly limited range of ideas and findings have fed such systems, which are monist rather than pluralist in respect of their intellectual origins (P/CBTE and the 'Keller Plan' are discussed in Chapter 8, and evidence provided as to their common indebtedness to behaviouristic ideas). What in a later chapter will be identified as the current and emergent model of teacher education in European countries is more pluralist in its origins, and thus more difficult to describe as a coherent system.

The trends that this model embodies are not the outcome of a systematic planning strategy, nor an attempt to apply a unified pedagogical system, but rather the untidy consequence of a variety of social, organizational and intellectual currents which produce common responses in countries at similar levels of development.

This pluralism is itself of value. To impose a single model of teacher education, however well based it may be upon research, is to rigidify courses and programmes, to make more difficult the adaptations necessary in the face of future social, political and economic circumstances. For example, in the United States, the tendency on the part of some state education authorities to make PBTE a mandatory basis for teacher education programmes (the claims that these are 'research-based' are extravagant if not entirely specious) is arguably just such a rigid and unimaginative attempt to find a simple answer to a problem that permits of no single solution. The alleged "inefficiency' and undoubted administrative untidiness of existing arrangements in many countries, whereby the explicit linkages between the activities of research workers and the practice of classroom teachers are tenuous or non-existent, does offer the researcher protection against political influence that would undobtedly be brought to bear should it be thought that the outcomes of research had direct, and possibly controversial, applications, It also projects the teacher from mistaken attempts to impose 'systems' which bear little relation to the unique realities of the individual classroom (Taylor, 1975a).

What the preceeding discussion suggests is that we should aim for the kinds of improvement that preserve the merits of pluralism, protect the freedoms of both researchers and teachers, and yet at the same time enhance the possibility of well-verified findings being brought to bear on the solution of educational problems.

If these desiderata are to be met, three sets of conditions must be fulfilled—adequate resources, appropriate structures and a sympathetic political, social and educational climate. Resources include both money and manpower. The rapid expansion of educational research in the Sixties— most marked in the United States, in Sweden and in the UK, but also visible in a number of other European countries—has since slowed down, and the overall volume of work may even have declined. Apart from the effects of economic recession and inflation, such a decline may have something to do with the false expectations current in some circles about the outcomes of research, expectations which researchers themselves did little to dispel. Disappointment with the results of research may have influenced the ability of education authorities to obtain money for new work and the funding of linkages of a kind that are essential if the results of research are to have an impact upon practice.

There is a now an active concern in several countries with the provisions of such 'linkage-structures', reflecting a more sophisticated appreciation of the way in which research influences — or fails to influence -- practice. Sweden was one of the first countries in Europe to concern itself with this problem. The National Board of Education has as part of its remit:

'....to ensure the continual renewal, development and improvement of the content and methods of education in keeping with the progress of research and developments in public and private administration, in commerce and industry and in the labour market and also in other sectors of society, due regard also being had to conditions abroad — to ensure that knowledge of educational development work is rapidly disseminated among public authorities and others responsible for activities' and among those who are otherwise affected by activities' (National Board of Education, 1974a).

Sweden has an impressive record of centrally-funded team research projects on a variety of aspects of teacher education. [Work undertaken up to 1974 has been summarized by Marklund and Gran (1974). A list of projects currect in 1976 includes work on the evaluation of teachers' roles, studies of pre-school and special school training, practical experience in schools, in-service training, training in school management and several specialist subject fields (National Board of Education, 1976).] About 12 per cent of all expenditure on educational research in recent years has been devoted to studies in this field. It is worth noting that responsibility for educational research was originally placed with the teacher education department of the National Board, since it was likely that most of the projects would be located within one or more of the Schools of Education located in Stockholm and other major university centres.

The aim of teacher education being "scientifically based" is promoted also by the concentration of educational research to the schools of education. The latter have been allotted research appointments. The institutions of educational theory are to attend both to research and to the teaching of educational theory to prospective teachers. This combination is designed to guarantee an immediate transfer of research findings to teacher education . . .' (Marklund and Gran, 1974, p. 40).

Even so, it is admitted that in Sweden as elsewhere 'educational research and teacher training do not necessarily or immediately stand to benefit from their mutual proximity' and that research is 'in constant danger of being isolated from matters of practical application' (ibid., p. 68).

As far as the employment of research findings in the improvement of teacher education is concerned, the teacher of teachers is the key individual. It is surprising, therefore, to find that very little research has been conducted in European countries on teacher educators as a specialist group within the education profession. This is in contrast to the United States, where in recent years a lot of work has been done on the selection, training and development of staff in college and university faculties of education, and the implications for such staff of current trends in teacher education policy and practices. (Summarized by Howey, 1975, on the basis of a National Institute of Education sponsored project. For earlier UK studies of the background of college of education and university staff see Taylor, 1969c.)

Trends in research support

There seems little doubt that there are some lean years ahead for educational research in general and research on teacher education in particular. For example, in common with a number of other European countries, the volume of real resources available in support of all kinds of research in France has declined in recent years as a consequence of inflation and government economy measures. It has been calculated that in 1975 state funding of research was only 70 per cent of that in

1967, and that the proportion of GNP devoted to scientific development had fallen during this period from 2.2 per cent to 1.5 per cent.

A keenness on the part of governments to stress research of an applied and 'useful' nature has hit universities particularly hard. As in the UK, only a very limited number of postgraduate research grants are available for those wishing to pursue third-cycle studies (doctorate de troisieme cycle). Such grants are available only for two years, whilst third-cycle studies often take three, and their value in 1975 was equivalent to only FF 6,000. At the end of 1975 the French government announced an increase in research spending amounting to approximately 8.5 per cent over the 1974 total, and the creation of nearly a thousand new research posts. This, of course, relates to all kinds of scientific research, not simply that concerned with education, and even with these increases, the amount of money set aside for university development is still regarded as inadequate in the face of increased costs. The 1976 budget provided for an increase of 15 per cent over the previous year, but new building projects and equipment grants were down by 7 and 9 per cent, respectively (Morgan, 1975b).

Similar cut-backs have taken place in Germany, where of 116 government sponsored research programmes administered by the German Research Association, only 54 in 1976 received as much as 70 per cent of the funds for which they applied and 18 received between 75 and 80 per cent. The average allocation was only 50 per cent of the sums requested. As in other countries, the real resources available for research are failing to keep pace with increases in salaries and the costs of equipment (Dungworth, 1976d).

In Norway the number of new jobs becoming available in research has been halved since the peak year of 1972. The Deputy Director of the Science and Humanities Research Council predicted early in 1976 that over the next fifteen years annual recruitment will be below the level of any year since the early 1960s. There seemed no prospect of an early return to the days of an annual increase of 5 to 10 per cent in the number of jobs when as half of the sociologists qualifying in universities went into some kind of research appointment (Duckenfield, 1976a).

All this means that opportunities for pursuing graduate studies in education at a high level are not increasing at anything like the rate consistent with the raising of qualification standards for entry to teaching, the increased size of the teaching force, and the growing scope and complexity of the knowledge base of teaching. In many countries there has been a tendency to hold constant or to reduce the number of postgraduate students. In the UK a fee structure was announced in 1976 which included a differential between undergraduate and postgraduate studies and, by substantially raising the general level of tuition fees, made it more difficult for employing authorities to release teachers for periods of full-time advanced study and research.

Despite cut-backs taking place in the funds available for research, doubts being expressed about the continuing viability of some of the large-scale linkage efforts created during the Sixties (e.g. the Schools Council in England and Wales) and something of a disenchantment among officials as to the usefulness of research outcomes, the availability of computerized methods of retrieval of research information, coupled with improved and cheaper reprographics and the manufacture of sophisticated but cheap personal calculators that much reduce routine statistical work associated with empirical studies, are tending to simplify some aspects of the researcher's task and of the dissemination process. It remains to be seen if improvements of this kind will counter the effects of reduced resources of money and manpower.

A model for the impact of research

Relevant to the questions raised in the preceding section are likely changes in six factors that help to determine the extent to which research influences practice. These can be labelled as volume, the adequacy of dissemination and diffusion mechanisms, motivation, the part that research plays as a credential, its professional, context and its problem situation.

If a large quantity of work has been done on a particular topic there is a better chance, other things being equal, for such work to be influential on practice. For example, during the past twenty-five years there has been much research on equality of opportunity in education, reflecting the priority that this objective has attained in the educational and social policies of most western governments. The impact of research is greater if its findings tend in the same direction. Conflicts of evidence, or a lack of clear-cut conclusions which inhibit popularization through the media, both diminish the attention and impact of work on a particular theme. This can be called the volume factor.

Research cannot be influential unless someone knows about it. There is now a substantial body of work on the ways in which research knowledge is diffused and disseminated among the community of researchers, practitioners and the public Diffusion studies, information science, mass media research and the sociology of knowledge have all contributed to our understanding of how ideas and information spread and become incorporated into the perspectives of students and practitioners. As a consequence, researchers have become much more sensitive to the importance of presenting their findings in a manner appropriate to audiences wider than their fellow investigators. A host of articles in the general and the educational press, in specialist journals, digests, abstracts, and in the form of papers circulated for conferences and meetings testifies to the importance now attached to dissemination. Funding agencies have shown themselves willing to pay for 'dissemination years' on the termination of a development project in order to ensure that those closest to the work have a chance to assist the processes by means of which it is made known and institutionalized. This we can call the dissemination factors.

Where an activity is highly valued, individuals are

motivated to undertake it. Research has traditionally enjoyed high status, particularly in the natural sciences It is expected of university teachers that they will continue to engage in research as part of their contract of service. If the possession of a higher degree or other advanced qualification is an important factor in determining prosfessional mobility and status, then research-based knowledge will have high rating and individuals will be highly motivated to acquire it. It has been a criticism of single-purpose teacher-preparing institutions that research has never had the attention it deserves. There have even been suggestions from time to time that an interest and involvement in research, as against teaching and pastoral work with students, reduced rather than enhanced opportunities for employment and promotion. Seen from another angle, governments have been reluctant to give formal research functions to newly-developed non-university post-secondary colleges and polytechnics, partly because of the costs that might be involved, and partly, again, because of the assumed dangers of an inappropriate stress upon advanced-level work. We can call all this the motivation factor.

Another consideration is the position within the education system of those familiar with research-based knowledge. We have to ask what part familiarity with such knowledge plays in helping people to acquire positions of power and influence. Do educational researchers end up as high-level administrators and policy makers, or is their influence exerted mainly in the academic sphere, in teaching future generations of senior staff? On the basis of such impressionistic evidence as exists, those in senior administrative positions seldom seem to have much time in which to attain a first-hand knowledge of research. The spread of their responsibilities beyond their original discipline or subject field makes it difficult to remain up-to-date with recent developments. But, in so far as such people have previously shared a commitment to research, they may be more sympathetic to its support than compatriots who have come through a different career line. Some educational systems provide better opportunities than others for research-oriented individuals to achieve positions of power and prestige. This we can call the credentialling factor.

Dissemination of research findings can be effective only if those for whom they are intended are capable of understanding the significance of what they hear and read. Thus the level of education and training of the practitioners expected to make use of research-based knowledge is an important consideration in determining its influence on practice.

There have recently been moves to incorporate courses about educational research in the basic and in-service training of teachers, not so much to produce more research workers as to encourage understanding of and sympathy for the researchers' efforts, and to help teachers to read and evaluate reports that reach them through the dissemination and diffusion processes. It is probably reasonable to suggest that the longer and deeper the education and training of the teacher, the better will he be able to appreciate the relevance of research for his own work. This is the professional context of research.

Finally, the impact of research is affected by the extent to which practitioners regard their work situation as problematic. Where changes are going on which create problems to which the teacher seeks answers, there is more scope for the results of research to affect practice than when change is slower and the situation stable. But it could also be argued that, if too much is uncertain, if there is too much that is problematic, then the sheer perceptual load that the teacher must carry, and the energies to be put into the task of surviving in a difficult environment, tend to reduce rather than enhance the prospects of research influencing practice. This can be called the problem situation.

Applying these criteria to research in teacher education, we can see a mixture of pluses and minuses as far as current trends are concerned. Resource problems, and a reduction in the size of the teacher education enterprise, make it unlikely that a large volume of new work will begin in this field during the next few years. But there is a substantial amount of completed and ongoing work yet to be assimilated to programmes and courses, and research will continue to be funded in the learning process, child development, the sociology of the school, and curriculum development in a wide range of subjects and interdisciplinary fields. All this has a potential impact on the way in which teachers are educated and trained. Furthermore, it is likely that new developments, such as systematic teacher preparation for secondary teachers in those countries where this is at present poorly developed, a systematic induction process for beginning teachers, and the introduction of a variety of new technologies and methods of training, will all encourage more detailed evaluation and appraisal of results, and help to ensure that teacher education research maintains and perhaps even increases its share of the total resources devoted to research in education.

The people who must need to know about relevant to teacher education are those concerned with the design and execution of programmes and courses. The numbers of such persons within the total ranks of educational, practitioners are small, and they do not always constitute an identifiable and self-conscious community of a kind that responds quickly to ideas and new findings. Indeed, the claims of classroom teachers to play a larger part in the education and training of their future colleagues may run counter to the development of such specialized expertise, and thus limit rather than enhance opportunities for effective dissemination. Yet it can be argued that there are specialized skills involved in preparing future teachers of a kind that not all classroom practitioners possess, and which repay development and a measure of specialized training.

The creation of new bodies of teacher educators, such as the European Association formed in Liege in 1976, is a hopeful sign, as is the appearance of several new journals directed to the educator of teachers and containing reports and summaries of ongoing and completed research. A proposal by a subcommittee of the United Kingdom Advisory Committee on the Supply and Training of Teachers that some of the teacher education staff who might be made redundant by reductions in the numbers of students in training should be given advisory and developmental duties in schools, and provide liaison between teacher-preparing institutions and classroom practitioners, constitutes an encouraging step. But in so far as it imposes a full 'teaching day' on those concerned, it is unlikely to provide opportunities for direct involvement in research, or for keeping up with new ideas and findings.

A reduction in the number of specialized posts for teacher educators, both as a result of contraction and because of new arrangements which give a more significant role to other practitioners, might serve to reduce the rewards associated with being familiar with research-based knowledge. On the other hand, for those who are still employed in this work, greater competition for senior posts may increase the likelihood of their undertaking advanced studies and personal research leading to a higher degree.

With a falling off in the number of single-purpose teacher-preparing institutions, and a trend towards their incorporation in larger units such as universities, polytechnics, district colleges and the like, there may be a possibility that more of those who at some time in their careers have been directly engaged in teacher education and training will obtain posts that embody broader responsibilities within the educational system, from which they may be in a position favourably to influence the development of work in their former field, Governments and providing authorities vary in the extent to which they seek and obtain academic advice, and in the qualifications and research knowledge of their own officials and inspectors. It is difficult to predict the effect on the research practice relationship of current changes in the organization and administration of education, but here again, if competition for the prime positions becomes stricter, then performance in publicly-assessable activities such as research and publication may become more rather than less important in legitimizing selection processes and decisions.

As far as what has been called in this section the 'professional context' is concerned, there are real hopes that a longer and deeper training for teachers, such as has been agreed or is under consideration in many countries, will give new opportunities for research findings to be made known to future and practising teachers, and for their implications and significance for individual classroom practice to be identified and worked out with those concerned. Those responsible for initial programmes of preparation have always been under pressure from the fact that there would be few subsequent opportunities in the teacher's career for any form of full-time systematic study.

3

Studies of Supply and Demand

The relationship between the scale and the character of a social activity such as teacher education is necessarily com plex. Both obvious and less obvious factors play their part. An obvious consideration is the size of the individual institutions in which teachers are trained. Less obvious is whether a particular scale of activity represents a point on the upswing or the downswing of demand for teachers and or for places in teacher education. Whatever the complexities, it is plain that no discussion of research trends in teacher education can ignore the demand for and supply of teachers, which provide the rationale for the existence of courses and institutions.

What are the factors that influence demand and supply?

The system's eommitment to educate

In advanced countries we take it for granted that between the ages of five or six and fifteen or sixteen children and young people will be legally required to attend school or college. Increasingly, we have added periods of more or less voluntary attendance at both the beginning and at the end of these periods of full-time schooling; 'pre-school' provision may be either full-or part-time from the age of two or three; 'post-secondary' provision includes voluntary staying on at school until eighteen or later, and full- or part-time attendance at college, university or vocational training establishment. The overall demand for teachers is determined by the numbers required to service such commitments.

The sheer scale of existing commitments inevitably sets narrow limits to what can be spent on innovation, especially if the overall sums available are static or increasing only very slowly. A UK Minister of State for Education and Science (Fowler, 1976) has drawn attention to calculations which show that whilst at the end of the Sixties the UK Government spent a total of £958m on pupils in compulsory education, some £730m went on those already in school or about to enter, £115m was spent as a result of population changes, £68m because of shifts in population, £4m on educational priority' (a policy of positive discrimination in favour of the least-advantaged areas and schools), £36m on the improvement of pupil/teacher ratios and £5m on other changes, 'This meant that only 4.7 per cent of expenditure went on areas that could be influenced by policy,' And' the Minister added, such limitations did not leave much room for great differences between the political parties on educational programmes.

The birth rate

Given the existence of a commitment to provide universal schooling, the birth rate is the most important single datum with which a society has to reckon in planning teacher supply, It is this that will determine the number of new pupils demanding admission in two to six years' time. Thus the accuracy of birth rate statistics becomes a matter of prime importance, Because of the time needed to design and erect buildings, to hire staff and to design courses, important also is the ability successfully to predict the trend of family formation, the numbers of births that will occur in future years. The weaknesses of such predictions have been a significant factor in determing both the shape and the development of teacher education in the past (Taylor, 1969c). In the UK, for example, it was the rush in the early Sixties to create new institutions, to recruit staff and to find economical ways of increasing supply in response to a trady perception of need that created some of the deficiencies in quality identified as a justification for more recent attempts at reform (Hencke, 1975). It follows that research which results in better predictions and helps demographers to provide more accurate calculations and to identify and to take account of hitherto unrecognized factors, is of some importance to the improvement of teacher education, (For examples of studies of this kind see, e. g., Population Trends, London, HMSO, quarterly.)

Birth rates have been declining in most European countries since the middle and late Sixties, and there are few signs of any substantial upturn, Figures published by the Department of Education and Science for England and Wales show that the number of children being born in the last part of the Seventies falls Well below net replacement rate (1.8 as compared with the necessary 2.1) and make clear that if these trends continue the school system might need to contract by as much as 25 per cent the end of the Eighties. The demographers have chosen a NRR of 2.2 as their 'central projection', which would not involve such a drastic contraction, but it remains to be seen if the combined effects of easier contraception and abortion, a high ratio of female employment, changing patterns of family formation and the effects of economic recession will chunge in time to make this 'central projection' realistic (DES, 1976).

A Netherlands Commission on teacher employment, reporting at the end of 1976, predicted that the number of children between the ages of four and six will decline by 25 per cent by 1982, and that junior school rolls will fall by 15 per cent over the same period. On the assumption that there will be no further fall in class size, and that numbers in teacher education are not reduced, only 45 per cent of newly qualified teachers would be able to obtain posts (George, 1976). Proposals made by the Danish government early in 1977 indicated that the demand for secondary school teachers would by 1990 be only 45 per cent of that in 1976 (Duckenfield, 1977b).

Retention rates and voluntary take-up

Within a given age-cohort, a greater or leaser proportion of children will elect to remain at school beyond the statutory leaving age, will achieve the necessary qualifications for various forms of post-secondary study and will seek entry to courses in post-secondary institutions. Factors of this kind can have a considerable effect on both the demand for and the supply of teachers, since it is from just these post-secondary groups that teachers are themselves recruited. They can also be very influential in the planning of post-secondary education as a whole. In the words of a recent UK report to the Council of Europe :

> 'These (downward revisions in student numbers) are not due to demographic factors since the size of the eighteen-year-old age group will increase between now and 1980. Fundamentally, the need for successive revisions to student projections of the numbers who will qualify to enter higher education. The main causes of these have been the slowing down in the previous growth in the proportion of the age group staying on at school, and in the 'proportion obtaining the required qualifications for admission to higher education.' (Council of Europe, 1975a, p. 1)

In this context it becomes important to know what considerations are affecting the decisions of young people to leave or to remain at school beyond the statutory leaving age, and to choose one kind of post-secondary education rather than another. Research again comes into play as an important element in decision-making. The UK Department of Education and Science financed a study at the University of Lancaster which confirmed the associations that have appeared in earlier work between pupils' intentions at sixteen and social class, attitudes to academic study and perceptions of average earnings for different career lines. It is interesting to note that the social background factor exerts its effect in comprehensive just as much as in selective secondary schools.

The authors pay particular attention to the way pupils' perceptions of their career and earnings opportunities are associated with decisions to leave or to stay on, and conclude that a causal relationship, although not estabiished, is at least a plausible hypothesis. Such a hypothesis could form a valuable basis for further and more detailed studies, particularly if it appears that the incidence of taxation and other aspects of economic reward exercises a disincentive effect on decisions about post-secondary education (Williams and Gordon, 1976, pp. 6—7).

A survey of current French statistics published in Le Monde de l'Education (reported in THES, August 15, 1975) is suggestive with respect to some of the sex factors that characterize decisions about staying on and the entry to post-secondary education, with a strong tendency for girls to choose 'A' series (literature, language and arts) Baccalaureat subjects, as against, 'C' series (mathematics and physical sciences). The proportion of girls in these two groups is 72 per cent and 30 per cent, respectively. But in terms of secondary retention rates, the girls have the edge. Some 72 per cent of the daughters of skilled manual workers, for example, stay on at school beyond the age of compulsory attendance, against 59 per cent of the sons, which is attributed to the greater ease with which boys can obtain apprenticeships and the difficulties girls have in finding suitable employment.

In some of the German Lander, the pressure to stay on into the upper forms of the secondary school is such that thought has had to be given to the introduction of a numerus clausus for upper secondary studies. The higher rates of retention are seen as the result of 'a growing awareness of the importance of educational qualifications for...,future career prospects and.... the increasing difficulty . . . in getting university places and apprenticeships' (Dungworth, 1975c).

Voluntary take-up of places is also important at the opposite end of the age range, and figures from several countries show a rapid increase in the number of parents who want pre-school education of some kind or another for their children. In the Federal Republic of Germany the number of places in kindergartens rose from 1,160,700 to 1,590,000 between 1970 and 1975, with a more than two-fold increase in staff, some half of whom have State qualifications (Dungworth, 1976b). The French pre-school development plan foresees the creation of some 11,000 new classes, and more than two-and-a-half million children between the ages of two and six were enrolled in pre-school in 1975.

As in the United Kingdom, the French Teachers' Unions are very interested in the way in which these nursery schools are staffed, and the idea of employing a larger proportion of non-trained teachers is strongly resisted (Farr, 1975).

In most of the Education Ministries of European countries, and in many universities, studies are being undertaken with a view to improving predictions of demand at the pre-school and post-secondary stages, which are of importance in relation to the level of teacher supply. Demand is not, of course, a passive variable. Government policies ore among the factors that influence the rate of take -up and the kinds of study opportunities that are sought, either directly through the operation of a positive private demand approach to planning, or indirectly through economic and income policies. There are rather few countries at present in which governments are actively encouraging an overall increase in staying on, although efforts are being made in some places (e.g. Sweden, the UK) to increase the numbers of those who go on to upper secondary and post-secondary studies in selected subject fields such as mathematics and the physical sciences.

The Netherlands is one of the few European countries to use a ballot system for selecting students to occupy the limited number of places available in the 'closed faculties,' which for the 1977 academic year included medicine, dentistry, veternary surgery, biology, pharmacy, agriculture, French, English, History, Art History and Dutch, eleven in all (George, 1977a, 1977c). Applicants are allocated to one of six groups in accordance with their leaving certificate grade. Those highest in the rank order are given a weighted chance in the draw. This system is justified—and apparently supported by many of the students themselves—on the ground that a substantial number of qualified professionals in Holland are already without work (4 per cent as compared with 5 per cent of the total working population) (Lissauer, 1976b). A report prepared for the Netherlands Ministry of Education and Central Bureau of Statistics predicted that, on 1977 trends, as many as 40 per cent of students who had followed academic courses might be unemployed by 1990 (George, 1977b).

Research undertaken by J. Wagemakers in the Higher Education Research Unit of the Catholic University of Nijmegen (Wagemakers, 1974) showed that, of a group of unsuccessful applicants, 53 per cent had wished to study medicine, 20 per cent history, 11 per cent dentistry, 7 per cent English and 7 per cent Dutch. Some 85 per cent of the group intended to make fresh application in the following year, and only 12 per cent felt that they would not be re-applying.

It appeared from this study that secondary school in Holland are not yet geared to providing the kind of advice useful to a candidate who wishes to seek a place in a closed faculty. Most of those who have been unsuccessful in the lottery had discussed their choice of subject principally with friends and with parents, and less than half had talked about the matter with their counsellors at school.

It is clear that under certain circumstances, a shortage of jobs for qualified manpower can increase rather than diminish the number of applicants for university places. This seems to have been the case in Italy, where in 1975 there was a 6.2 per cent increase in first-year student enrolments, indicating student intention of using the universities as a 'parking area' in which to wait for an upturn in the economic situation. The problem is made worse by the existence of certain educational and other fringe benefits for students, which are not available to school-leavers who are without work (Hallenstein, 1975).

New selection procedures had to be introduced into West German universities following a ruling during 1975 that the system whereby the marks of individual candidates are scaled up or down according to the average of the Lander from which they come in relation to the Federal average (the Bonus/Malus) was unconstitutional. It is interesting to note that this decision led to a demand for a nationally-based Abitur in order to ensure equality of treatment. This tendency towards greater centralization in the name of equality is clean contrary to the arguments put forward by educationists and by the more radical student groups in favour of school-based assessment procedures and forms of assessment other than traditional three-hour examination scripts. Some of those who advocate these radical changes admit that what they propose is not well suited to the needs of a competitive technological society.

Their proposals reflect a larger vision in which competitive pressures are much less in evidence than to-day. In an effort to meet the wishes both of those who demand greater fairness in selection procedures and those who would like to see the schools relieved of competitive examination pressures, a former Minister of Justice in the Federal Government, Gerhard Jahn, produced during 1975 a proposal to allocate places on the basis of a lottery among three groups of candidates, Group One, comprising the top decile of qualified applicants, would ballot for 50 per cent of the available places.

The next 50 per cent of applicants would comprise Group Two, but only 30 per cent of the places would be open to them. The remaining 40 per cent of candidates would compete for only one-fifth of the available places. Admission criteria to be taken into account would include such additional factors as military service, a record of voluntary social work undertaken between school and university military training, vocational experience and further education, as well as the average Abitur mark.

This ingenious scheme, which has similarities to that which operates in the Netherlands, proved unacceptable, although it commanded support in some Lander, and at the end of 1975 agreement was reached that from 1977/78 admission to numerus clausus subjects would be on the basis of two-thirds of the available places allocated in proportion to each Lander's number of young people aged 18-21 in that year, and one-third according to that Lander's proportion of the total number of applications for a particular subject (Dungworth, 1976a).

Some falling off in applications in 1976 made it possible to lift entry restrictions in a number of subjects, and only archi-techtune, biochemistry, biology, dietetics, domestic science, food chemistry and technology, medicine, pharmacy, psycho-logy, social science, veterinary surgery and dentistry were then still subject to a national numerus clausus (report in THES, October 8, 1976). New allocation procedures, including the introduction of quotas for each Land, form part of the Hochschulrahmengesetz or General-Framework Law for Insti-tutions of Higher Education, to come into effect from 1977-78 (Kloss, 1977b).

There are already a large number of unemployed profes-sionals in Italy, and it was reported at the end of 1975 that a state competition for middle school teachers produced half a million applications for a total of 23,000 places.

Teacher supply in Italy has been complicated by the large numbers of teachers with temporary status in both primary and secondary schools. During 1974-75 the Italian govern-ment conferred permanent status upon one hundred and sixty thousand such teachers, but it appears that delay in the assign-ment of teachers to permanent posts in school at the begining of the year led to a continuing pattern of 'displacement', where-by after a few days or weeks in front of a class, a teacher with only temporary status has to make way for someone with tenure.

> 'Although usually aware that a degree is now virtually worthless, school-leavers crowd into the universities—now open to anyone who has completed their secondary educa-tion—simply to fill in time and postpone for another three

or four years the disheartening search for a job' (Clough, 1975).

Stock and flow

The implications for teacher supply of the current and predicted birth rate, the tendency to stay on beyond the statutory leaving age and the demand for better pre-school provision must be reckoned in terms of the current teacher stock and the flow of teachers through the educational system. Some factors that need to be laken into consideration in such calculation are well illustrated by a paragraph from a Report of the Department of Education and Science (London, 1974):

'The survey suggests that if . . . turnover is expressed as a percentage of the stock of full-time teachers at the beginning of the year, 10.8 per cent of the September stock moved during the year to other teaching posts in the maintained primary and secondary schools (5.3 per cent on promotion, 5.5 per cent on transfer; 5.0 per cent to another school in the same Local Education Authority (area), 5.8 per cent to a different LEA); a further 7.8 per cent gave up teaching in the maintained primary and secondary schools, if only for the time being; and 2.1 per cent retired or died . . .'

If planning is to be useful, there needs to be detailed information available about the characteristics of the teacher stock, in terms of age, experience, qualifications, specialist skills, career profiles, turnover and wastage, and type of current employment. (For a discussion of some of the difficulties of calculating wastage see Perry, 1971, p. 153.) The quality of this data, and the extent to which it can be used in making decisions about teacher demand and supply that bear upon the way in which teachers are trained, varies considerably from one country to another. In some European countries, for example, teachers are civil servants and, within certain limits, can be sent-to those schools where it appears they are most needed.

In others, teachers are state employees, and although they can be 'posted' by administrative decision within the state, their qualifications also entitle them to consideration for employment as qualified teachers in other states, between which there is a good deal of movement. In the UK, a large proportion of the teaching vacancies are nationally advertised, and teachers are free to move from post to post as they see fit. In most countries efforts are being made to refine and to the range of available information about teacher stock and flow, with a view to improving predictions about the demand for and supply of teachers.

To the extent to which such refinement and disaggregation of data serves to identify sectoral weaknesses and deficiencies, so it complicates the planning process and tends under certain circumstances to encourage tighter control from the centre. As a reaction to this, it has been argued that the strictly manpower approach to teacher supply that has been the policy of most countries, whereby only enough teachers are trained as seem likely to be able to be employed, should be abandoned and students preparing for teaching should have neither explicit nor implicit guarantees of employment at the end of their course. More competition would mean a better choice for employing authorities and schools, and a margin of safety in supply would avoid the necessity to exercise tight control over the numbers admitted to particular courses and programmes within the teacher-preparing institutions. But such ideas are seldom favourably received by the teachers' unions, and they are also inappropriate in those countries where student salaries are paid to intending teachers.

Staff/student ratios

However important it may be to obtain data that permit detailed disaggregation of teacher demand and supply, national policies are usually based on cruder assessments of staff—student rati os, either overall or for types of school. There is no research-based optimal SSR to which policy-makers work. In the context of greater variety in teaching methods and patterns of school organization—team teaching, open plan, group work, computer-assisted instruction—such a figure would have very little meaning, as the abandonment of such aims as 'no class larger than thirty' has indicated (although some teachers' unions persist in their claim that the continuing reduction of class sizes should be the objective, believing no doubt that SSR conceals as much as it reveals).

Policy is nearly always made in relation to a ratio that is historically rather than theoretically determined. Research comes into the picture in guiding decisions about where additional resources are best placed in relation to the improvement of teaching and learning. The opportunity cost of further improvements in SSR as against additional in-service training, more books and equipment, better financed resource centres and libraries and more ancillary help, constitutes the important calculation. Unfortunately there are severe limitations on the extent to which research-based knowledge can inform such calculations. A certain amount of research has been done on the size of teaching units in relation to a limited number of educational outcomes.

Interesting evidence concerning the relationship of class size and educational outcomes was produced by a study undertaken by Cherkaoui and Lindsey involving 3,500 children in 125 schools in France. The authors argue that middle class children worked better in small classes, and working class children in large ones. They relate this finding to patterns of control that characterize working class family life and large classes, where contact between adults and children is 'irregular and intermittent'. In the smaller classes, working class children who used what Bernstein (1971) calls a 'restricted code', more often qualified for teacher criticism, were more readily identifiable, and found themselves in more direct conflict with the values of their teacher and schools (Cherkaoui and Lindsey, reported Gretton, 1976).

Whenever there is teacher unemployment, pressure arises for a reduction in class size. In the Netherlands, opposition moves in Parliament early in 1976 to reduce the size of primary and infant classes were defeated on the ground that such a measure would be impossibly expensive. The Minister stated that this would still be the case even if unemployed teachers were given 80 per cent of their normal salary. Some £10 m of initial expenditure would be required to cut primary classes by only one pupil. At the time of the debate, there were 2,500 nursery and 1,800 primary school teachers without posts in the Netherlands. By 1979 the number of unemployed primary teachers is likely to reach 2,000, and the number of unemployed primary teachers is likely to reach 2,000, and the number of unemployed infant teachers 3,000. By the beginning of the Eighties, as a consequence of declining birth rates, the number of posts available will have gone down by some 5,000 (Lissauer, 1976a).

It needs to be noted, however, that not all European countries are experiencing a surplus of teachers. In Sweden, following sharp cut-backs in training, supply and demand had by 1976 been balanced (Duckenfield, 1975c, 1976c). In Spain the Minister of Education stated in October 1975 that there was a shortage of teachers at all levels. It was hoped to increase the number of teachers of 6- to 14-year-old children (the basic school) from 100,000 to some 111,000. Teachers of 14- to 17-year-olds would rise from a mere 2,000 to no fewer than 10,000.

It is also worth noting that, as was made clear at a UNESCO/IBE Conference held at Geneva in September 1975, the 'teacher surplus' is very much a characteristic of the developed world. Within the next ten years, African societies would require some 51 per cent more primary teachers, 55 per cent more would be needed in Asia and 49 per cent more in Latin America. To achieve universal primary education within the same period, the increases in numbers would have to be even more striking—200 per cent in Africa, 147 per cent in Asia and 92 per cent in Latin America.

There is little likelihood of developing countries being able to afford to train teachers and equip schools on a scale necessary to overcome these shortages, or of the countries now moving into teacher surplus being able to offer large numbers of teachers within their programmes of overseas aid. Indeed, they are already having difficulty in funding home-based employment for all the teachers they train.

Some estimate of the difficulties that shortages of money cause were clear in Germany during 1974-75, when the target figures for teacher recruitment approved by some of the Lander were considerably below the numbers of qualified entrants expected to present themselves for employment. ('The Bavarian Ministers of Education and Finance . . . decided to drastically limit new teaching posts. Unless the Bavorian parliament alters its target figures, 15 per cent of all teachers qualified in Bavaria to teach in Volksschulen (primary and upper-primary schools), 33 per cent of fully trained Gymnasium (grammar school) and 80 per cent of qualified Realschule (intermediate school) teachers will not get jobs.

This means that of the 960 graduates expecting to be employed in Realschulen in 1975 and 1976 only 200 will be able to teach. The situation is similar in other Lander. Hamburg, Baden-Wurttemberg and Rheinland-Palatinate have all cut recruitment' (Kloss, 1975). As a result, the Ministers of Education in several Lander have sought to reduce the number of students preparing for teaching. It was reported in March 1977 that the University of Munich, the largest in the Federal Republic, would be required to cut a total of 11,000 teacher training students to no more than 3,923, a reduction similar in magnitude to that proposed in the United Kingdom, where by the early Eighties a 'minimum system' is to be established with some 40,000 students in training against the 115,000 of 1972-73 (Kloss, 1977c).

As in most countries, the numbers of students training for teaching in Germany showed a very sharp increase during the late Sixties, and in the light of economic difficulties and a falling birth rate this will undoubtedly cause embarrassment to employing authorities in the years ahead. The number of university students in the Federal Republic increased by a third between 1966 and 1972, but during this period there was a 93 per cent increase in the number of students training to be teachers in the Padagogische Hochschulen and a 93 per cent increase in university undergraduates with this intention. Current projections suggest that by 1985 there will be a teacher surplus of between 140,000 and 210,000.

As we have seen with respect to the UK and other European countries, these forecasts do not command universal agreement, and the teachers' unions, in particular, have been active in demanding improved teacher/pupil ratios (those in Germany are claimed to be among the worst in Europe, with 42 per cent of classes in North Rhein-Westphalian Gymnasien containing more than 35 pupils, and Bavarian Volksschule and Realschule classes having an average of 34 pupils). Furthermore, shortages still persist in some subjects and some areas.

Just as in England there is a chronic shortage of teachers in science and mathematics, heavy crafts and some other subjects, so it is claimed that in Lower Saxony three hundred grammar school classes during the school year 1974-75 received no instruction in sport and mathematics, four hundred had none in German, three thousand none in religion, a thousand none in history and seven hundred none in physics. The Lander Ministry has admitted that staff shortages have resulted in a shortfall of 30 per cent of the lessons given in Gymnasien in country towns and 24 per cent of those in Gymnasien and Realschulen (Dungworth, 1975b).

The major factor in causing such shortages of teachers as still exist is economic rather than due to any lack of qualified applicants. In some of the German Lander drastic measures had to be taken during 1975 to reduce the number of lessons timetabled in grammar schools for subjects as fundamental as mathematics, English, German and physics, and in Hesse the Ministry of Education suggested at one point that parents might make voluntary contributions to enable schools to employ additional teachers.

Another aspect of the same problem is the shortage of alternative employment for graduates in the humanities and social sciences, who thus tend to seek qualifications as teachers. In Denmark, for example, enrolments, in the fifteen years prior to 1975 in the 'open' faculties (i.e. those other than medicine, agriculture and law) have increased by 540 per cent as against 250 per cent in the faculties that maintain a numerus clausus. It is unlikely in present economic conditions that a 34.5 per cent increase in social workers, 31.8 per cent in mathematics graduates, 29.8 per cent in science graduates and 28.9 per cent increase in psychologists can be absorbed by either the public or the private sector.

Shortfalls of between 10 and 25 per cent are also reported from German Lander. The main reason appears to be a shortage of money to employ staff with the necessary qualifications.

In this context, any proposal to reform teacher education in a way that upgrades the entrant to primary school work is likely to be resisted on economic grounds.

Given the complexity of the variables involved, it would be optimistic to believe that research will ever yield information of a kind that enables us fix upon that precise mix of learning resources needed to secure a particular result with a given group of pupils. What research can do is better to inform those judgmental and political processes that policy makers, administrators, heads and teachers will employ in reaching decisions about how much to spend on wha and where.

The supply of suitably qualified candidates

It is no accident that ten years ago much of the discussion of teacher numbers was about the supply of suitably qualified candidates for training, whilst now it is focused on the number of teachers who can be employed. In many European countries at the present time there is a more than ample supply of secon-

grasp the ongoing negotiated and processual character of reality definition as social action is accomplished and social actors generate adequate performances during the negotiation of their own status and role behaviours in situated settings' (p. 20).

Linguistics provide a third source of ideas from which students of classroom interaction have obtained insights and upon which they have sought to base their theories and techniques. The work of, for example. Bellack (1966), Gumperz and Hymes (1972) and Sinclair and Coulthard (1975) has encouraged studies of a kind that endeavour to satisfy Hymes' claim that :

> 'Studying language in the classroom is not really "applied" linguistics; it is really basic research. Progress in understanding language in the classroom is progress in linguistic theory' (Hymes, quoted Sinclair and Coulthard (1975), p. 6).

The corpus of research referred to here depart from the mainstream of linguistic study by using larger speech units than those which preoccupied may linguists in the past. The focus is upon discourse, what Hymes again has called an 'ethnography of speaking.' By anylysing classroom discourse, it is claimed that greater understanding can be achieved of the ways in which particular forms of language use exercise a controlling function upon behaviour. The following example from a study of the English used by teachers with pupils of varying ages draws attention to how single statements can both embody factual information intended to add to the pupil's knowledge, and also serve as means of social control.

> ' "Shouting out" or "calling out" was proscribed even when the answer was correct. Pupils who made an answering move when a preliminary bid followed by a teacher nomination was required, were told "Can't hear you if you shout out". The importance of this example is that it shows how linguistic and social behaviour are linked, although as usual we are only aware of this when something goes wrong. In this instance, learning to speak and learn-

ing to behave are inseparable, and the discourse acts that we have identified as cue, directive, and evaluation show this particular teacher instructs his eight-year-olds in making appropriate contributions to the discourse in a way that is apparently unnecessary in the recordings we have of the same teacher working with ten-and eleven-year-olds. A study of teacher—pupil interaction in the reception classes of junior schools and nursery schools could shed more light on what the rules for discourse are, as well as how they are established and learned. How does the five-year-old who speaks when he wants to become the ten-year-old who waits to be nominated ?' (Sinclair and Coulthard, 1975, p. 113).

The preceding examples show that studies of teacher and student relationships that rest upon symbolic interactionist, ethnomethodologist or linguistic bases do not, by virtue of their concern with the micro-sociology of the classroom, lose their links with broader theories of the role of teachers in society. Such theories often demonstrate a strongly Marxist orientation (Sharp and Green, 1975; Bowles and Gintis, 1976; Taylor, 1977). Liberal-bourgeois theories of society no longer provide the framework of assumptions within which most discussions of the teacher's role take place, and much research effort is devoted to exposing the inconsistencies between liberal educational ideology and the practice of teachers and the schools.

It was suggested at the beginning of this chapter that we can usefully distinguish between statements about changes in teachers' roles that are :

(a) prescriptive;
(b) based upon teacher and non-teacher analyses; or
(c) reflect expert observation of teacher behaviour and role performance.

Prescriptive statements vary in the extent to which they take into account, for example, the results of studies on pupil learning, statements about teacher role conceptions derived from questionnaire and interview data, and classroom behaviour reported upon in terms of the great variety of instruments and category systems that have been devised or adapted for this purpose.

Much observational data are of very recent origin. However useful such data may be in facilitating more accurate descriptions of what goes on in classrooms, there are difficulties in using them on the basis of judgments about changes in teachers' roles. For this purpose a strategy is required which takes into account a broader mix of factors. An example of such a study was the 'Education in Teacher Training Project —PIL' undertaken in the University of Malmo School of Education under the direction of Bertil Gran (1974) where that part of the research concerned with occupational analyses and training needs took into account.

'. . . comprehensive information . . . on the ways in which different groups formulate the demands they make on the teacher and also on the difficulties encountered by the teacher in the situation concerned. The methods used are :

(a) analysis of official texts (over time);
(b) interview surveys;
(c) critical incident studies;
(d) questionnaires;
(e) systematic observations.'

There have been few studies to adopt such a wide-ranging approach as this. Most of the work that has been done (partly, no doubt, because it is on a relatively small scale and undertaken by ingividuals rather than teams) involves single-track rather than multiple-track methodology, The need for the latter is, however, increasingly being recognized (see Harre and Secord, 1972).

It is not intended in this report to undertake a full-scale analysis of the teacher's role, but merely to indicate aspects of how it may be changing that have implications for the way in which teacher are educated and trained. Having examined some of the trend that characterize empirical studies of teaching, we now turn to a number of features of teaching roles emphasized in contemporary literature on education—the teacher as an upholder of cognitive standards, the teacher as a moral and political agent, the teacher as innovator, the cooperative role of the teacher alongside representatives of other social agencies, and the teacher as an agent of social and educational equality. The choice of these headings emerges from inspection of the available literature from a number of European countries, supporred by studies that have been made of teacher role performance and role conceptions (Rodhe et al., 1974; Fritzell; Marklund and Gran. 1974).

5

Roles for the Future Teacher

The teacher and cognitive standards

From the time when pen was first put to paper on the subject of the teacher's role, it has been acknowledged that his prime task is to pass on to the new generation the societal heritage of knowledge and skills. It is this instrumental aspect of the teacher's work that is frequently given pride of place by parents in their assessment of the teaching role, and, by implication, by the wider society in respect of any deficiencies in literacy, numeracy or other skills that are displayed by teachers and students. King and his associates (1974), in a valuable study of post-compulsory education in Western Europe, showed that in England, France, Italy, Sweden and Germany a substantial proportion of both teachers and students attached importance to the part the school played in preparing for employment, despite considerable differences between countries in respect of other goals. Pupils, too, display strongly instrumental attitudes, as is illustrated by research carried out by the Danish Research Council for the Humanities by Mogens Jansen et al. Although small-scale, involving some 250 pupils in 25 classes in four schools—a village school, a school of a minor provincial town, a Copenhagen city centre school and a suburban school in a newly developed area—the study brought out very clearly the same instrumentalism as has shown itself in similar research elsewhere. As the investigators put the matter, 'To an outsider the school may be primarily a social institution. To the pupils it certainly is a teaching institution. Their opinions of subjects and teachers were closely related to learning' (EUDISED, 1975). One finding that related to claims for greater involvement by parents in the work of the school was that 'most pupils think that parents should definitely not have more influence on school—especially as long as they are not better informed'. Respondents also felt that parents lacked 'skill and time' for school activities.

The pupils who responded to the questionnaire saw teachers in general very much as teachers of a subject. 'They demanded, from a good teacher, an ability to engage the attention of pupils and to control the classes for which they were responsible. The older pupils were satisfied with the arrangements whereby they received specialist teaching, but would have liked to have had the same teachers for a longer period. Substitute teachers were valued for the variety that they brought, but were also seen as a source of indiscipline and interruption of learning.'

As human knowledge has increased in scope and complexity, so the selective process by means of which curricula are constructed have become more difficult and problematic. Research on learning and child development has introduced important discriminations into the analysis of learning and teaching behaviour, which make what was once straightforward at least as far as the preparation of the future teacher was concerned, a matter for dispute among and between theorists, researchers and practitioners. That which in many accounts goes under the title of 'cognitive learning' is broken down into a number of important sub-sets, the differences between which assume significance in relation to particular curricular offerings. The teacher is seen as responsible for identifying and developing relevant intellectual skills and cognitive strategies, as well as communicating the necessary information out of which bodies of knowledge are constructed. Psychologists conduct detailed investigations into the nature of the skills and strategies, and on the teaching procedures best calculated to develop them. Curriculum developers attempt to take this new knowledge into account in producing proposals for the teaching of subjects, and in the design of teaching kits, packages and audiovisual aids. The main trends in this aspect of teachers' work have been

(a) a great increase in the volume of knowledge that has a legitimate claim for inclusion in the school curriculum;

(b) much greater refinement of our understanding about what this knowedge comprises, and how children may best acquire it;

(c) much sharper disagreement than heretofore about the priority that is to be attached to one form of knowledge rather than another, and the place that cognitive learning itself occupies vis-a-vis other purposes performed by the school and other aspects of a society's expectations concerning the work of its teachers.

Now that overall teacher shortages are receding, it is being argued that an opportunity exists to raise the quality and standards of teacher education, as a contribution to dealing with what is claimed to be a massive 'cognitive deficit' in industrialized societies. Before looking at some of the implications that this may have for the teacher's role, it may be useful to examine the concept of standards in more general terms.

'Standards' is one of the most potent symbols of educational discourse. Like all condensed symbols, it can be employed in many verg different contexts and is open to a wide variety of interpretations. To sustain high standards (of professional performance, of pupil achievement, of classroom order) is one of the chief moral imperatives of the teaching task. Complex social arrangements exists by means of which standards are defined and monitored, foremost among them the processes of formal examination and evaluation of pupil and student learning. To claim that a teacher or an institution has low, standards' is the most serious form of task-specific condemnation that education knows.

Standards serve to order particular social relationships within educational institutions, and to structure the linkages between such institutions and the social, political and economic organization of the societies within which they operate.

As a result of undergoing prescribed forms of training and acquiring relevant experience, relatively small groups of people in society are designated as the guardians of standards in their respective fields, qualified to make judgments on the work and achievements of others. Their authority to do this derives from recognition of superior knowledge of a specific literature, language and technique. The process by which individuals are so accredited as guardians of standards is never 'pure', never frees of the complexities that enter into all human and institutional relationships, and which sometimes threaten the integrity of the activity they purport to sustain. Mechanisms exist to ensure that structures of reward among the guardians are such as to encourage rather than undermine their commitment to high standards. The means by which this is done, e.g. the referee system, the development of agreed criteria for academic promotion, the distribution of honoured status, and the legitimation of paradigms of accepted knowledge at particular phases of institutional history, have all been extensively documented by sociologists of science.

The development of professional self-government and codes of practice, together with control of entry, has also been urged as contributory to the maintenance of standards. The ratio of qualified persons to available employment opportunities should not be such as to make fear of loss of employed status greater than fear of loss of professional membership.

Within many fields there is a high priesthood, in the form of a learned society or parallel body, which by its direct access to the forms of knowledge that sustain the enterprise, e.g. through research activity, is granted high status and features prominently in the reward system. Examples include the Royal Society, the Universities of Oxford and Cambridge and many specialist departments elsewhere, the Royal College of Surgeons, the Grandes Ecoles in France and a multitude of other bodies.

It is by invoking standards that movement between strata in society and status and reward groupings in professions and institutions is controlled. From their earliest days, even in the most progressive and examination-free environment, children's performance is monitored and assessed, and some kind of value is placed upon it by individuals who either immediately or later will have power to influence the child's future. Examinations of educational achievement and competence are central to the means whereby a complex advanced society proceeds to classify and categorize its members, and to legitimize unequal distribution of status and reward. Such processes inevitably attract considerable political attention. It is in the interests of particular groups to exert influence over the modes of categorization employed in a society. The intricate interconnection between examination systems and the structure of advanced societies helps to explain why the introduction of new techniques of assessment and changes in the criteria employed to assign particular gradings tend to take a very long time, sometimes in the teeth of political and lay opposition.

In most systems, control of the processes of assessment and evaluation is not wholly in the hands of professionals. There are lay councils or boards to which professional groups are formally accountable. Where the proper performance of a function is of significance to society as a whole, there are often arrangements whereby elected representatives play some part in the control of standards, either directly or through specialists who owe first allegiance to the central or local body rather than the profession or the institution itself. Examples include the work of the Education Inspectorate in the UK and in France, and the extent to which governments have sought to exert greater or lesser influence over the selection, education and certification of e.g. doctors, teachers and airline pilots.

Between educational institutions themselves, devices such as formal accrediting by some central body or the use of 'external examiners' drawn from cther institutions than the one responsible for granting the award, are extensively employed.

The right to set one's own standards, and to claim public recognition of awards made in accordance with these, is only grudgingly admitted. The award of a charter to a university the right of professional certification, the credibility of an internally set but externally moderated school examination are only conceded following satisfaction of stringent criteria. The system of external examining, widely used between universities and colleges in the UK but not so common in systems that have central accrediting agencies or where government control over certification is still maintained, raises questions of considerable sociological interest which deserve more detailed analysis and appraisal here. The means by which such external examiners are selected, the way in which they undertake their task, the independence or otherwise of their assessment of candidates' work, the extent to which they share a common paradigm of knowledge in a particular field with those responsible for teaching the course the students of which are under examination, all deserve exploration.

Because standards in most disciplines and techniques are both norm-referenced and criterion-referenced, the right of entry to a course is often rigorously safeguarded. Arguments that the equity principle is best satisfied by open entry coupled with stringent examination at a variety of points during a course of education and training and at its termination, are countered by the claim that the standards deemed appropriate to a particular course of education or training are in part set by the groups to whom such education is addressed. (It is in this context that evidence that pass rates within particular institutions tend to remain stable over time, despite changes in clientele, assumes significance.) If the setting of standards has something to do with the patterd of social relationships within an institution, and is not simply a reflection of the 'forms of knowledge' to which teachers have access, then it is not easy to ignore consistencies of this kind, and harder to believe that if we only tried we could introduce a genuine objectivity into assessment and evaluation. Proposals to introduce alternative modes of examination, such as course work, open book examinations, the assessment of practical work and credit for field experience, although much more common now than in the past, tend still to arouse anxiety. Expressed in doubts about the validity and reliability of such measures, such anxiety also has something to do with the difficulty of snsuring standardization and with the ease with which such methods can be subverted by, for example, plagiarism ond the trading of essays.

In seeking to maintain stendards, comparisons are made not only between the performance of individuals within a defined group, but also over time. Standards are essentially conservative, drawing much of their force from the ability of accredited individuals to cite traditions of performance which constitute a minimum basis for the appraisal of new work, and below which individuals and groups must not fall.

In common with symbols of comparable potency, standards generate their heroes. League tables are published showing schools that have obtained the largest number of university open scholarships. It is not long since local newspapers in the UK published comparisons of the performance of individual primary schools in the eleven-plus allocation procedure. Oxford and Cambridge colleges are rated in accordance with the number of first-class degrees their students achieve. Individual teachers are celebrated for their capacity to enthuse reluctant learners, and to obtain out-of-the-ordinary results from run-of-the-mill material.

The symbolic significance of standards is also reflected in the rituals associated with processes of assessment and evaluation. At ancient universities it is still necessary to wear special formal clothing whilst sitting examinations. In schools and colleges mock examinations, revision, the three-hour written test, the grading of performances and the posting of results, all exhibit a strongly ritualistic character. That standards have elements of the holy, and are the responsibility of specially accredited guardians, is reflected in the awesome formal apparatus of assessment, intended to instil initiates with a sense of the significance of the process they are undergoing, its importance for their personal lives, and the dignity and values of the award they seek to maintain.

Although standards—of performance, achievement, conduct—are important in all human cultures, they take on a special significance in advanced societies, first, because of the diversity of their often highly technical performance and achievement criteria, and second, because the application of such criteria clashes with the equity principles adopted by many such societies, which seek to diminish the incidence and importance of failure and rejection. This clash between meritocratic and equity principles is at the heart of many of our contemporary educational disputes, including those which have to do with the standards of attainment achieved by pupils in different types of school, the merits of various teaching methods and the importance of teacher quality for educational outcomes.

Concern with the principles that shall govern the distribution of educational opportunity is but one aspect of the broader question of equity that dominates contemporary social and economic policy. For a time, at least, economic growth and its attendant affluence can prevent the necessity of having to face up to the sharper issues to which this gives rise. When growth slows down or stops, when the demands of hitherto subordinate or disadvantaged groups cannot be met by redistribution at the margin, these issues can no longer be put aside. Being both norm-referenced and criterion-referenced, the intrinsic and the market aspects of most so-called standards are inextricably mixed—not least tn public discussion. Hence the agonizing about the relative merits and status of different levels of course and type of qualification, and anxiety about the tendency for the value of certificates and degrees to decline as access to them is opened up. As Hirsch (1976) has pointed out, the attractiveness of some goods (including educational qualifications) is partly dependent upon their scarcity; seen thus, such scarcity is an object of consumption rather than a factor of production.

There is thus considerable interest in research that bears on changing standards, as has been shown by the publicity given to findings about the relative merits of 'formal' and 'informal' teaching methods in the primary school (Bennett, 1976), and in the possibility of comparisons between countries of the kind attempted in the large-scale International Educational Achievements Project. Governments have responded quickly to suggestions that standards of literacy and numeracy are not what they should be.

A Swedish study, sponsored by the National Board of Education and published in 1975 (Grundin, 1975) suggested that one in five of the sixteen-year-old school leavers have attainments commensurate only with those of thirteen-year-olds, and 25 per cent of these 20,000 'functional illiterates' have the reading, writing and numerical skill of eleven-year-olds. The effect of this, combined with a simultaneous report by the NBE adult literacy project which estimates that 100,000 of the six million adult population of Sweden and 40,000 of the 406,000 immigrant population are almost totally illiterate, was to produce reaction described as 'alarmed and rapid':

> 'The Association of Swedish Teachers . . . has demanded a new programme for teaching Swedish in schools, the office of the Chancellor of the Universities has proposed a lengthening of teacher training and . . . the junior Education Minister in charge of schools . . . told Parliament that measures for improving Swedish teaching would be included in legislation next year' (Duckenfield, 1975b).

A further survey among thirteen-year-olds carried out at the end of 1975 indicated weaknesses in numeracy that provided further ammunition for those in Sweden who were arguing the need for a return to the basics, including members of the new Liberal/Centre Party/Conservative government (Duckenfield, 1977a).

Recent years have seen criticism in several countries of teachers' competence in language skills, and their ability to secure adequate levels of spoken and written performance by children. There is little evidence to sustain the view that standards in this respect are now lower than in former times (Department of Education and Science, 1975) and comparisons between countries present serious difficulties of interpretation. The orientation of teacher training in recent years, especially for those preparing to teach younger children, has been experientially oriented, rather than placing high priority on the development of linguistic competence. Yet there is a sense in which language is essential to the very concept of the school.

> 'Increasingly, then, language in its decontextualized form becomes among human beings the medium for passing on knowledge. And, of course, the emergence of written language—a very recent innovation from an evolutionary point of view—gives this tendency still further amplification. Once this mode of transmitting knowledge has become established, the conditions for the invention of school —a place where teaching occurs—are present. School is a very recent development in evolutionary terms, even in historical terms . . .' (Connolly and Bruner, 1974, p. 38).

Concern for greater competence in language use has now begun to affect the work of schools in many countries, and this trend is showing itself in the content and organization of teacher education programes. In this, the work of cognitive psychologists such as Bruner combines with that of developmentalists such as Piaget to stress the active role of the teacher and the school in promoting linguistic skill. The stress in education for the younger age groups on providing an adequate experiential basis for learning is still present, with its roots in Froebel, Dewey and the child study movement. But it is currently overlaid by a fresh emphasis on principles of cognitive organization and the need for a carefully structured curriculum. The structure can be explicit—in the form of timetabled subjects and skilled specialist teaching in each of them—or implicit—in the sense that the skills and forms of knowledge that contribute to interdisciplinary studies and projectbased work are identified and systematically woven into an 'integrated' approach. The important consideration in the view of many educationists is that the structure should be there.

Systematic monitoring of educational achievement within individual countries is now being attempted, and in England an 'Assessment of Performance Unit' has been set up in the Department of Education and Science. As we have seen in the preceding discussion, there is a sense in which 'standards' are essentially conservative, and from time to time it has seemed that a concern for standards of achievement in the basic school subjects has been the prerogative of right-wing interests. There are many progressives and radicals, however, who emphasize the importance of raising the achievement levels of minorities and the disadvantaged if members of these groups are to have opportunities for full self-development. Whatever the outcome of research on these topics now under way, it seems likely that more emphasis will be placed on the 'subject' element in the teacher's preparation, and on those method courses that relate to the acquisition of basic skills.

We can define the outcome of any teaching act as the product of the interaction of four main elements :

1. The motivation and the ability of students.
2. The content of what is to be taught and learnt.
3. The skills of the teacher in relation to the type of tramsmission involved.
4. The teaching materials available to facilitate the transmission.

In much of what has been written about teacher education in recent years there is to be found a new concern with the role of the teacher as a motivator of student learning. Pupil interest can no longer be taken for granted. Increases in the statutory leaving age are keeping in school many young men and women who would prefer to be elsewhere. The home environment of many younger children is not conductive to the development of those learning strategies that create a ready response to sehool regimes. As doubts increase about the scientific of 'measured intelligence', and the latent political and cridibility social cousequences of basing school organization upon such psychological assumptions, so greater emphasis is placed on motivation. With this is associated the view that one of the teacher's major tasks is to develop the individual capacity of each child and to maximize intellectual and affective potential. Although it has its roots in the classical ideal and in some of the writings of the philosophers of the Enlightenment, this view has come to the fore in the practice of training institutions and school only within relatively recent years. Improvements in the length and depth of the education and training of those who were to teach young children gave scope for such ideas to become incorporated in the curricula of normal schools and colleges, and rellected the emphasis on individual rights that has characterized the rhetoric and, perhaps less often, the reality of social practice during the present century. Types of selection and school organization that, as we have seen, clash with some of the most deeply held values of late twentieth century society, were introduced into European educational systems in the period between the two World Wars as means whereby the ability of the individual could be fully recognized and developed, and opportunities provided for social mobility irrespective of origins and parental background. That such selection and streaming were ineffective even in securing these ends is by now well known. Less obvious are the links between such features of school organization and that strain of romantic humanism that ran from Rousseau through Froebel and Montessori to the Child Development Movement in Germany, France and Great Britain in the first three decades of this century, and emphasized the need for children to be viewed as

individuals, for the pupil to be as important in the teacher's eyes as the subject, and for 'child-centredness' to be the dominant ideology of educational provision at least up to the beginning of the teenage years. The influence of this ideology on teacher education has been documented and criticized by, among others, Taylor (1969c), Peters (1969) and Dearden (1968) and, from a somewhat different standpoint, by Bowles and Gintis (1976).

The teacher as moral and political agent

The role of the teacher as a moral agent of society has been stressed since the earliest times, and in the nineteenth century sometimes seemed to take precedence over other functions concerned with literacy, numeracy and the development of cognitive skill. Indeed, such skills were themselves conceived as part of the process of moral education, since it was widely believed that the well-informed and literate citizen would be less likely to become criminally deviant or to promote undesirable forms of civic disorder. The 'discovery' on the part of Marxist critics that the organization and content of education serve to bolster the values and practices of capitalist and technological society represents nathing very new. The language and codes of curricular transmission employed, the nature of the teaching transactions encouraged or discouraged, the modes of evaluation applied, all necessarily reflect negotiated settlements of greater or less stability in relation to predominant values and beliefs within national and to a lesser extent regional and local communities. But with the realization that despite compulsory education from 5 to 15, almost universal literacy and numeracy, and the existence of a well-trained teaching force, the moral objectives of education remain unfulfilled has underpinned a substantial reappraisal of the role that the school performs in this respect. This reappraisal has both drawn upon and stimulated greater sophistication in the conceptualization of moral and political processes in education and encouraged empirical studies to explore the relationship involved. Thus today we have a large and growing literature concerned with the part that the teacher plays in socializing the young, the limitation of the school's contribution in this respect and the steps that should be taken to ensure what one of those concerned has called the development of 'political literacy' (Crick and Lister, 1974). Anyone with the intention of making student teachers aware of the language and literature of this field has now an extensive range of source on which to draw. This has a number of different and not always compatible elements, e.g. the work of Kohlberg (1963) and of the former Farmington Trust Unit at Oxford (Wilson et al., 1969; McPhail, Ungoed-Thomas and Chapman, 1972).

Interesting as many of these analyses are, few of them are adequately worked out at a level that makes inclusion in a relatively short period of initial teacher training a possibility. And as yet, there are few sources which bring together the findings of the empirical work that has been done in moral and political education in a form that makes for ready assimilation by the student teacher and implementation in the individual classroom. Growing anxiety about order and control, and about the activities of teachers held to possess radical and even subversive views, will encourage more work of this kind. In this context so much interest has been shown in the ideas of Stenhouse and his collaborators on the former Schools Council 'Humanities' projects and their subsequent work within the Centre for Applied Research in Education in the University of East Anglia. In focusing upon the necessity for the teacher to assume a 'neutral' role in stimulating pupil discussion of controversial issues, and providing materials for this purpose, Stenhouse's work holds out promise of enabling policy maker and practitioner to avoid difficult questions of influence and indoctrination.

That the identification and correction of stereotypes forms an important part of the teacher's task is clear from a study carried out in Norway by Brock-Utne of the College of Education at Tromso. Completed in March 1974, the survey of children's impressions of various nationalities concerned 494 children in the 7th grade of the Norwegian elementary school. The findings were as follows :

. . . on the whole the attitude towards the Russians had not changed much over the last twenty years. This was not the case when it came to the opinion of the Americans. This opinion was more negative than in the previous study. The adjective "aggressive" was used often. The children made comments on the Vietnam War, Nixon and Watergate. The stereotype which had earlier been attached to the Germans was now being applied both to East Germans and to West Germans. They were hard-working, industrious. But the opinion as regards the East Germans was definitely more negative that as regards the West Germans. The East Germans were even given the whole blame for the Second World War ! . . . ' (EUDISED, 1975).

At thc beginning of the century it was still possible for Durkheim to speak without self-consciousness of the teacher as the moral agent of society in terms such as the following :

'Just as the priest is the interpreter of his god, the teacher is the interpreter of the great moral ideas of his time and of his country. Let him be attached to these ideas, let him feel all their grandeur, and the authority which is in them, and of which he is aware, cannot fail to be communicated to his person and to everything that emanates from him. Into an authority which flows from such an impersonal source there could enter no pride, no vanity, no pedantry. It is made up entirely of the respect which he has for his functions and, if one may say so, for his office. It is this respect which, through word and gesture, passes from him to the child' (Durkheim, 1956, p. 89).

As Elvin (1964) has suggested, sentiments or this kind now have a totalitarian ring that was no doubt absent at the time when they were originally uttered. 'Society' is no longer a homogeneous concept, or one in which there inheres significant moral force. Attempts to find a basis for the teacher's moral authority are now more likely to be rooted in the 'public traditions' of subjects and scholarship which the teaching role serves to pass on to each new generation. At the same time, it is stressed that teachers need to be trained in critical reflection, and to apply this in their selection of teaching materials and to the habit formation that their teaching will generate. Teacher education is not merely the induction of the future teacher into an established and unproblematic moral order, an education in means and technique. Thus it is argued that such education should not take place in institutions which stress the application of knowledge and its technical usefulness, but in those which place their emphasis on critical thought, moral autonomy and development of the creative imagination.

> 'If one takes what I would call broadly the democratic view, teacher education belongs basically in the context of the debate on the intrinsic, on the openness of ends. And this is what university education too is about. It may well be the concern of many in many polytechnics, too. If so, so much the better. But it is not central to their tradition' (Thompson, 1974, p. 16).

At the broadest level, we can distinguish two positions about the task of the teacher as a moral and political agent. The first stresses his responsibilities to the 'social heritage', his obligation to induct children into public traditions of knowledge and to obtain their adherence to agreed procedural principles, fairly to represent the range of existing points of view on controversial issues, and to act as a stabilizing influence in a world of flux and change. This conception of the teacher's role is to most of its advocates essentially 'non-political'.

For their opponents, such a stance seems merely to gratify and endorse the values of a consumer-oriented, capitalist society characterized by coercion and the ideological trickery of the false consciousness. The claim that teachers have an obligation to act as agents of change within such a society is by no means new, or restricted to those of Marxist persuasion. In an article very influential in its time, and which has continued to be quoted frequently during the years since its first appearance, Jean Floud (1962) argued that :

'The teacher's task is to "iron out swings in the trend cycle". This is an ambiguous brief, but one thing is clear; the powerful contemporary vogue for bringing life into the classroom, imitating it and preparing for it in school, effectively ties the teacher's hands behind his back before he starts. Education is a moral activity; "life" as lived anywhere is not good enough. What is the teacher's brief in the affluent society if life as his pupils meet it on leaving school is a long carnival of moral, intellectual and artistic mediocrity? He must search for "excellence", fighting a "strong rearguard action in defense of high intellectual and artistic standards", protecting the "long-term intellectual and humanistic interests" of his pupils. Here then is another role for the teacher in the affluent society; he is to be not only a missionary in the slum but a crusader in the suburb, dedicated to the war against mediocrity and to the search for excellence.'

More recently, however, as we have seen from quotations earlier in this chapter, the notion of the teacher as an agent of social change has taken on a new and more strident tone, closely allied in some countries to Marxist analyses of society and to doctrines of revolutionary upheaval. The trend is towards the politicization of teachers' tasks, and the polarization of debate in terms of radical and conservative alternatives. To some extent the teacher's role requires that he takes up positions, as has been noted by Flechsig (1975) :

'He (the educationist) does not primarily select the information which he wishes to convey because of the value it had for earlier generations : his material is chosen chiefly because it is seen to be of probable relevance and value to the growing generation . . . The educationist is . . . caught up in the tension that exists between present and future.'

It was in Germany that the radical movement in colleges and universities of the late Sixties took on some of its most dramatic forms, and secured a measure of success in influencing constitutions and decision-making. This has inevitably produced a reaction, with university decision-making now in the hands of the bodies in which professors and senior staff have an absolute majority, and a clear swing to the right in the voting behaviours and preferences of universities and school students.

The Schulerunion, a right-wing pupil group, increased its membership by a third during 1975. In the words of one commentator :

> 'This rate of growth is remarkable in view of the publicity and popularity hitherto enjoyed by the left-wingers. It springs partly from the natural opposition of young people to authority, in this case in the form of Marxist teachers not much older than themselves who use the classroom to preach the virtues of the class struggle and attack the capitalist structure of society' (Dungworth, 1975a).

There is provision in Germany for the exclusion from public office, including teaching, of those who are through membership of extremist organizations or by virtue of other activities regarded as 'politically unreliable', although Social Democratic and Opposition controlled Lander tend to interpret what is sometimes called the 'Extremists' Decree', which dates from 1972, somewhat differently (Dungworth, 1976d; Kloss, 1977a.) Apparently, several hundred candidates for public setvice employment have been rejected on political grounds since the agreement between the Federal Chancellor and the Lander Premiers came into force (Dungworth, 1976c).

Germany is not the only country in which there has been an attempt to persuade the authorities to face these issues directly. The head of the INRDP in France, Louis Legrand, has written :

> '... it is essential to investigate the value of the political and ethical aims whics governed the creation of the primary school under the Third Republic. The present texts are silent on this point, as though maintenance of traditional aims went without saying and as though the new edifice

merely responded to the same values while allowing for the new socioeconomic context. But this implicit continuity is not unambiguous. The absence of official precision is more a reflection of the lack of clear and consistent thought in this respect than confidence in traditional values. And this confusion is not only in the minds of the political authorities. It is widespread in public opinion and among teachers themselves; . . . this absence of explicit ideology in the state school of to-day is perhaps the fundamental educational problem' (quoted Belbenoit, 1974).

Belbenoit refers to the way in which, in France, a suggestion made by a speaker at the National Seminar on Education of November 1973 thar the school should concern itself with the development of 'a new form of citizenship' evoked something of a shocked surprise 'in a country where the training of the citizen, which has always been solemnly inscribed, together with the training of the man and the worker, among the school's essential tasks, has long since ceased to be the subject of any activity specifically relating to the acknowledged importance of the stakes involved'. But despite Legrand's plea for an explicit consideration of the ideology that underlies educational provision, Belbenoit admits that, in attempting to throw light on the 'complicated and largely contradictory reasons for an aloofness which is undoubtedly prejudicial to the functioning of a Republic', it has to be taken into account that 'since 1968, we dare not completely evade the dabate on aims but dare not face the reality covered by words whose ambiguity camouflages the disagreements and excuses us from taking sides'. As has been urgued elsewhere (Taylor, 1969d), the ambiguity of the terms employed in much educational discourse is functional for the social and political integration of the groups to which such messages are addressed. To pursue all questions as hard and as far as possible is inevitably to exercise a potentially or actually disrupting effect on existing structures.

The teacher as innovator

The social, economic and political climates in terms of which decisions about teacher education are being made by European countries in the mid-Seventies are very different from those of ten years earlier. There is no unanimity about the nature and implications of the changes that have taken place over the last decade in society, economy and policy, the factors that have brought such changes about, and the direction that future events will take. Description and analysis of what is going on around us constitute a substantial proportion of contemporary academic and popular writing; the nationalities, political predilections, social philosophies and personal dispositions of the authors produce a bewildering variety of ideas, matched by an equally varied pattern of responses. Thus any attempt to identify and to categorize those elements of contemporary life that have implications for the way in which teachers have been, are, and are likely in future to be educated and trained, is inevitably somewhat arbitary.

Yet, arbitrary as it may be, such an attempt is necessary if we are to avoid that style of educational discourse that celebrates the merits of change and produces vigotous advocacy for the increase in the innovatory capacities and skills of teachers, without once stopping to spell out what kinds of change are being held up as desirable, which particular innovations the teacher must be trained to implement, and what is the content of the teaching in which innovatory, change-conscious teachers are expected to engage.

This unwillingness to enter into specifics is understandable enough. The analysis of educational change has become something of a sub-specialism; few of those concerned are at the same time specialists in a particular area of the curriculum that might provide some substance for their schemata. Those who are well qualified in one or more subjects sometimes avoid referring to these in order to ensure the largest possible audience for their ideas. The broader educational and social contexts of many types of educational change are hard to identify, the interactions of education and society complex and difficult to tease out into manageable strands. And if change is a reality, then how can one predict the conditions under which teachers who are being trained today are likely to find themselves working five, ten, twenty years hence? Better, perhaps, to borrow from old-fashioned ideas of mental training (without drawing too much attention to the fact) and claim that innovative capacity, once developed and trained, can be applied in whatever set of circumstances a teacher finds himself. To commit oneself to a particular philosophy or methodology is to invite criticism and disagreement.

Another prop for discussions of content-less change has been the tendency for subject teaching, especially at the secondary stage, to be associated with conservative attitudes and an unwillingness to consider new organizational arrangements at both system and school level. Critics of the schools, faced with the accusation that teachers trained on the basis of radical ideas will politicize the classroom, respond with the argument that the traditional organization of knowledge itself embodies political bias. From time to time educational systems in Western countries find themselves having to cope with disputes such as that which flared up in the UK during 1975 about the controversial ideas that it was alleged were being taught to primary-age children in William Tyndale School, London, or the kind of English teaching which a radical critic of society, Christopher Searle, was providing in another London school. This involved children in studying 'land speculation, profiteering, cuts in public facilities and destruction of community life and class solidarity by forces totally opposed to the well-being and social and political health of these children and their families . . .', together with a study of oppression in the Third World and the struggle by rank and file trade unionism in England (Searle, 1975, p. 10).

Few of those who write so persuasively about the ubiquitous nature of educational change and the need for educational innovation would go this far. Indeed some, especially those whose writing embodies a technocratic model of society, see their advocacy of change as contributing not to the overthrow but to the support and continued existence of bourgeois capitalist democracy. It is possible to detect a sense among some teachers that despite the current demand for information; justification and public discussion of nearly every aspect of our social, political and economic arrangements, there are some questions which are best not asked—or at least not too often. Even in an information-rich world such as our own, the continued ability of societies to sustain a high level of political and economic freedom, individual autonomy and respect for persons is recognized as being dependent on a willingness to live within a rich web of ambiguity, to accept many apparent inconsistencies. As a leading article in the Times Educational Supplement seated with respect to the Searle book (October 17, 1975):

> '. . . (it) will shake a little more the fragile base on which the professional teacher's curricular autonomy stands, force reluctant censors out of their corner and further complicate the debate on the separate but overlapping domains of the Government, l.e.a.s, governors and managers, parents and teachers in respect of the school curriculum.'

But to suggest that some of the social structures and agreements that support political freedom, the rule of law, the potentiality of greater personal equality, and the possibility of orderly, non-violent change, are fragile, mysterious and vulnerable to over-critical exposure is to invite the scorn of the radical, and also to risk appearing to contradict some of the major imperatives of academic life. The radical sees such acceptance of 'mystification' as merely another way of obfuscating the issues and preserving existing structures of power and influence. Academics commit themselves to principles of rationality that demand the explosure of latent functions and of hidden motives. To do other than pursue one's questioning as hard and as far as it will go is to betray the academic ethic.

For all these reasons, much contemporary discussion of educational change and of the preparation of teachers is marked either by the absence of social, political and economic dimensions, or by bland and anodyne statements that add little to the analysis or to our understanding and insight. Sometimes there appears to be an omission of the social dimension. Take, for example, the following statement from a paper entitled 'Social Science and Humanistic Education' in the 73rd Yearbook of the National Society for the Study of Education (Chicago, Chicago University Press, 1974) (italics added) :

> 'Contemporary industrial society is organized around values which require persons to acquire "objects" by means which others consider legitimate. These objects may be described as empirical indicators of concepts which, through their symbols, shape our lives. These concepts are status, security, acceptance, affiliation and privacy. Most persons, during most of their lives, are seeking those states of being or objects which either provide or maintain them in the circumstances that these conceptual ideas indicate . . .
>
> An alternative consciousness would be one in which reduction of those same needs or drives could be sought in the personal experience, independent of socially valued attainments. This would mean, for example, that an individual's sense of worth would evolve on the basis of his own sense of accomplishment or productivity, separate from other evaluations of him' (p. 104).

Leaving aside the issue of whether a sense of worth that 'evolved' on this basis would have desirable or undesirable social consequences, a prior question is whether there is any meaning in a sense of worth that does not at some time depend upon interaction with other people. In assessing our accomplishments we use ineluctably social categories, acquired from our cultural experience. Without such experience, our self-concepts would be non-existent. Which is not to say that alternative forms of consciousness are not possible, or to deny the close relationships that these have with the nature of our social and economic arrangements. Marx, Durkheim and Veblen had important things to say about all this many years ago, and more recently authors such as Berger, Berger and Kellner (1974) have attempted systematic analyses of the ways in which specific forms of consciousness are shaped by and in turn help to perpetuate particular kinds of society. But we cannot remedy the alleged deficiencies of existing social structures and social processes by pretending that the problems with which these structures and processes attempt to deal no longer exist.

Another weakness in the style of thought under discussion is an all-pervasive eclecticism, an ability to see every side of the question, coupled with a willingness to lean for support upon mutually contradictory sources of ideas. The result reflects the enormous range of more or less relevant materials on which anyone who sits down to write on anything other than the most esoteric and narrowly-defined educational topic can draw, and produces both information overload and indigestible prose. Whilst, for the reasons indicated, this is more apparent in writing about education than in some other fields, the problem of organizing large quantities of information in readable and useful form is common to all disciplines. Speaking of the study of history, Bensman and Lilienfeld (1973) state: 'The constant search for accuracy in recording and describing events creates the possibility of assembling an almost infinite amount of materials of such complexity and volume as to overwhelm all but the professional specialist' (p. 129). Indeed—but why exclude the professional specialist? What is true of the discipline of history is even more true of a multidisciplinary field of study such as education. Bensman and Lilienfeld go on to suggest that there are four main responses to the need to secure order and meaning among this mass of material.

The first is to leave the reassembly of historical unity to the journalist or the popularizer. "The latter, in order to achieve the dramatic values that are possible in any recording of human activities, will personify, dramatize and stress the spectacular and the unexpected, and so seek to violate the expectancies of everyday life. In this latter respect, he will take the norms of prevalent public opinion or historiographic assumptions and attemp to invert them in order to introduce the idea of novelty, excitement and "news" into the writing of history.'

A second approach is to 'boil down' into a textbook. ' . . . he simply compresses, orders and balances the universe of monographs. Such history usually has the professional virtue of being competent, dull and empty. If there are distortions, they are the distortions that come from a lack of ideas rather than from their presence.'

There are two other strategies. One is to take a broad sweep; to attempt—as Wells and Toynbee in their different ways attempted—to write 'universal history'. The other is to order the material around a particular theme or organizing principle, or to confine oneself to what can be done within the framework of a distinctive theoretical orientation. Provided that the orientation concerned is sufficiently rich in concepts, has historical and philosophical roots of adequate depth, and provides opportunities to participate with others in intellectual effort within a coherent universe of discourse, this is the solution much preferred by academics. It helps to explain the appeal, in our own time, of Marxist ideas, and their tendency to penetrate deeply into many areas of the social sciences and education.

This discussion began as an effort to justify the necessarily selective and arbitrary nature of any attempt to identify and describe those elements in contemporary societal change that bear upon education in general and studies in the education and training of teachers in particular. The principal justification for such an attempt rests in the fact that if the values that characterize present-day teacher education are to be examined and understood, this can be done only in the context of the wider society within which they take on meaning. There are several features of present-day social, political and economic life of particular importance in grasping the way in which the teacher's role and preparation for the performance of that role have changed.

One of these is changes in the pattern of economic growth. It has become part of the conventional wisdom of education that innovation and growth go together. Expansion in size and in the range of activities of institutions and systems encourages and facilitates planned change to achieve educational objectives. This assumption is in part rooted in experience of theyears between 1945 and the beginning of the Seventies, which in many European countries divide into two clearly marked periods.

Up to about 1960, despite moves in some coun tries (e.g. Sweden, the UK) to reorganize secondary education, and the steady proliferation of the 'progressive' ideas and practices in primary schools that had already been in evidence pre-war (e.g. Denmark), there was little change in the technology of teaching or in the main features of educational discourse.

It was not until the Sixties that the stimulus of increased numbers, and a more sophisticated awareness of the weaknesses of existing provision in relation to ongoing technological change, encouraged large-scale efforts to reform curriculum and school organization, to devise new kinds of courses and programmes at post-secondary level, and to create institutions and roles explicitly concerned with the promotion and evaluation of educational change. Not all countries experienced these pressures simultaneously, and there were also variations in the time at which they were felt in relation to different levels in the educational system; e.g. for reasons that were only partly to do with an explicit desire for educational reform on the part of governments and authorities, changes in higher education in the Federal Republic of Germany took place somewhat earlier than the reform of secondary schools.

All this had a considerable effect on the nature of educational discourse. Political preoccupations and elements from social science disciplines combined to produce a vocabulary and agenda that took their character from the technological

Zeitgeist at the time, and were distinctly different from those of the immediately post-war decade.

The Sixties were in many cases years of unparalleled expansion at nearly every level of education. Increasing numbers in primary and secondary schools exposed chronic teacher shortages, which colleges and universities sought to meet by doubling and redoubling their student intakes. The setting up of new universities, and the full force of higher education expansion, together with the diversification of institutions, the designation of polytechnics, Fachhochschulen, Institutes Universitaires de Technologie, etc., changed the face of higher education.

It was during this period that interest began to be shown in the phenomenon of innovation itself. National and international organizations arranged conferences and working parties, research workers tried to establish by empirical inquiry the conditions favourable and unfavourable to innovation, and whole book began to appear on the subjects. In one of the best known, Matthew B. Miles, Innovation in Education, the author had little doubt about what constituted the most significant causative factor. In his words : '. . . the sheer size and growth of the educational establishment itself is exerting perhaps the most profoundly innovative effect of all' (p. 9). Within the educational establishment, Miles argued, the higher schools were influencing the lower in the direction of innovation with 'the apogee of influence turning out to be the graduate department in the university, which not only influences lower programs but also produces new knowledge, controls admission to itself, and trains related practitioners.'

The links between growth and innovation were not difficult to establish. Growth meant the recruitment of new staff, many of them young, and the desire (which must sometimes be separated from the ability) of the young to innovate is supported both by commonsense observation and by evidence (Carlson, 1965; Miller, 1967).

Growth produces a regular increment of additional resources, which can be applied to new purposes without having to meet the political costs of reducing allocation to existing activities or ceasing to support ongoing work. So people can be hired, departments and units established, equipment purchased, buildings erected and programmes funded, without too much pain for those who do not wish to, or cannot, participate in the innovation. And if innovation is not as rapid as some of the providers and some of the customers and clients might wish, then growth also provides an alibi, a set of plausible reasons why in the face of continuing demand for taking on additional students, hiring inexperienced staff, commissioning new plant, it has proved impossible to undertake the fundamental modifications in programmes and technology that 'everyone' agrees are necessary and desirable.

Size, too, is also associated with diversification, in student interest and ability, teaching methods, course options and organizational forms. Such diversity, in breaking down the tight collegiality and control that often characterizes the smaller, more self-contained institution, facilitates interaction of a kind directed to the achievement of particular objectives. Within large schools, departmental and other working groups sometimes achieve a commitment to cooperative action through sustained face-to-face contact in lunch-time meetings, curriculum projects, planning sessions and so forth that goes beyond what could have been achieved in the less differentiated framework of the smaller school, where staff meetings were rare, teachers were isolated from one another's practice, and control if benevolent was often autocratic.

In colleges and universities, growth enables new units and departments to be financed within traditional structures, and complete institutional frameworks of a non-traditional kind designed without too much anxiety being generated about threats to the excellence of the mainstream of university activities. Growth yields money to back projects and programmes and units in educational research and development, and to see that the results of their efforts are disseminated widely through materials and the media, and by innumerable conferences and meetings.

It is hardly surprising, therefore, that we have come to associate innovation with increases in the size and scale of educational operations. Such an association is part of the biographies of very many of those who now occupy major positions of influence and power within the education system.

Nor is it surprising that growth in numbers of teachers and pupils, lecturers and students, courses and programmes, books and journals, conferences and meetings, and in all the processes that contribute to the rate of turnover within the system, have come to be causally associated with effort to achieve planned change in the service of particular educational objectives. Over a period of some ten years from the end of the Fifties, national and international organizations in the field of education promoted the idea that educational development actively contributed not only to economic growth but also to the attainment of those broad social objectives that most countries and most political parties within each country espoused, such as the extension of educational opportunity and the easing of access to upper-secondary and post-secondary education for women, rural youth, ethnic minorities and other identifiably 'under-privileged' groups in the societies concerned.

By 1970 the tide had begun to change. One empirical analysis after another seemed to show that education played a somewhat less direct role in the economic achievements of society and in the attainment of societal goals than had been thought to be the case. Pressure on resources mounted. The willingness of electorates to give mandates for unlimited educational expansion was seriously eroded by the actions of activist students and, in some cases, by greater political and industrial militancy on the part of teachers.

Before the Seventies were many years old, the metaphors had changed. Educational discourse was strewn with refere ences to steady state, zero growth, the beauties of smallness, the advantages of not having to spread one's net too widely, the need to assess priorities and to identify and protect the essentials of one's own particular activities. Associated with such sentiments was a new interest in the part that individual teachers might play in the process of curriculum reform. If change would no longer ride in or the back of growth and technological innovation, then it might come from smaller-scale, teacher-directed efforts; references to the 'teacher as innovator' became common in the literature of education and the conference agendas.

The formal responsibilities of the teacher for innovation in curriculum, teaching method and evaluation vary a good deal from one country to another, in line with differences in central, regional or local control exercised over teacher decision making in the schools. But there is a common rhetoric in many countries concerning the need for more responsibility to be given to the individual teacher, and for him to assume the role of innovator in curriculum, pedagogy and evaluation. Increasing stress is being placed upon the teacher's capacity to act as an organizer of learning resources, as the one person able to put each child in the way of those means and materials of learning that are suited to individual needs and interests.

In some cases the idea of school-based curriculum development is being pursued, based on the assumption that 'the best place for designing the curriculum is where the learner and the teacher meet' (Skilbeck, 1974; see also Menck, 1972).

A project in line with Skilbeck's ideas about the school-based nature of innovation is the 'autonomy project' condcted by Blichfeldt at the Oslo Labour Research Instituted at the request of the Norwegian National Council for Innovation in Education, the aim of the project was to contribute to increased self-management for teachers, students and administrators in schools, in particular :

> partitions by the individual pupil in the classroom situations in a setting of relevance to the society he

lives in, which can increase his ability to raise questions and to make choices which affect his whole life;

2. the development of flexible role relations in the school, so that the teachers too can learn continuously from each other and from the learning process itself, so that institutional learning can more easily come into effect;

3. improved cooperation between school and local social settings' (EUDISED, 1975).

The research is still operated with a business school and a vocational school, with additional contacts with other school regions, and work with the staff and students at the school, observing learning processes and 'developing trust in the local area'. The research team are continuing with work elsewhere 'to investigate the conditions which facilitate cooperative problem-solving by pupils and cooperation between teachers and the conditions whereby both pupils and teachers are able to extend their range of autonomy'. One of the sets of institutional relationships which the project is continuing to study involves a junior school in Oslo and a local college of education which uses the school for purposes of practice teaching.

A number of factors, additional to the wish to give teachers greater autonomy and independence, help to account for the stress upon the school as the centre of curriculum development. Doubts about the centre-periphery models of curriculum development and about some of the assumptions of rational curriculum planning (RCP) have become commonplace in recent years; a sense that a curriculum imposed from above or presented in the form of 'teacher-proof packages' has failed to secure its objectives; the influence of universities and colleges where teachers are encouraged to develop their powers of independent and critical thinking; the anti-hierarchical and participatory mood of many teachers' organizations, and recognition of the need for a continuous adaptation of curriculum to changing external conditions, have all helped to encourage the movement. It has taken different forms from one country to another. In France and in Sweden, where traditionally curricula have been handed down from on high, periods of 'optional time' have been introduced, in which teachers may determine for themselves the content and organization of what is taught. In the UK, teachers are being encouraged to adopt 'Mode III' styles of examination, which place a greater emphasis on the paper and test set in the school, marked by teachers and moderated externally.

Another factor that has encouraged the conceptualization of the teacher's task in terms of organizing learning resources is the greater availability of books and other forms of printed materials, of reprographic aids, of audiovisual materials and all the other equipment that helps to extend the teacher's educative capacity.

But claims that the past few years have seen a substantial decentralization of decision making in matters of curricula and pedagogy in many countries need to be treated with caution. It is important that the realities of what has occurred be separated from the aspirations and wishes of those concerned with advocating policies of curriculum renewal and change. It is also important that crude distinctions between 'centralized' and 'decentralized' systems be avoided, and the complexity of the real, as opposed to the apparent arrangements in each country recognized. For example, White (1973) has shown how the 'tradition' of curriculum freedom in the UK is of somewhat less antiquity than is often claimed, going back no further than the years between the two world wars. Furthermore, in the UK as well as elsewhere, there are many influences on teachers' decision-making in curriculum matters that have nothing to do with the presence or absence of 'central direction' by legislature or administration.

In some cases, 'democratization', involving the creation of bodies such as the administrative council of French Lycees and colleges which include, in addition to administrators, teachers and supervisors, representatives of parents, pupils and citizens, may have rather little influence on the content and methods of teaching a curriculum the broad outlines of which have already been determined centrally. Moreover, as Belbenoit (1974) points out, under existing arrangements French teachers expect and are generally granted considerable autonomy in interpreting the centrally approved curricula. In Belbenoit's view :

> '. . .the redefinition of curricula is not a task with which teachers should be associated as a matter of priority. The result would, on the contrary, be to plunge them still further into their traditional way of thinking' (p. 4).

There is an important difference in 'teacher participation' in a consultative and advisory capacity at the time that syllabus guidelines are produced and approved, and the freedom of the teacher in his own classroom to determine what he or she will or will not teach within a particular subject or interdisciplinary area.

Whilst some decentralization has taken place in Italy, with the setting up of Centri Didattici Nazionali, the model of curriculum decision-making is still basically centralist. Inevitably, a federalist system produces a considerable variety of patterns, and in Germany there are quite marked differences between the extent to which the syllabuses issued by the various Lander are regarded as binding and act restrictively upon teachers' freedom to determine their own methods and content. In nearly all cases, teachers are free to select their own textbooks and methods of work, and in some Lander syllabuses are regarded as provisional and subject to fairly rapid amendment—Jackson (1974) reports that in Saarland and Bremen they are issued in the form of cyclostyled sheets.

It is sometimes argued that the slowness of curriculum and organizational reform is due to the conservative orientations of teachers themselves, particularly subject teachers in the secondary schools.

A study carried out by Lauglo (EUDISED, 1975) on the

Norwegian uppersecondary teacher at the end of the Sixties failed to confirm this view. In terms of the attitudes of this group to the changes that were then ongoing or proposed in the Norwegian secondary school, the results did not support the oft-quoted view that such teachers are strongly opposed to educational reform. Whilst most teachers were opposed to changes which might be seen as a threat to the traditional function of the gymnasium as a secondary school with a clear-cut academic function, they were in favour of a variety of oher reforms, including granting students greater autonomy and influence over their education. What the investigators called 'reform-mindedness' was associated positively with age and with certain school characteristics, e.g. small size, and students drawn from a more middle class background.

There was apparently no relationship between reform-mindedness and the teacher's sex, social origins and early commitment to a teaching career.

The attitude of Austrian teachers towards innovationh as been investigated by Knapp and Kowalski at the Oesterreichisches Institut fur Berufsbildungs forschung in Vienna—on the basis of hypotheses suggesting that young teachers are more ready for innovation than their older colleagues, and that readiness for innovation is influenced inter alia by the status of the initiator and the source of information. Further hypotheses, based upon a study of relevant literature, suggest:

'—there is a negative correlation between individual stress caused by professional work and the readiness for innovation, and there is a positive correlation between professional engagement and readiness for innovation.

'—readiness for innovation correlates with the social position which the teacher concerned feels he is occupying within the staff. On the other hand, participation in innovation improves the social position of the teacher among his colleagues and the local community.

'—there is a positive correlation between the readiness for

innovation and the awareness by the teacher of discrepancies in the aims of the school and the school practice' (EUDISED, 1975, p. 35).

So far we have examined three aspects of teacher tasks in relation to which there appear to have been major shifts of emphasis in recent years, i.e. cognitive learning and the development of individual potentiality, the teacher as innovator and his contribution to moral and political education. Two more aspects remain that require brief attention—the teacher as a cooperator with other internal and external agencies, and, finally, his role as an agent of social and economic equality.

The cooperative role of the teacher

The terms cooperation and collaboration appear with great frequency in recent discussions of the teacher's role. There are several reasons why this should be so. First, the conventions, rituals, institutional frameworks and social expectations that once sustained group and community action have lost much of their capacity to control and direct behaviour. Hence, as we have seen, emphasis is laid upon individual acquisition of the skills that make social life tolerable. Second, on the narrower base of the schools themselves, what Bernstein (1971) has called 'classification' and 'frame' have been weakened, and teaching is a much less private activity than was once the case. Team-teaching and the open classroom are only two of the most obvious manifestations of this trend. Third, the lack of success that schools and teachers have had in satisfying many of the social objectives of education, together with evidence on the limited part that schools can play in the achievement of such aims when other influences in society are either passive or working in contrary direcctions, have underlined the importance of cooperation between teachers, social workers, welfare agencies, parent associations, and other groups within the community.

For all these reasons, it is maintained that teacher education should give greater attention to the development of cooperative and collaborative skills, and, indeed, it is maintained that these may constitute important predictors of teaching success. Strom (1971) has argued that the orientations towards individual achievement that make for success in college may be counter-productive when the teacher starts work in schools.

> 'However necessary learning to collaborate may be, it is unlikely to eventuate in the absence of proper training. Yet for most undergraduates, teacher preparation seldom includes working with colleagues. Instead, common practice dictates a competitive, individual orientation. Collaboration is forbidden and the talent of others is viewed as self-misfortune. This procedure which produces self-adequate loners perhaps made sense in the days of one-room schools. Teachers then had exclusive responsibility for their students and found it unnecessary to get along with colleagues in faculty or curriculum meetings, because there were no colleagues. Today, however, the knowledge explosion, availability of resource personnel, and the viability of group-initiated change combine to make unreasonable any teacher preparation program which excludes the principles of shared responsibility' (p. 164; see also Strom, 1976).

Just as team-teaching and the open classroom represent two aspects of the general trend towards collaborative learning, so there is now acceptance in some places of the principle of students helping one another, from the first stages of the primary school up to and including Preparation of theses for doctoral degrees. It is difficult, in relation to contemporary claims on behalf of the 'cross-age relationship' collaborative classroom, not to see affinities with nineteenth century patterns of monitorial instruction (Briggs, 1975).

In Denmark, the tradition of the Folkeskole 'from-master', with responsibilities for liaison with parents and the community, has in recent years been amended by decrees that permit the appointment of a variety of consultants to undertake specialist tasks. School psychologists, school medical officers and dentists have been employed for many years, but it is now possible to have additional help in respect of, e.g. elementary instruction, mother tongue instruction, orientation on vocational and educational possibilities, social studies and science (history, geography and biology), school library activities, audiovisual work, and educational research. In the words of a recent report :

> 'this area is growing rapidly and an increasing number of persons are employed' (Jansen, Hansen and Leerskov, 1975).

A recent survey of these cooperative services shows that changes have taken place not only in the way in which the role of the teacher is defined, but also in how some of the longer-stadding ancillary professionals define their tasks.

> 'From being originally somatically oriented, the school medical service is now of a mental hygiene nature . . . (sociomedical). The focus on risk children demands close cooperation with the teachers, the remaining service personnel at school, and the parents. The school dental service no longer tries to "drill and avoid problems", but aims at prophylatic work, teaching children and parents healthy dental care. This task can be accomplished in cooperation with the school (i.e. with the form-master) and must be regard as a general educational task.' (ibid).

The Danish investigators found that the function that has been traditionally exercised by the form-master is by no means redundant in the face of this increase in specialist help, but has in fact expanded and needs more careful organization than before, given the larger size of schools and the greater range of ancillary help that must now be coordinated in the interests of children and their families.

The implications of democratization of decision-making in education for the cooperative role of teachers was brought out in the report from Finland to the OECD Conference on Teacher Policies of 1974, which states :

'Teachers of today have to share their decision-making and their responsibilities with other adult persons and with their pupils. There is a remarkable trend towards wider distribution of responsibility, democratization and establishment of representative organs at all educational levels. In the reform of teacher education a new emphasis has to be laid upon developing the future teachers' capability to cooperate with their pupils, their fellow educators and various groups of persons outside the school. This necessitates a placing of emphasis on behavioural sciences in teacher education curricula'

The Finnish report also states, in a way that is reminiscent of the findings of the Danish investigators to which reference has just been made, that teachers must be trained to cooperate which other specialist personnel in the school, as well as with their teacher colleagues, pupils and parents.

In France and Belgium this is reflected in the emphasis being placed upon 'T-group' teacher education, and on an understanding of the socio-dynamics of social life. In many discussions about the changing role of the teacher these is a certain ambiguity between the demand for performance of specialist functions, and need for teachers to have an overall responsibility for the development of their pupils. The latter has always predominated at the primary stage, whilst specialist teaching has been characteristic of intermediate and upper-secondary education. But as we have seen in the case of Denmark, the skills and knowledge required to undertake various forms of teaching even with the younger age groups now call for separate personnel to undertake distinctive tasks. This is reflected in a statement concerding recent developments in Austria :

'. . .the new concept of the Austrian teacher-training course for primary-school teachers foresees the introduction of a system in which certain teachers concentrate specially on these creative artistic subjects (musical education, handicraft, drawing, physical education) . . . the introduction of this system is justified because in each of these fields great demands are already being made and it can no longer be expected that every teacher master each domain' (OECD, 1974b).

Whilst there is a good deal in the literature about increases in the number of ancilary staff in schools and the educational services generally, the methods of classification used in some countries make it difficult to assess the qualitative significance of this trend. In the UK, for example, the 10 per cent sample census figures published at the end of 1975 indicate that the number of full-time educational administrators and ancillary workers employed by local education authorities has risen since 1964 in about the same proportion as the number of those classified as 'teacher'. Between 1964, and 1974, the numbers of full-time teaching and non-teaching staff both rose by about one-half. There was, however, a considerable increase in the number of part time non-teaching staff. The ranks of the non-teachers included in these figures covered a wide range of occupations, including part-time ballet tutors, industrial training officers, a 'crane and hoist operator' and 'two female bargees' (Times Educational Supplement, November 28, 1975). In 1975, the local authorities in Great Britain spent some four per cent of their educational budget on 'administration and inspection'.

What would be of greater interest both for the UK and for other European countries would be figures showing the proportion of those classified as 'teachers' who are in fact engaged in such activities as curriculum development, as teachers' centre wardens, in advisory capacities, and as specialists in guidance, counselling and careers advice.

The Finnish authorities have drawn attention to the difficulties that heavy teaching timetables cause in arranging cooperation between teachers and other personnel working either directly or indirectly for the school. It is felt that teachers might be freed for more cooperative activity if additional auxiliary personnel could be appointed to take care of some of the routine functions, such as preparation of materials administrative chores and similar tasks. As far as cooperation with pupils and parents is concerned, legislation has existed since 1973 which requires a school council to exist in every secondary school 'to supervise and facilitate instruction and education in general' (OECD, 1974c, p. 7).

> 'The councils are elected by the school's teachers and students for one year at a time. Teachers and students have an equal number of representatives. Depending on the size of the school, the number of representatives in the council varies between six and ten. Class meetings and subject meetings are sub-organs of the school council '(ibid., p. 7).

The school councils have wide powers and responsibilities and represent a greater degree of democratization of decision-making in the school than had been customary in many other countries.

> 'The secondary school councils tend to advance school democracy. The aim has been to change the common passive attitude to responsibility and co-influence. The council has the right of decision on matters pertaining to discipline and undisturbed working conditions. It confirms the rules of various school clubs and decides on joint school activities. Its most important task, however, is to coordinate general educational planning and to initiate and continue planning connected wiih classroom instruction. It may submit recommendations on curriculum development as well as on the textbooks used. Together with the implementation of the school council system the parents' opportunities to participate will also improve' (ibid., p. 8).

Along with other aspects of the cooperative tasks of teachers a press towards more cooperative relationships with pupils. University unrest at the end of the Sixties was reflected in the setting up of organizations in a number of countries for pupils of secondary school age, which in many respects matched the radical opinions and actions of their university counterparts.

Not all educational authorities were hostil to the aspirations of their students. In Sweden, at the end of 1969, the central organization of Swedish pupils was given a week in which they were.

> 'allowed to present totally pupil-orientated activities, such as general meetings to which representatives of different branches of society were invited. A list of questions for discussion in class had been drawn up in the hope of creating a more critical attitude towards textbooks and the content of the teaching. The idea was also that proposals for changes in the school should be put forward in order to influence the conditions in the school' (Rodhe, 1974).

The resolutions passed by the students after the final day of discussion included the following :

'1. *Marks*

We demand a discussion of the marking system, because of the following criticisms that have been made of the present system :

(a) the marks create a competitive situation which makes cooperation and solidarity between pupils difficult;

(b) the marks create a gulf between teachers and pupils;

(c) the marks lead to a fight for points which overshadows the interest for the subject.

2. *Textbooks and curricula*

We demand that

(a) the study material should devote more space to different opinions;

(b) the source material should to a greater extent be rendered as an account;

(c) the curricula and study materials should be subject to further penetration on a central and local level.

3. *The relationship between teacher and pupils*

There is an unnatural antagonism between teachers and pupils which must be overcome. It arises above all because of the marking system. The antagonism makes it difficult for both teachers and pupils to enjoy the degree of freedom of speech that would be desirable.

4. *School democracy*

The school is our place of work. Therefore we demand that

(a) all those working in the school should have an equal opportunity to participate in decisions;

(b) this right to participation should apply to all school levels;

(c) we are given full insight into all questions and decisions that affect our situation.'

Here can be seen the same pressures towards a romanticized group solidarity, embracing all categories of educational personnel, that has been in evidence in universities and colleges over the past decade. Any form of evaluation or assessment is seen as divisive, and there is a stress upon the educational experience for its own sake, rather than as preparation for some form of subsequent employment, least of all for the hierarchical, status-conscious social world outside the school.

Staff at the Malmo School of Education who have been concerned with a number of parallel investigations into teacher education and the role and function of the teacher, suggest that teacher functions, defined as 'the main type of tasks connected with the job', as against the teacher's role, by which is meant 'those expectations that different persons, including the teacher himself, have about his job' are divided into two main groups—primary and secondary.

The primary functions of the teacher include tasks connected with pupils' cognitive development, which takes in motivating the individual, introducing relevant knowledge, individualizing instruction and creating a positive learning environment. A second primary function is with tasks relating to pupils' social and emotional development, including experience of diagnosing pupils' needs, the ability to diagnose and to deal with group situations, and the ability to function cooperatively with children. The third and final primary function takes in what the teacher has to do by way of developing teaching aids and teaching media.

Among the secondary functions identified by the Malmo team are the cooperative or communicative functions, which have so do with the way in which the teacher interacts with his colleagues, with heads of schools, with specialists (which requires knowledge and understanding of both the possibilities and the limitations of such specialist assistance), and the development function which has to do with teachers' own personal and professional growth, as well as in-service activities that bear upon the development of the school as a social institution. As a result of the experimental work undertaken, it is claimed that the isolation of the teacher has to a substantial extent been broken down :

> 'A rather narrow view is often found among teachers: my class, my classroom, my teaching aids and so on. Working together with others has taught the teacher to listen more to others, not only teacher colleagues but also to many other adults within and outside the school. A more broad minded attitude to others people's ideas and views is a natural consequence of this. Attitudes towards cooperation with other adults have been found extremely positive in the evaluation of teaching in Malmo' (Rodhe, 1974, p. 48).

The teacher as agent of social and educational equality

The educational goals that people profess are, in part at least, reflections of the major roles and complexes of roles that they play in society. The fact that a great deal of human activity is concerned with getting and making a living that the individual's social position is dependent on his wealth, income and occupation, and that the range and style of his familial, cultural, political and interpersonal activity are closely associated with such occupation and social position means that many statements of educational goals are inevitably concerned with the performance of economic roles of one kind or another. Educationists have frequently seea a conflict between such goals and those which relate to the spiritual and emotional needs of the individual.

> 'Any educational system has two primary responsibilities—the first to society at large, the second to the individual. Its duty to society at large is primarily an economic one—to provide an appropriate educational background for the men and women who will be required at various levels to administer and develop the total economic system of the country. The second duty—that to the individual—is to develop his full potentialities, to equip him, in all ways possible, to meet the demands which life will make upon him, and to help him towards a satisfying individual life. In its first role it is on the side of Humanism. These two duties of the educational system to society and to the individual will nearly always pose conflicting requirements . . .' (Mumford, 1967).

It is not difficult to argue, as Durkheim, Mannheim and many other sociologists have done, that in an industrialized and market-based society, the facts of economic life are essentially related to the possibilities that exist for individuation and cultural and political pluralism, and that the distinctions made in the preceding quotation are ultimately unreal. But this may not help very much at the school and system level, where decisions still have to be taken about vocationalism and specialization, about the relation of various kinds of educational provision to the individual's post-school life.

Analyses of educational policy indicate that one of the most pervasive themes of the past three decades has been the part that the educational system might play in fostering social equality. Conceptions of the teacher's role have been influenced by egalitarian policies, and these have implications for the way in which teachers are educated and trained.

In the fifteen years from 1955 to 1970, a demand that the educational system should facilitate greater equality of opportunity played a part in educational policy-making in a large number of European countries. In the UK, every major educational report since 1944 has been concerned with it in one way or another, the sociology of education as an organized discipline virtually owes its existence to it, it has become de rigueur for educational statesmen to include references to its implications in their statements and speeches. Debates about the future of the independent and direct-grant schools, the reorganization of secondary education, the structure of higher education, streaming, banding and school organization, home/school relationships and parental choice in education, all show its influence. In a valuable review of debates about equal opportunity, Silver (1973) goes so far as to claim that 'the discussion of education and social class has been the most prolonged educational issue of the twentieth century in Britain'. He goes on :

> 'In its early phases, particularly in the 1930s and 1940s, it was related closely to psychological views of intelligence. From the 1950s it was the essential concern of the rapidly growing sociology of education. Philosophers have been engaged in the discussion of the concepts, and the arguments in favour of wider opportunity have sometimes been conducted in economic terms. Given the political repercussions of the discussion, some of the most interesting recent literature has been produced by political scientists. The record of the discussion is of major importance to the historian.'

Towards the middle of the Sixties, it appeared that virtual consensus had been achieved between the political parties on the issue of fostering equality of opportunity. One of the two quotations that follow is by the then leader of the Conservative Party, the other from the election manifesto of the Labour Party for the same year :

> 'Our educational aims are two-fold: to give the highest possible standard of education to all children, and to ensure that those with special abilities have the opportunity to develop them to the full.'

> 'Our purpose is to improve the opportunities for the average child and at the same time to ensure that the ablest are not held back. So that all children can develop to the utmost of their abilities and have every opportunity to fulfil their potential.'

The first of the two quotations is that from the Labour Party manifesto, the second by the leader of the Conservative Party. But the sentiments are practically interchangeable.

Kogan (1975) has classified educational policies as 'educational, social, economic and institutional'. He identifies thirty-five main policy themes that showed themselves in parliamentary debate and government policy during the period 1960 to 1974, and among these 'those associated with the social value of egalitarianism have been, perhaps, the most important in our period' p. 62).

In Sweden, there has been similar concern with the pursuit of egalitarian educational policies. Following a number of official inquiries, the previously divided pattern of education has been replaced by a nine-year 'common school', within which the selection of programme and options that nave implications for social advancement is deferred until a comparatively late stage. Similarly in Finland, and in those German Lander which have Social Democratic majority governments, there have been attempts to reform the structure of education in such a way as to maximize the opportunities that boys and girls from less advantaged backgrounds have to secure academic and professional qualifications and to become socially mobile.

Much of the research associated with the equal opportunity debate during the Fifties and Sixties was concerned to demonstrate the impediments to success that faced the child from a disadvantaged home. Studies in a number of countries documented the part that education had played in the distribution of life chances. The cumulative impact of this research was considerable. Study after study in which measured intelligence was controlled against educational performance and social outcome showed that middle class children and those from other advantaged backgrounds continued to be over-represented in the ranks of the upwardly mobile and the academically and occupationally successful.

The main implications of all this for teacher education lay in ihe new demands made on the teaching force by the coming into existence of all-through comprehensive schools. the gradual disappearance of ability grouping, streaming, setting and banding at the primary/elementary level, and the introduction of new types of external examination (e.g. the CSE in the UK) designed for those less able pupils who hitherto had not been candidates for any form of public examination. As the schools became comprehensive, so there was a demand for teacher education to follow suit. Debate and policy-making in teacher education began to stress the need for a unified profession, and for entry requirements and length of education and training for teachers in primary and lower secondary schools to be equated with those that had traditionally applied to the selective Gymnasien and grammar schools. There was pressure to lengthen the course of training from two to three, four or five years, and to ensure that all students, not just those intending to teach the younger age groups, had some acquaintance with psychology of learning and motivation and the disciplines that facilitate understanding thc social background of pupils who might not hitherto have stayed on at school.

As we have seen in other chapters, these trends, reflected in the upgrading of institutions and courses, in new ideas about the content of teacher education, in the introduction of compulsory professional training for graduate and specialist teachers and in the emphasis found in some systems on social science disciplines, are still working themselves out in current policies and planning.

By the mid-Sixties the egalitarianism debate took a new and sharper turn. As Bowman (1975, p. 74) has pointed out, its aims were never very clear. She suggests that

> 'the most casual perusal of what is being written in our day about "equity" in the provision of education reveals confusion and inconsistency, infused often with incoherent fantasy',

and goes on to suggest some of the diverse definitions of equity that had been employed in recent debates :

1. 'Giving equal amounts of schooling (equal schooling "inputs") to every individual.
2. Bringing every individual to a stipulated minimum level of performance, whatever happens thereafter.
3. Bringing every individual to the same level of performance.
4. Ensuring that each individual receives the schooling that will enable him to realize his full potentialities.
5. Bringing each individual to the point at which his margidal ratio of added-learning to inputs matches that for other individuals.
6. Providing equal opportunity for access to education, whether individuals utilize that opportunity or not.

7. Ensuring proportional representation from every ethic, social status, sex, or other relevant category of individuals.'

Bowman's list identifies several of the themes that have preoccupied educationists concerned with problems of equity during the past decade. For present purposes, it is sufficient to mention a number of themes that have implications for the organization and content of teacher education beyond those already identified as stemming from the earlier 'equality of opportunity' emphasis.

1. Attempt to identify and to meet the specific need of 'disadvantaged' groups;
2. the application of policies of positive discrimination;
3. the effects of new research evidence on the part played by schools and teachers in the determination of life chances; and
4. Utopian and revolutionary value-orientations.

Among the categories of persons that it is claimed are 'disadvantaged' under our present educational arrangements are the lower paid, rural youth, members of certain religious denominations, the inhabitants of remote and/or economically and socially deprived regions, immigrants, members of minority ethnic groups, and women.

The kinds of educational provision designed to help the members of such groups were at one time defined as 'compensatory'—

> 'special educational provisions or adaptations designed specificially to overcome learning difficulties or handicaps in school associated with poverty, class, status, nationality, race, cultural background, home conditions or adverse environmental conditions generally, as distinguished from organic causes' (Burke 1969).

The concept of compensatory education has since been challenged in terms of its assumptions of cultural homogeneity and hegemony. In Bernsteins's (1970) words :

> 'The concept "compensatory education" serves to direct attention away from the internal organization and the educational context of the school, and focus our attention on the families and children . . . the school has to, "compensate" for the something which is missing in the family and the children are looked at as deficit systems. If only the parents were interested in the goodies we offer, if only they were like middle class parents, then we could do our job.'

The debate in recent years about concepts of compensatory education, the part that the teacher might play in meeting the specific needs of disadvantaged individuals and groups, and the relation of this efforts to so-called middle-class values reflects some of the central problems of the relationship of education and society. As such, these issues have important implications for the education of teachers, not all of which have yet been fully grasped, let alone translated into coherent programmes of action.

Educators recognize that the value and significance of what goes on in schools, colleges and universities must not be reckoned in accordance with the social origins or occupational destinations of students. Market forces and the cash nexus provide no criteria by which we may measure the worth of the child's first poem, the slow learner's halting attempt to read, the nervous, unathletic boy's first home run, or the adolescent's struggle towards emotional maturity. Coupled with this is an awareness that, as things are, the scales are weighted from the start in favour of the child from the advantaged home, and that, contrary to the impulses of educators themselves, underprivileged families often measure the quality of the education their children receive by the extent to which social mobility is made possible. In conventional 'equality of opportunity' terms:

> 'The empty-belled migrant from the land moves to the

city in search of employment for himself, but for his children he is in search of education, the fulfilment of the twentieth century city dream, in which each of his sons will be an urban professional, a lawyer, a doctor, an engineer, a politician or a university professor' (Lewis, 1969).

In the face of evidence that the underprivileged view education in largely instrumental terms, the reformer feels himself trapped. He wants to provide an education valid in its own terms, that provides life-enhancing experience, opportunities or personal growth, a proper sense of individual and group achievement. He judges that some of the values represented in the life-style of the disadvantaged are by no means morllay inferior to those of the middle classes, that to 'succeed' in terms dictated by stratified, status-conscious society may involve substantial losses not only for those who correspondingly 'fail' but for the successful themselves. At the same time he knows that to provide an education more directly relevant to the personal and cultural needs and immediate interests of the majority of students may be to deprive them of opportunity to compete for the rewards and privileges characteristic of advanced technological societies. He knows, too, that these rewards and privileges arise form the operation of a system which, for all its faults and disfunctional features, has made possible longer life, less burdensome work, greater leisure and a wider choice of goods, services and styles of living than at any other time in history. If he is politically sophisticated, he may also have views on the extent to which the achivement of greater equality is possible only at the cost of a certain measures of liberty.

It has been in struggling with these dilemmas that educators have at one time or another embraced doctrines of intelligence which claim to provide a morally neutral legitimation for the selection, rejection and allocation that a meritocratic system requires; supported the provision of 'separate but equal' kinds of secondary education for the so-called non-academic child; participated in campaigns to stress the social importance and individuals dignity attached to manual and technical occupations; underwritten the attempts of governments to create and to obtain status for the non-university sectors of higher education; designed programmes of compensatory education and endeavoured to enlist community resources in the improvement of both rural and urban educational provision.

More recently, educationists have sought to reconcile on the one hand the demands of minority groups for 'recognition' on their own terms with, on the other, the provision of a form of education that will facilitate the assimilation and integration of such groups into society. The time required to design and to implement programmes of black studies, to teach migrant languages in schools, and to undertake activities of a kind that express a claim to cultural equality, may all be at the cost of action to facilitate the assimilation and integration of minorities into the wider society, and the penetration of power and clite groups by successful minority representatives. To some extent such penetration has become devalued by the assertion that such successful individuals all too easily take on the values and assumptions of the established elite, and by the claims made for cultural and group activism. The political and social consequences of the kinds of pluralism implicit in the views of those who asert claims for the recognition of separate identities are poorly worked out.

Both conservatives and radicals are interested in these issues, if for rather different motives. For radicals, the lessening of educational disadvantage is an essential step towards reducing the material and cultural inequalities that categorize our society. For conservatives, it reduces the threat to civil order and property posed by the existence of ghetto conditions and by the attitudes spread in the slums, and frees the members of minority groups to take their full part in the operations of a market economy.

Whereas structural and institutional solutions to these problems were those that attracted most attention ten years ago, recent trends have been both more individual, in that they placed greater stress on the subjective consciousness of difference and of blocked opportunity, and collective, in their emphasis on the possibilities of group self-help.

Whether the problem is that of community breakdown in the urban area, or the removal of educational handicaps for migrant workers, or greater opportunities for women, recent years have seen a shift away from externally-imposed remedies and solutions, towards approaches designed to help individuals and groups to learn to help themselves. Interventionist strategies are being evaluated more in terms of their positive multiplier effects than with respect to immediate pay-offs.

Those who advocate these approaches still give education a key place in efforts to promote economic, societal and community development. But it is a very different kind of education from that traditionally embodied in the activities of schools and teachers and examination boards. It seeks, first and foremost, to identify and to enlist the existing educational resources of the groups concerned. It tries to start from where people are, and to construct its goals and objectives in terms of subjective perceptions, rather than by imposing standards and aims from without. It places the highest value upon participation at each stage and at all levels, of those involved. It recognizes that the availability of new technologies will do little to solve problems unless they are congruent with existing or emerging community values and attitudes.

The teacher's part in all this is to be played as much outside as inside school. So students in training undertake community projects, spend evenings, weekends and sometimes periods of several weeks in youth clubs and community centres, and in doing so satisfy the validating bodies' requirements for specified periods of 'practical experience', read the works of Paolo Freire and try to understand the diverse needs and problems of disadvantaged groups and minorities.

6

The Emerging Model of Teacher Education

The European Context

Over the past decade teacher education has been a subject for discussion and reform in most developed countries. No single reason accounts for attention being focused on the ways in which teachers are selected, educated, trained and inducted into their profession. As in most areas of human activity, the factors that help to focus attention upon a particular set of issues and problems at the given time are complex and have diverse origins. Some of the influences to be listed in the following pages cannot be clearly distinguished from one another, and overlap both in their origin and in the way in which they manifest themselves within the system. Nonetheless, it may be useful to tease out some of the stands that have contributed to recent and ongoing movements for reform and change.

Over the past twenty-five years, problems of teacher supply have been endemic in many countries. These derive salience from difficulties in predicting variations in birth rate and in the demand for pre-compulsory and post-compulsory education, together with the cash and opportunity costs involved in financing growth. As we have seen, overall shortages have recently, in some countries, turned into sectoral and regional surpluses. All these issues receive greater prominence because of the difficulties of forecasting and planning in situations of demographic, economic and, sometimes, legislative uncertainty.

The past quarter-century has been one of growth in nearly every aspect of educational provision, not least in the size of the teaching force and of the institutions and courses by means of which future teachers are prepared. Large-scale and expanding enterprises command greater attention than those that are small, stable or in decline. From being a relatively insignificant aspect of post-secondary education, the preparation of teachers became in the 1960s a large-scale enterprise, employing substantial capital outlay, large numbers of staff, and an increasing proportion of the resources devoted to post-secondary studies.

A willingness on the part of governments to find more money for education during the Fifties and Sixties was linked to a widespread belief that education and economic affluence were causally related. At least on casual inspection, it seemed that those countries with the best educated populations were also the most wealthy and prosperous. At every level, from sophisticated and economic sociological analysis, to vulgar assertions about the movement from the 'muscle-driven' to the 'mind-driven' society, the economic importance of education was urged upon politicians, administrators and the general public—not least by educators themselves. Many educators were willing to use economic arguments to sustain their belief in the non-economic values of knowledge, understanding and scholarship. Inevitably, as faith has declined in a simple one-to-one relationship between economic and educational growth, so have the arguments—and the credibility—of such advocates, who have lost their power to muster legislative effort and resources. In their day, those who argued that for both individual and society the route to prosperity lay through education, could also assert the importance of there being adequate numbers of well-qualified teachers available for work in schools, an assertion that took on added point against what was in many countries a chronic shortage of adequately trained staff.

To the economic arguments that sustained the importance of education in general, and teacher education in particular, there were added after the mid-Sixties a number of political impulses, deriving from the anxiety and interest caused by student involvement in the social and political disturbances of that period in Europe.

'May 1968' has achieved its own place in the hagiography of student movements. Whether the events of that period, especially in France and Germany, will in the context of history be seen to be as significant as they may appear today and to those directly concerned, is difficult to predict. Nonetheless, the activities of students at the barricades and the widespread publicity given to occupations and disruptions in universities and secondary schools throughout the world served to focus attention on the part that teachers play in the political socialization of their pupils and students.

It became clear that there was at least a minority of teachers in both universities and schools whose commitment to the values of bourgeois capitalist society was less than total, and a smaller number with an active revolutionary engagement. Some people within teacher education, and a number from outside, began to scrutinize the courses and academic style characteristic of the colleges and departments of education in terms of their implicit or explicit political content. Critics tended to concentrate their attention on those more recently developed aspects of programmes, such as studies in the sociology of education, that could be held to 'undermine' traditional values. The need began to be urged for society to exercise a closer control over what went on in such institutions. Given the importance attached to academic freedom, this was seldom expressed by direct government action. Its significance can, however, be inferred from action that has taken place in a number of countries to bring the selection, training and certification of teachers under the control of bodies more broadly based than those of the academic community.

Dissatisfaction with the work of some of the institutions hitherto responsible for the personal and professional education and training of teachers also played its part in the movement for reform. An increasingly unionized and self-conscious profession was in some cases vocal in its condemnation of the inadequacies of the preparation of its members. Demands were made in some countries for more professional involvement in this work. It was argued that the colleges, admittedly sometimes for reasons outside their control, such as the need to double and redouble the number of students in training and thus to recruit large numbers of less well-qualified and able staff, were failing to meet so-called 'needs' of schools and of society. In some countries political leaders committed themselves to the investigation and reform of teacher education as part of their electoral platform. Academics and university men condemned the poor intellectual standards of the training provided for the majority of the teachers. Students complained about being over-taught, without at the same time being intellectually or professionally stretched, and drew attention to the failure of many college staff to refresh or renew their experience of the 'real life' of the classroom.

All this dissatisfaction was given greater emphasis by reforms simultaneously taking place in many aspects of primary and secondary education. In some countries (e.g. Sweden, the United Kingdom) there was a strong commitment to the all-in secondary school and to 'comprehensive' principles, which made legal or de facto separation between training for different types of secondary education no longer appropriate. The period of schooling was being lengthened at both ends—by more widespread provision of pre-school opportunities, by the raising of the statutory leaving age, and by increases in the proportion of those who remained at school or in some kind of continuous full-time education beyond the statutory leaving age. These and other factors implied changes in the teachers' roles with important and consequences for the ways in which teachers were trained. As we shall see in later chapters, reforms in primary and secondary school organization have been among the most significant factors in bringing attention to bear on the means and methods of teacher preparation.

With changes in school organization went a new interest and concern with curriculum development, with ensuring that the growth of knowledge and of the range of skills relevant to life in a post-industrial society were reflected in the contents and methods of teaching in schools. Whether in centralized or decentralized systems, subject to explicit curriculum direction (e.g. through guidelines issued by the Ministry of Education, as in France or Sweden) or implicit control (e.g. by common voluntary adherence to national or regional systems of examinations, as in England and Wales), the teacher has an increasingly important role as a curriculum innovator. This has inevitably required modifications in training, with particular reference to the importance of in-service provision.

Within teacher education itself, the availability of a wider range of relevant techniques—micro-teaching, simulation, audiovisual methods of presentation, field-based courses, computer-assisted instruction—required additional expenditure, the appointment of suitably qualified and experienced staff, and all the steps necessary to ensure institutionalization. In some cases, the costs of the apparatus and equipment required meant that small units were no longer economic, and the enhanced importance of technology supported the case for larger units.

Alongside the introduction of new techniques, new knowledge was becoming available about how pupils and students learn, new theories were current about the processes of professional socialization and induction, and larger numbers of well-qualified psychologists, sociologists, philosophers, historians and other specialists were available to teach in the colleges and departments. For some of these people, teacher education became a study in its own right. Journals were started, flourished or died, professional associations of teacher educators were set up, conferences arranged, and the interests of the international agencies aroused. More people writing about how teachers were educated and trained, more individual and team research on different aspects of the process, all helped to put the subject closer to the centre of educational attention.

Some aspects of what involved gained from their relation to wider movements of educational reform, e.g. the stress upon life-long education, education permanente, and recurrent education, on the obsolescence of skills and knowledge obtained during initial periods of preparation and the importance of an institutional and personal commitment to learning and skill development a career. The recent emphasis upon in-service education and training is one of the most significant developments in teacher education of the past decade, and one to which due attention will be given in the chapters that follow.

Alongside these factors that have helped to gain attention for teacher education, there are others which, in a work of broader compass, would also require attention. For example, the pressure towards greater participation in decision-making by elected representatives, by parents and students, alongside a movement for regional devolution, by means of which the political tensions characteristic of the contemporary state are contained, plus a related concern with accountability, which limits the professional autonomy of practitioners in the interests of client and public, have all had their effect on the values of teacher education and the institutional arrangements and programmes that characterize different countries. We shall see some of these strands appearing in various places during the analysis that follows.

The interest of national authorities in problems of teacher education has also stimulated activity by the European-based inter-governmental organizations, and in the past five years a number of major conferences and meetings have taken place, reports commissioned and new initiatives displayed.

In a statement in May 1973, the then Commissioner for Education of the European Community (Ralf Dahrendorf) outlined what the Commission saw as the 'major problems of education . . . common to all developed industrial countries' :

(i) How to give effect to the citizen's right to education and to achieve equality of opportunity for all;

(ii) How to cope with new problems of scale . . . in secondary and tertiary education;

(iii) The relationship between education and occupation (content of education, structures of demand, career prospects, etc.);

(iv) The exploration of new technical and organizational methods of opening the way to adult education;

(v) Qualitative changes in the content of education and in the organization of the educational system in the light of the demands for democratization and the tendency to adopt a critical attitude towards the economy and society' (Dahrendorf, 1973, p. 101).

The quality of teacher education is relevant to a number of these themes, and the Communities have been active in fostering the exchange of teachers between member states, encouraging a European dimension in the curriculum of both schools and colleges (Janne, 1974, p. 50), and working for the greater mutual recognition of certificates and diplomas. A number of countries have thrown open their post-experience, in-service courses to nationals from other states, and in the United Kingdom bursaries have been made available to enable several hundred teachers from other member countries of the Community to study alongside their English counterparts during vacations and at other times.

Strictly within the terms of the Treaty of Rome, the Communities' contribution to educational policy-making is somewhat limited. In fact, the Commission and the Education Ministers have sought to go beyond a strict interpretation of the Treaty, and towards the end of 1975 Ministers approved a seven-point educational action programme which included such objectives as the establishment of an inquiry into education and unemployment among youth in the Community, the promotion of European language learning, and the facilitation of youth and student interchange. The sum set aside for the support of this programme was relatively modest—some three hundred thousand pounds—and there was comparatively little emphasis placed on students in the field of higher education.

Among member governments, the French have been active in persuading the EEC to take a larger part in the development of higher education, and it was proposed at the end of 1975 that a large independent fund should be established, administered by a Board composed of government, private sector and higher education interests to aid suitable projects.

The former Minister for Universities in France underlined the importance of such a programme to his own country when he revealed that less than one-fifth of all the students from abroad who are studying in France are from other EEC countries, that only 282 members of higher education institution staff were from the EEC, and only 67 academics from France were working in higher education elsewhere in the Community (Times Higher Education Supplement, December 12, 1975).

The European Communities have been joint sponsors of work undertaken by the recently established Institute of Education of The European Cultural Foundation, in the work of which the Carnegie Council on Policy on Studies in Higher Education has also played a part. Although several of the major studies planned by the Institute, including work on the policies and problems of paid educational leave, quantitative trends in higher education, response to the need for 'non-traditional' forms of higher education, constraints on the free movement of students at undergraduate level and the organization and financing of youth services of countries of the Communities, are relevant to problems of teacher education, none of them is centrally concerned with this aspect of educational provision. A Conference held at Liege in June 1976 under the auspices of the Institute, and with the support of the Council of Europe and other European agencies, resulted in the establishment of an Association of European Teacher Educators, with headquarters in Brussels.

But it is UNESCO, OECD and the Council of Europe that have so far sponsored the bulk of the work more directly related to problems of teacher education. A nine-day international conference was organized by UNESCO in Geneva in September 1975, which had as its theme the changing role of the teacher and the effect of such changes on preparation for the profession and on in-service training. The OECD sponsored a meeting on Teacher Policies in November 1974 that resulted in the production of a very large number of papers and reports from participating countries. The Organisation is currently working on analyses of teachers' tasks. The Council of Europe (Council for Cultural Co-Operation) has lately collected information from its twenty-one member countries on continuing education for teachers and its relation to pre-service training, and through the work of a number of its committees is continuing to examine these and related problems.

Although efforts are made to ensure adequate cross-representation at meetings and in the planning of programmes, there is inevitably some overlap between the activities of the various European bodies. The EEC, for example, in their action programme agreed in December 1975, committed the Commission to a study of ways to enable teachers to spend some time working in other Community countries. (The automatic transferability of professional qualifications under Article 57 of the Treaty of Rome does not include school teachers.) The Commission also committed itself to improving documentation and statistics on European education, and to collecting data on educational cooperation.

The extent of links between European countries in the field of teacher education is by no means restricted to the activities of the inter-governmental organizations. For example, an association of teacher education institutions exists in the United Kingdom with a view to stimulating links with similar institutions overseas. There are many colleges which have direct links with European universities or teacher education institutions (e.g. S. Martin's, Lancaster with colleges in Sweden, Didsbury College with Norwegian institutions) as well as many contacts between individuals in respect of exchanges betweed students and lecturers.

By studying statements and reports provided by European authorities in support of teacher education activities of OECD, the Council of Europe, the European Communities and other inter-governmental and international agencies, it is possible to discern a number of trends common to the development of ideas and practices in several countries. Substantial differences in organization and approach remain, and are likely to do so for a long time to come—for example, the more or less sharp distinction that many countries make between preparation for primary and for secondary teaching is showing itself resistant to the efforts of reformers—but there is enough common ground to make an effort to outline a general model worth while.

To outline a general model of teacher education is, of course, to theorize, and for an activity so large in scale and of such importance to the societies in which it is carried on; teacher education has been surprisingly atheoretical. This is not to use 'theory' in the same sense as practising teachers sometimes employ it to refer critically to the predominance of theory over practice in actual courses of training. What they mean—and students often echo their complaints—is that there is too much philosophy and psychology and history and not enough practical advice and help and opportunities to work with children.

But as Bernard Crick has noted, those 'who have no time for theory commonly hold the most interesting, sometimes arbitrary, often quite fantastic, general views on how things work and should work'. Any properly conceived course of teacher education gives students opportunities to become aware of the assumptions and beliefs that underlie their practice, and to acquire knowledge of a kind that will underpin the improvement of teaching. It is not, however, this kind of theory with which we are here immediately concerned, but with the theory of teacher education itself, with what we are about when we set out to educate or train a teacher to do a particular job in the classroom and school.

Outlines of a model

There is now no lack of descriptions of what goes on in colleges and schools of education, or of prescriptive statements about what should be included in the training of teachers for different age levels. There is also a growing body of research findings about the classroom behaviour of teachers and students, about what methods are most effective in achieving particular ends, and about the personal characteristics of serving teachers and new recruits. The sheer volume of all this writing is intimidating. Two examples will suffice.

In the United States two authors have collected together the instruments—tests, schedules, category systems—used in recent years to explore the interaction of teachers and pupils in classrooms. These fill sixteen volumes (Simon and Boyer, 1967, 1970). Reference has already been made to the Conference of the Organisation for Economic Co-Operation and Development (OECD) at the end of 1974 on policies for the training, recruitment and deployment of teachers. The forty-nine papers prepared in connection with the Conference ran to just under two-and-a-half thousand pages.

The efforts that all this material represents are to be welcomed if they throw more light on what we are about in the teacher training business, if they enable people from many different countries to profit from the knowledge and experience of their neighbours, and if they help us to take a few more faltering steps in the direction of improving the quality of education. But these things are going to happen only if somehow we can get all this effort and all this paper into manageable form.

We have to enable those who chair committees and devise syllabuses and assess students' performance to feel that there is at least the possibility of grasping the main elements of what is going on. This requires that we devise categories and identify variables that help them make sense of what they see and hear and read, and to communicate economically and profitably with others in the same business as themselves.

To do this, and to stimulate new research that will enable progress to be made, requires theory. It requires both the limited kind of theory that in the context of political science David Easton (1965) has described as 'any kind of generalization or proposition that asserts that two or more things, activities or events co-vary under specified conditions' and the general theories that he sees differing from other kinds of theories with respect to their scope and their coherence. The main objectives of such general theory in the political sphere are threefold :

> '. . . to establish criteria for identifying the important variables requiring investigation in all political systems; to specify the relationship among these variables; and to achieve these goals through a set of generalizations that hang together with greater rather than lesser logical coherence and interdependence' (Easton, 1965).

Teacher education is seriously short of both kinds of theory. The reasons are not far to seek. Systematic description and research in this field are of relatively recent origin; most of the relevant work has been done only during the last ten years. A good proportion of what has been done has been with the object of comparing the advantages and disadvantages of one kind of training with another, and has had limited and practical ends. Most recent studies are small-scale. Much of the more general literature on the subject is inspirational rather than analytical. The disciplinary bases of a great deal of the efforts of the past decade have been in experimental, developmental and social psychology; sociology; philosophers, historians and comparativists have displayed only limited interest, political scientists almost none at all.

The rate at which, in the Sixties, teacher education expanded to meet the shortage of teachers in most developed countries absorbed the energy and attention of many of those who might otherwise have been in the best position to monitor the process in which they were engaged and to theorize about it. More recently, the institutional diversification that has characterized the higher education provision of many European countries has begun to blur the lines between teacher education and other kinds of general education and occupational preparation. There is now a tendency for student choice of programme to be wider, occupational selection to be delayed, for training programmes to be undertaken in universities and polytechnics rather than in single-purpose colleges. Teacher education is becoming less easily identifiable as a specific academic and institutional process than was once the case.

All this helps to account for the paucity of theory about teacher education and for its relatively poor quality. The confusion that in this situation might be caused by a growing pile of books and research studies is reduced because, first, many of them are based on roughly similar sets of (often unexamined) assumptions about society, about child development and about the objectives of education, and second, because such experimental work as exists seldom permits generalization to classrooms in the real world or has specific and clear-cut implications for the content and organization of programmes of teacher education. Thus while there are difficulties in propounding anything that might have claims to be a theory of teacher education, there are certain trends discernible in European countries which reflect a measure of agreement about the characteristics of an ideal-type programme.

1. Potential teachers should be recruited from the same ability cohorts as the members of other professions,

should have successfully completed secondary education, and should be limited in number according to how many teachers it is expected in future years will be required and are capable of being employed.

2. The style of teaching for which the student is to be prepared will be more pupil-centred and interdisciplinary than in the past, will be innovative, geared to a continuous process of curriculum renewal, and will reflect a trend towards more open and flexible forms of pupil assessment. There will be more emphasis on various forms of cooperative teaching, and a broadened concept of the teacher's role, requiring some of the skills and knowledge of the diagnostician, the group leader, the guidance counsellor, the resource manager, the therapist and the community worker as well as those of the instructor.

   Such skills and knowledge will be of particular significance in relation to the educational needs and problems of children from under-privileged homes and those who do not respond readily to the regime of the school.

3. Potential teachers should follow a course which includes, either on a concurrent or consecutive basis, study of both the subject or subjects they will teach in school, and professional courses in education and the social sciences. The weight attached to subject as against professional courses will differ both between countries and among students preparing to teach particular age groups in individual countries.

4. The means of instruction employed and the organization of the courses should permit the continuous interplay of professional studies and professional practice. To this end full use should be made of TV, film and videotape, micro-teaching and other forms of simulation, interaction analysis and multi-media

presentation. There should be opportunities for a variety of group and individual work with students, both in classroom and non-classroom settings, and for appropriate supervision, feedback and evaluation in respect of more continuous periods of practical experience.

5. The processes of pre-service education and professional preparation, certification, induction, post-experience study and career development will constitute a continuous and interrelated sequence; staffing ratios and secondment arrangements will permit teachers to take advantage of in-service study opportunities without prejudice to the work of the school or of their classes. These opportunities will include further education and training that permits transfer to other kinds of work in schools or to specialist tasks in the education service.

6. Training institutions, certificating and employing authorities, members of the teaching profession and students need to be involved in the design, implementation and evaluation of teacher education programmes at all stages.

These groups of ideas do not say all there is to be said about trends in the education and training of teachers in Europe, but they constitute a model of the process that would be readily recognized in most European and other developed countries.

A diversity of influences has helped to shape this model. The educational ideas of Rousseau, Froebel, Montessori and Dewey, the researches of Piaget and Bruner, and the writings and practice of Hahn and Neill have played a part. So have the demands of students for greater democratization, and the opportunities that cheap travel has brought for educationists from many countries to take part in international conferences and to observe at first hand what goes on elsewhere.

At the same time, the model reffects a particular pattern of technological and social change, the acceptance of which has characterized the recent intellectual climate, efforts that have had to be made to come to terms with institutional inertia and occupational vested interest, and the flowering during the Sixties of a belief in the importance of education on the part of the family, for whom it spelled greater social mobility and improved life chances, those responsible for the economy, for whom it promised faster growth and greater efficiency, and the guardians of the local and national polity, for whom it held out hopes of more responsible and ordered social conduct.

This is a framework of ideas and assumptions which secures the allegiance of large numbers of those professionally concerned with teacher education, as legislators, school and system administrators and trainers. As a result of systematic and effective popularization it has permeated the thinking of parents and the lay public to a remarkable degree. It is a model that is essentially liberal, moderate, democratic and evolutionary. It tends in many countries to be somewhat in advance of what actually goes on in colleges and schools, but in recent years practice has been rapidly catching up with theory. Underlying the model is a loose, untidy assemblege of maxims, morals and beliefs' often internally inconsistent, sometimes too easily bent in response to strong winds of disapproval from left or right, but all in all displaying a remarkable resilience and capacity to assimilate new notions and to sustain liberal educational practice. It is exposed to the more systematic and often revolutionary doctrines of the de-schoolers, the Marxist intellectuals and social and political Utopians, the significance of whom is often exaggerated because of the dialectical nature of media presentation, in which good news is no news and there is a high premium on dissent. Bourgeois ideology, the rhetoric of socialization and a dash of hard-headed empiricism are combined in a way calculated to achieve the broadest possible basis of agreement.

Perhaps the most significant of the trends so far identified is the wish to organize the education and training of teachers as a continuous sequence, from the initial process of student selection up to and including retirement from the profession. It may be useful to discuss this process in a little more detail.

Teacher education as a continuous sequence

Such a sequence has five main elements.

Selection is the process by means of which applicants for training who possess the statutory minimum academic and personal qualifications are chosen or rejected in accordance with more or less explinit criteria and predictions of ability, potentiality and subsequent classroom success. In countries that have suffered chronic teacher shortages, especially for primary and lower-secondary schools, there has for some considerable time been very little real selection. Practically all those with basic minimum qualifications have been able to obtain a place in a normal school or college.

This has not, however, precluded selection within the total range of applicants by the more prestigious and better-placed institutions, which have often been able to pick and choose amongst first-choice candidates. In many countries there is now a supply of classroom and non-specialist teachers greater than the demand and institutions lower down the pecking order have better opportunity to be selective in filling their places. In some countries, such selection is strictly in accordance with academic criteria, with the cut-off point on the performance scale determined by the ratio of applicants to vacancies. Elsewhere, there is an effort to employ criteria based upon personality and character assessment, on interests, non-academic activities, commitment to teaching and other non-cognitive factors.

A strong identification by psychologists with the mental testing movement during the first half of this century encouraged a substantial number of projects on student selection (for reviews see Taylor, 1969b; Lomax, 1972). A realization that little real selection was taking place led to a decline in the significance of such work during the 1960s, but if pressure on places for teacher training grows during the next few years, we can expect renewed interest in the development, testing and validation of selection criteria. Such interest may remain small in countries which already have clear-cut criteria of acceptability, usually related to high-school graduation Elsewhere, where selection criteria are problematic, the findings of research may have a larger part to play.

Pre-service education and professional training has hitherto largely been conceived as 'figure' against the 'ground' of prior educational experiences and subsequent career, at least by those professionally concerned with such training. Increasingly, however, there is a willingness to see such education and training as no more than one element—albeit an important one—in a multi-stage process.

Thus conceived, and with some assurance that opportunities will exist for later systematic study, geared to the gradual enrichment of the teacher's experience, it is easier for teacher-educators to concede that some traditional course content is out of place in the pre-service sequence, and can safely and beneficially be left until later. Some have gone as far as to suggest that the main purpose of pre-service professional training should be directed to the needs of the students' first post (Hirst, 1975). Commissions responsible for recommending reforms in teacher education have either given considerable emphasis to the articulation of pre-service and later stages or have been able to assume the existence and partial implementation of appropriate in-service arrangements, e.g. the Joxe Commission in France took into account the existence of the law of 16 July 1971 which covered continuous training and education for employees.

But it is probably fair to say that the full effects of looking at pre-service education and training in the context of a process of continuous professional renewal have not yet been felt in most countries. In part, this is due to lack of structural means of articulation between the various elements in the overall training and career development sequence. To see the pre-service stage as part of 'recurrent', 'permanent', or 'continuous' teacher education is to argue for a clearer identification of those forms of knowledge and skill that are appropriate to this particular part of the teacher's career. Thus perceived, there is no longer a compulsion to crowd everything in to initial training since opportunities exist for more advanced forms of training to be provided later in the teacher's career.

Certification involves the conferment of recognized or qualified teacher status by the national, state or other teacher-employing authorities. In some countries this has traditionally been by means of a state examination, in which the academic and professional staff of the university or training institution have played only a minor role. Elsewhere, employing authorities accept the award of a university or college diploma or degree as constituting a sufficient claim to qualified status, although there is sometimes the requirement that the recommendation by the institution on behalf of a student should include a statement about his 'personal', as distinct from academic, suitability for teaching. Where the qualifying examination is set by employing authorities, it inevitably has a washback effect on the syllabus and methods of instruction employed in the training institution. This has sometimes had the effect of laying stress on what could be argued are for the primary teacher 'inappropriate' approaches to learning and efforts are now being made to encourage teaching styles in the training institution relevant to the approach that a student might use in his contact with children.

The induction sequence. Initial certification is commonly on a probationary basis. The former 'probationary year', during which a beginning teacher had to provide further evidence of his suitability, and on the successful completion of which long-term certification was granted, has now in some places been reconceptualized as the induction sequence, with a stress on positive training and learning aspects rather than on assessment functions. During the induction year or years, teachers have a lighter timetable, and are either required or encouraged to take part in classes and discussion groups under the auspices of the employing authority, a training institution, or both, with a view to maximizing the learning potential of this critical period and minimizing the problems—disciplinary, curricular, personal—that young teachers commonly encounter. In some cases, stress is being placed on the role of a 'professional tutor', a senior teacher with special responsibilities for the guidance of newly-joined members of staff. In the United Kingdom, the preparation and training, function and role of such professional tutors has generated a literature of its own since the idea was originally mooted in the James Report (see Chapter 10).

Continuing education. Reference has already been made to the importance of seeing each of these elements in terms of its place within a continuous and interrelated sequence. Decisions as to the content and organization appropriate to each element must take account of what has gone before, and what reasonably can be expected to follow. On this basis, post-experience study (often referred to simply as 'in-service training') must reckon with the varied age and experience of its potential students, and the kinds of expectations and demands they will make.

There is a tendency to limit the consideration of post-experience study opportunities for the teacher to such courses, conferences and other events as are provided by universities, colleges, employing authorities, specialist associations, teachers' unions and other bodies active in the in-service field. In fact, teachers are among the most frequent partakers of general and non-vocational adult and continuing education of all kinds. In the early years of the UK Open University, teachers accounted for a high proportion of the registrations, not just for professional courses and those in education, but the full range of subjects offered. It is probably fair to say that almost any experience that provides the teacher with fresh information about himself or the world he lives in, that increases his understanding and enhances his judgment, can make a contribution to the improvement of teaching and learning in schools. Elite schools in many countries have traditionally sought as teachers the graduates of high-status colleges and universities, with extensive knowledge of particular subject fields, a highly-developed sensibility and understanding, but without professional training. It has been assumed that most people of this kind have a commitment to the continued improvement of their own education, which is not necessarily the same thing as a willingness to attend courses and meetings arranged specially for teachers.

The man or woman who is widely read, has informed and cultured tastes in art, music, literature, and a civilized life style, brings qualities to the classroom which advanced professional training may focus and enhance, but for which it can never substitute. This commitment to self-improvement needs attention during initial training as well as at the in-service stage. As has been noted elsewhere (Taylor, 1970a) teachers trained to make proper use of print materials, and who have access to a good general and professional library, need never lack for ideas and inspiration. Thus the aim of any national system of post-experience provision should not be simply to make available courses, conferences and other professional study opportunities, but also to develop the teacher's own responsibility for learning and to encourage such self-educative efforts as the teacher is able to make on his or her own behalf.

Career development. Post-experience study takes its place within a broader concept of career development. Experience can be educative, but it is not always so (Wilson, 1975a). There must be opportunity for teachers to reflect upon their experience, to make use of the feedback they receive from colleagues, pupils and other professionals, and to find their proper place within a community of fellow teachers at the level of department, subject group, division or school. There is growing interest in many countries in the concept of 'staff development in the education service' (Pratt, 1973), and in the responsibilities that administrators and heads of institutions have for ensuring that the school is an environment in which not only children, but teachers can grow and mature.

The need for counselling and guidance facilities does not end with the successful completion of the induction stage, but is needed at many points in the teacher's career, especially when a change of employment or career direction is contemplated or planned. With the diminution in the range of promotion opportunities that accompanies the increasing size of units and the declining birth rate, it is important that individual educational institutions should give as many teachers as possible a chance to exercise personal initiatives in the development of their own work, and to assume responsibility, if not on a long-term career basis, at least in respect of short-term activities such as working parties and curriculum groups organized to undertake specific tasks.

Again within the context of career development, the needs of the teacher for advanced study opportunities have to be assessed and provided for. Such advanced study includes courses and programmes that lead to postgraduate awards and advanced specialist qualifications, research leading to doctoral degrees or their equivalent, and other academic or professional training at a high level. I have tried elsewhere to set out some of the objectives for work of this kind (Taylor et. al., 1974) :

'1. To advance, by means of both empirical research and reflection, knowledge about the process of education.

2. To bring the fruits of research and experience in the humanities and physical and social sciences to bear on educational problems.

3. To improve and extend the educational acuity, professional understanding and competency of individual practitioners in the field of education.

4. To provide initial preparation and training and appropriate further professional study opportunities for an increasing variety of specialist educational roles.

5. To stimulate a critical dialogue with the profession on matters affecting the structure and organization of the school system, the values and beliefs embodied in teaching procedures and practices and the continuous evolution of curriculum, pedagogy and evaluation.

6. To elaborate and sustain, among colleagues, professionals and the public, an awareness of the university's responsibility towards and involvement in the work of educational institutions at all levels.'

Finally, there is an aspect of the professional sequence that is often forgotten or neglected, and for which little explicit provision yet exists in any developed country, namely, preparation for retirement. This, one of the most significant watersheds in any individual's life, is traditionally little regarded, and only recently has begun to receive attention from social scientists and those concerned with personal growth and development. Whilst there has been no great increase in recent years in life expectancy of either males or females, there are some indications of a pattern of earlier retirement, especially in countries that are moving towards teacher surplus and wish to encourage older teachers to leave the profession and create opportunities for their younger counterparts.

The fact that resources devoted to preparation for retiremeut produce no demonstrable pay-off for the educational system or for society may help to explain neglect of this topic. Equally, it may have something to do with the denial of ageing that characterizes the ethos of modern Western society, and the cult of youth evident in advertising and the mass media. In any event, a shift in population balance towards older age groups, and the tendency for the period of post-retirement life to be prolonged, all indicate a need for schools and educational authorities to make appropriate provision for those who are about to give up full-time work. In a few countries it possible, without loss of salary or status, and whilst remaining in employment, to step down from more responsible and demanding positions some years before retirement is due, and to develop interests and activities essential to a satisfying post-retirement life, which have often been inhibited or denied by the demands of contemporary educational activity in school, college or university.

To conceptualize the education of the teacher as a continuous sequence from selection to retirement and beyond is not to suggest that a monolithic structure should exist within which all the various stages are planned, controlled and executed. Nor is it to argue for records of a kind that accompany a teacher from the beginning of his initial training through to the end of his career. Records may be valuable, but individual freedom requires that they contain only essential information, and that there are opportunities for every individual to make many fresh starts. Nonetheless, it is useful to think of the sequence in the terms discussed above, in order that authorities ensure that some agency exists at each and every stage by means of which teachers may be helped to identify and to satisfy their professional and personal needs. It is in these terms that the impact of research on teacher education must be assessed, not simply to the extent that it makes findings available which can be 'used' by the teacher in the classroom, or which contribute to the theories that both reflect and help to shape the teacher's experience, but for the light that it throws on the processes involved in the stages that constitute the entire sequence of teacher education and training.

7

Curriculum Change in Teacher Education

The context of school and post-secondary reform

As we have seen, while there is a tendency in several European countries for single-purpose teacher preparing institutions to become smaller in number and play a less important role in teacher supply, two fairly distinct patterns are being followed in the adaptation of teacher education to new post-secondary structures. In some countries integration is taking place with the university (e.g. Finland, West Germany), whilst elsewhere it is non-university institutions of higher education, such as the polytechnics in England and the regional colleges in Norway, that are chiefly involved (Ford, 1974).

The pattern being adopted in Finland would seem to have something in common with that which existed in the UK between the publication of the McNair Report in 1943 and the reorganization of the early Seventies. The teacher training colleges in Finland are being brought into the universities as teacher training departments, under the direction of a university professor. Within the departments, 'class teachers' follow courses for a degree in teaching; whilst those preparing to work in secondary schools follow subject and professional studies on a consecutive rather than on a concurrent basis, with the professional element occupying one full year. The authors of the report establishing this pattern maintain, however, that a four-year programme of study for all teachers should be the aim, and thus align themselves with the movement to establish a common basis of Preparation for those preparing for teaching all age groups and levels.

As in all European countries, arrangements for the education and training of teachers in Germany have been influenced by changes taking place in the organization of higher education as a whole. During the next few years, developments of higher education in the Federal Republic are likely to be within the terms of the Hochschulrahmengesetz (framework law for institutions of higher education), parliamentary approval for which was finally obtained in the last weeks of 1975. In various forms, the Bill had been under discussion for some five years, Earlier versions required that the Gesamthochschule (Comprehensive University) should become the universal form of higher education organization, but this is modified in the Act by agreement that institutions can instead be related as 'joint bodies,' rather than constitutionally merged.

Ministry of Education and university representatives are to cooperate through 'course reform committees' in the design of new programmes and methods of evaluation. The trend towards a highly participatory form of internal government is to some extent halted by the requirement, first. that each university must have a full-time head, who holds office for not less than four years, and second, that professorial and senior staff must have at least 51 per cent of the votes in all the institution's decision-making bodies.

In an attempt to limit the number of 'permanent students', normal periods of study have been laid down as comprising six to eight semesters (half-years), with the requirement that if a student does not register for the appropriate level of examination by due date, his registration will be null and void.

In some Lander, colleges of education are already being merged with new or existing universities, whilst elsewhere they have formed consortia with other higher education institutions, and are being designated cooperative comprehensive universities (Geissler, 1973). Elsewhere the Padagogische Hochschulen still exist to train teachers for primary and upper primary schools, and some of those who will take up posts in Realschulen.

Although higher education in Norway will continue to expand during the next few years, nearly all the growth will be in the new district colleges, which offer a mixture of basic university and other two-year vocational courses, and bring together a variety of institutions within each of seventeen regions of the country. At the end of 1974 there were 54,000 students in Norway, 35,800 in universities, 2,900 in regional colleges, 9,800 in teacher training and 4,500 in technical schools, with another 2,800 undertaking their studies overseas (Vaigo, 1975).

It is intended that by the late 1980s there will be some 80,000 places in higher education, taking some 20—22,000 students every year, which constitutes in excess of 30 per cent of the relevant age group. The 25,000 new places required to house this increased student population will, however, mainly be in the new district colleges, with only a small rise in the number of students in the existing universities (Duckenfield, 1975a).

This pattern of development is reflected in expenditure patterns, with the bulk of new money going to the regional colleges, which in 1976 had an increase of 26.3 per cent in their budget, compared with an increase in universities of only 11.4 per cent, most of which went on improved pay for academics (Duckenfield, 1976b).

The decision to implement a system of regional colleges followed a period of 'action-research' in which a number of institutions of regional college form were established on a trial basis in selected areas. It is intended that the regional colleges will eventually have some 40,000 students as compared with 50,000 in universities. Selection is still applied to students coming straight from school, although as is the case in most other countries, 'mature students' with work experience are given access without possession of the normal pre-requisites.

During the trial period, the six regional colleges operated autonomously alongside other institutions providing post-secondary education, but in terms of the goals earlier formulated by the commission on post secondary education :

1. To qualify matriculation candidates or others with an equivalent educational background for work in their chosen careers.

2. To qualify matriculation candidates or others with an equivalent educational background for further studies at university college.

3. To qualify stuents who have already taken more than the matriculation examination, e. g. part of a university course, for certain vocational tasks.

4. To satisfy the need for insight into certain subjects, without necessarily aiming at qualifying for a career or further studies (Skard, 1975).

It will be some time before the outcome of the Norwegian attempt to organize non-university higher education on a comprehensive basis can usefully be evaluated. It could be that the political situation will develop in a way that will preclude the full integration of institutions of a specialist and vocational character within the regional college structure. In this case, it can be expected that the existing colleges will continue to function, although not fully exercising their role as study centres within the larger regional structure.

Patterns of post-secondary reform in European countries

are very diverse (Taylor, 1970b) and this diversity is reflected in proposals and arrangements being made for relating teacher education institutions to new and emerging forms. It is noteworthy that where universities are largely free of central direction as to curriculum and internal organization (e. g. the United Kingdom) or are the province of a separate Ministry (e. g. France) there has been a trend towards retaining teachers colleges as part of the 'controlled' sector, either by mergers with what in England and Wales have come to be called 'public sector' institutions or by continuation as separate colleges. Since polytechnics and colleges do not have such a well-defined research role as universities, this may have effects on the volume of educational research in general, and teacher education research in particular, undertaken in the countries concerned.

Course structure and curriculum

Those countries taking steps to integrate the preparation of teachers for primary and for upper schools face problems in respect of the very different curricula that these two groups have followed hitherto. In Denmark, teachers for grades 1 to 10 have been prepared in colleges, which they enter after passing the upper-secondary leaving examination. The college course includes both subject and pedagogic studies. Secondary teachers have followed a university degree course, extending over some six years. Within the framework of proposals for the establishment of University Centres, which would bring together post-secondary institutions of different types, it was proposed that some of the modules forming part of the primary school teacher training should be integrated with those for secondary teachers. But these plans have still to be implemented (OECD, 1974e).

In countries like Denmark, where teaching duties, conditions of service and class sizes are all specified in legislation, there is a problem about reforms of teacher education that do not take account of intending or likely changes in the structure of schooling. Different sets of proposals for the recognization of upper-secondary and vocational education are under discussion in the country, and these plainly have implications for the structure and qualifications of the teaching force required.

Under present provisions, teachers trained in the colleges of education and working of primary and lower-secondary school- take a maximum of 45-minute lessons each year, averaging out at 28 lessons a week over the 40 weeks of term. The time allowed for the prepration and follow-up work required in connection with each lesson 1.6 hours. Teachers above the age of sixty work reduced hours, and there are also reductions for those teachers who have particularly heavy marking or preparation loads, who act as school psychologists, librarians or consultants. Administrative work and in-service training commitments also entitled the teacher to a reduction of teaching hours. The numbers of hours per week required of upper-secondary teachers is twenty-two. Not more than twenty-eight pupils may be taught in each primary, lower-secondary and upper-secondary class, and in 1973—74 the average in primary and lower-secondary schools was twenty to twenty-one and upper-secondary schools twenty-four.

Although a committee sat from 1972-74 to analyse the demand for teachers, and made some recommendations about the different lines of teacher preparations, there is no evidence at the time of writing that these proposals will be implemented in the near future (Torpe, (1972).

The Danish colleges of education (seminaria) provide a, curriculum that bears closer resemblance to that with which students in the United States or Great Britain might be familiar. Ford (1976) identifies six main categories of study :

1. Compulsory pedagogic subjects.
2. Compulsory studies in the teaching of basic subjects (e.g. Danish, religious knowledge, arithmetic, etc).
3. Music, physical education and home economics.

4. Civics.
5. Two main subjects chosen from a range of those appropriate for teachers up to the tenth grade.
6. One pedagogic specialism for teachers of the first five grades, or grades six to ten or those who are to teach children who are handicapped.

All this is in addition to periods of block school practice, and 'study practice', undertaken during the normal college term.

The course for those who have followed a six-year programme of study for their master's degree in the university comprises a single semester 'pedagogicum', which is essentially school-based, and; during which a salary is paid. Especially for those students practising in schools located a long way from the university, training is the responsibility not so much of university professor of education, but of experienced teachers in the Sohools. A different of training for secondary teachers is being tried at the University of Roskilde which involves a two-year basic education coure followed by group studies oriented towards the work of a teacher (Christensen, 1974).

As has been noted elsewhere, a unified system of teacher education is usually dependent upon a prior decision to implement a school reform that modifies or abolishes traditional distinctions and patterns of institutional separation, and in some countries also involves major problems with separately established teachers' unions. A Committee that reported to the Norwegian Minister of Education during 1976 recommended the intergration of teacher education, at present divided into that for laerer. or class teachers for the younger children and in practical subjects, for adjunkt, who teach thirteen-to sixteen-year-olds, and for secondary teachers, or lektors. The last of these are typically university graduates whose professional training has been limited to six months following a full academic coure, often of six or seven years in duration Duckenfield, 1976d).

Curricular issues and those relating to the control of teacher education are often associated. In proposals for the tecorganization of teacher training made by the then Minister of Education, M. Haby, early in 1976, which would involve the selection of teachers after the two-year general studies diploma, the DEUG, rather than as hitherto at the stage of CAPES and Agregation examinations, have important implications for the curricular content of the teacher training course.

It was proposed that students successful in the "free-recruitment' examination would continue their teacher training in specialist centres for this purpose, rather than in the universities as such. Responsibility for running the centers would thus fall to the Recteurs, appointed by the government, rather than to the academics. In the new centres, students would follow courses in their area of academic epecialization and also in didactics and pedagogies. This proposal, strongly resisted by teacher and student interests, as well as, by the universities, is also linked to supply considerations, since the numbers successful in the 'fre-recruitment examinations would be limited to the number of teaching vacancies likely to be avilable in the local Academie—

The new professional centres, although housed in universities, would not be subject to university control, and the Minister is reported as having said the university teachers are not competent to train those who are to work in the schools (Morgan, 1976b).

These proposals are linked to the reforms in the curricula of all stages of French education that came into effect in 1977. In the words of one commentator, these show the Minister's

'. . . concern to find ways of giving all children equal opportunities by providing common programmes with some options while deferring specialization and by adapting structures and teaching methods to diffeient needs and rhythms instead of insisting on unifrom treatment for all' (Farr, 1976).

The proposals attempt to achieves a closer reletionship between nursery and primary provision with work in the primary school based more closely on the assessment of individual capacities and needs. To some extent this will involve the grouping within classes the some critics have seen as a from of streaming and grading. Such grouping will continue into the secondary school it where heads will be free to adjust the curriculum to the progress of groups and individuals. A single secondary school will be provided for the age range of twelve to sixteen, with some optional programmes in the last two years, a common core of French, a common language, mathematics, human sciences, economics, natural and physical sciencesthe arts, manual and technical, skills physical education and sports making up the first two years of 'observation' Cycle.

The post-compulsory stage will be bassed upon a two-year common programme, undertaken either in conventional lycees generaux or in lycees techniques. The full three-year lycee course its first two years will comprise six of the courses followed between the ages of twelve and sixteen—French, a foreign language, mathematics, natural science, human sciences and physical education, plus some optional subjects, with these subjects or other specialisms being continued into the second year and a free choice involving specialization being postponed till the third year, the classe terminale de specialisation, in which only philosophy, physical education and sports remain obligatory. Admission to the third year will be dependent upon success in the Baccalaureat (Neave, 1977).

University studies in France are now organized in three cycles. The first cycle lasts for two years, and leads to the award of the Diploma des Etudes Universitaires Generales (DEUG). While the general framework of the DEUG is laid down on a national basis, universities have a substantial amount of choice in allocating sections of the curriculum to, e.g. consolidate basic disciplines, provide extra choice, or create additional functions. But the eight programmes of multi-disciplinary study leading to the DEUG, with teaching hours allocated to the main and supplementary disciplines, is laid down nationally and must be followed all universities. Similar programmes are to be established for the Licence, the examination for which is taken at the end of the first year of the second cycle, and the Maitrise, which is sat at the end of the four years. Students who have not completed all the requirements for the DEUG will be permitted to start their study for the Licence, providing they make up the necessary number of credits during the year.

In contrast to the UK, where independently-chartered universities are free to award their own degrees, those in France must submit their proposals to the government in order to obtain accrediation for their awards. The groups set up to appraise-the proposals by the Secretariat d'Etar aux Universities include a majority of academic members, but with one-third representing the 'cultural, social and economic' interests of France. Furthermore, where professinal elements are involved in second-cycle studies, these have to be looked at in relation to the needs and interests of the professions concerned.

The third cycle cf French university education leads to the award of a doctorate, and as in most countries, is pursued only by an elite minority of those originally enrolling for the first cycle. Research undertaken for third-cycle qualifications will as far as possible be geared to the perceived needs of the French economy, and the thesis originally required for the Maitrise will be replaced by more practical studies directed towards the achievement of skill in specific fields of business and industrial activity. Greater control is being exercised over the preparation of theses for the doctorate, including a Diplome d'Etudes Approfondies, taken after one year is a central stage in work for the doctorate. More supervision will be required, and a limitation placed upon the number of years over which the thesis may be prepared (Morgan, 1976a).

The proposals for the reform of teacher education introduced by M. Haby early in 1976 would give complete control over the content and curriculum of university courses for teachers to the central authorities. The teaching provided by the universities would be controlled by a contract between them and the Secretary of State.

In considering the reforms being introduced into French higher education, careful account must be taken of wastage rates, which in some faculties can reach as high as 80 per cent after three years of study. Over half of all students who enrol at university leave without obtaining a diploma. It is in this context that the Secretary of State for Universities proposed early in 1975 to introduce new admission requirements, which would turn the final year of lycee study into a period of orientation for university, and would require all potential students to pass in all three of their chosen subjects. Greater emphasis would also be placed on the admission of mature candidates, with some years of experience in commerce or industry, who would not be subject to the same tests as lyceens who go direct from school to university (Morgan, 1975a).

The division between the preparation of teachers for primary and secondary school seems likely to remain well marked in France for some time to come. The Ministry of Education has agreed with the National Primary Teachers Union that from 1978 all new primary teachers must, following the Baccalaureat spend at least two years in programmes of teacher preparation.

The professional course in the Ecoles Normales comprises two years of full-time study of subject and education courses, plus school attachments and block practice.

Intending secondary teachers follow the first and second cycles of the standard French university course, for the Diplome d'Etudes Universitaires Generales and for the Maitrise, and then take the CAPES examination for entry to a Centre Pedagogique Regional or CPR. But this is not the only way in which secondary teachers can qualify. Some can obtain entry after the first year of DEUG course to an Institut de Preparation aux Enseignements de Second Degre or IPES, whilst others still obtain entry to the Ecoles Normales

Superieures where a three-year course, mainly in science and arts subjects and with little pedagogical content, is provided.

In most of the German Lander, an intending teacher's professional training is also mainly school-based, undertaken in the Studien-seminar and comprising some eight to ten hours per week of teaching, observation of experienced teachers and a certain amount of theoretical study, mainly under the direction of experienced school staff (Ford, 1976). It is intended to retain the seminar system after the likely reorganization of basic teacher education into three types, comprising a three-year period of study in a primary college for primary teachers, three years in a university or college of education for those who will teach the 10 to 16 year age group, and four years in a university for the upper secondary teachers. Pedagogical studies are better established in the teachers colleges than in the courses provided by universities, although the latter are currently under review.

Ford (1976) has also noted the highly stratified character of teacher education in the Netherlands with several more or less distinct categories of training appropriate to particular types of school. Broadly speaking, the length of the course and the prerequisites in terms of secondary or university education correspond to the type of work the future teacher will undertake, from kindergarten at one end to pre-university preparation at the other. Pedagogical studies are well established in most forms of training, and the recent establishment of institutes of teacher training for secondary teachers associated with universities has served further to encourage the development of such work. Nonetheless, the proportion of such foundation and practical study is small in relation to continuing subject work, and can be taken alongside an appropriate stage of the latter. For example, the statutory content of the course comprises 48 hours of 'special method' undertaken by teachers in the respective faculties, and a period of teaching practice which varies markedly in length from one university to another.

The detail with which the curriculum for primary and secondary teachers in some countries is laid down is illustrated by the programme for those preparing to teach in pre-primary schools in the Netherlands :

> Throughout the training (lasting three years) students attend a total of at least 2,360 periods of 50 minutes duration, including preparation periods. The training . . . comprises at least the subjects and the number of periods given on the following table :

Subjects		*Number of Periods*
Pedagogics and psychology		240
Didactics and teaching methods		360
Dutch language and literature		240
Speech		80
Civics) History) Road safety)		160
Biology		120
Hygiene) Child care)		120
Music		200
Drawing Manual Skill	160) 160)	480
Physical education		240

For the higher general secondary school leaving certificate (HAVO), which is one of the requirements for admission to the first year of a teacher training programme, courses are provided in the teachers colleges themselves, in special departments which teach the fourth and fifth year of the HAVO course. The training course itself is for three years, at the end of which successful candidates are awarded the Certificate of Efficiency as a fully qualified primary teacher which also qualifies them to teach certain subjects, such as Dutch, arithmetic, geography, history and biology in the lower and intermediate general secondary schools.

Proposals have been under discussion in the Netherlands for the association of colleges preparing students for primary teaching, hitherto classified as 'vocational schools', and the universities. A draft Bill announced by the Minister of Education in the Netherlands in 1973 would have given vocational colleges the status of higher education institutions if they entered into a contract of cooperation with the university, by establishing a joint body in which the colleges and the university participated on a basis of parity.

University reaction to the Bill was muted, but the vocational schools strongly objected, on the ground that co-operation within the joint framework would be on terms dictated by the university, the values of which are not necessarily consistent with those of the vocational school.

'There is . . . a general conviction that university courses and the more practical courses of the vocational schools fulfil different, but valuable functions which must be safeguarded in a new system. Especially the function of the vocational school is seen as a vulnerable one. The higher prestige of theory and research may easily lead to a transformation of the practical courses, the more if their teachers (lecturers) have had a university education and have, in an increasing proportion, never entered into practice' (Moor, 1975, p. 76).

As in some other countries, the vocational school diploma that confers qualified teacher status also gives an individual opportunity to enter appropriate faculties in a university, irrespective of his or her possession of the customary entry qualifications. If and when the vocational schools are fully integrated with the universities, their most able students will no doubt transfer to university studies after the end of the first year rather than on the basis of their diploma.

In all this we have evidence of trends characteristic of several European countries—anxiety about the power of the 'academic' model in relation to the recognization of post-secondary education, concern about the respective role of government and university authorities in shaping the reform, a desire to upgrade teacher education and to bring it within the orbit of higher education proper.

On 18 June 1975, the Netherlands Minister of Education issued a discussion document (Contours of a Future Education System in the Netherlands) which proposed that a reform of the education system should take place along the following lines :

(a) A new primary school for the -—12 age group to take the place of the present nursery school for 4-and 5-year-olds and for primary school for 6-to 12-year-olds;

(b) A middle school for all 12 to 15-year-olds;

(c) A high school for those 16 and over, with 3 departments :

  (1) a two-year academic department which gives direct entry to higher education;

  (2) a vocational department with three to four-year course, offering training for employment in medium grade positions:

  (3) a vocational department with a two to three-year course, offering training for lower grade functions;

(d) Higher education on the principle of the coordination of the universities and higher vocational education;

(e) The introduction of the open school as the last link in the educational structure;

(f) Raising of the school leaving age to 18;

(g) Special education; fewer types of school and more attention paid to the educational needs of the child.'

As a consequence of reform based upon such principles, it was proposed that a new training course should be introduced for all primary school teachers instead of the present separate courses for those who are to work in nursery and primary schools respectively (Moller, 1972). The integrated course could contain a choice of two specialisms, one for young children from 4 to 8 years of age and the other for those who wish to teach the 8-to 12-year-olds.

New non-university teacher training courses would provide staff for the middle schools, and for teachers of practical subjects in the high school. Finally, there would be other courses to qualify teachers (presumably university graduates) for the two-year academic stream of the high school and for certain sectors of higher education. Some teachers from this group would work with the more senior and academically orientated pupils in the middle schools.

As far as the conditions of teachers' work are concerned, it is suggested that more aides should be appointed, to take over some of the present duties of teachers, especially in respect of organization of the supervision of pupils. Teachers should be represanted on the governing body of the school; and teachers' councils should be established, the duties of which would be 'to arrange the acquisition of material within a certain budget, and to decide on methods of assessment and on teaching methods. The teachers' council should also be involved or consulted in decision on appointments and the setting out of the school building'.

Finland is one of the few countries where specific qualifications are laid down for those who teach the teachers. There are also specific regulations concerning the qualifications of teachers in the practising schools associated with the teacher training departments, and staff of both groups are required to undertake one term's study every seven years on full salary.

A committee set up in 1973 to make new proposals for the reform of teacher education suggested in its interim report that all teachers should qualify by means of a single basic degree examination, following different curricula in accordance with their particular needs. This basic course would last four years, each of 34 weeks, and each group of studies—general studies (one year), specialized subject studies (two years), and differentiated studies (one year)—would include practice teaching, seen as 'a multi-stage process consisting of various kinds of teaching and work experience' (p. 24).

The process of reorganizing teacher education in Finland has highlighted the lack of information available on some issues.

'The reorganizing of teacher education has turned out to be a complex task. Its reform and continuous development call for large scale research work. Research is directed at the information need which has arisen from the reform of higher education. The central problems in this connection are the examinations reform and the realization of the general principles of the examinations reform in teacher education. This leads to at least three problem areas :

(1) Information is needed about educability in general and especially educability in teacher education.

(2) It is necessary to study the professional image of teachers and needs for its change.

(3) The reform of teacher education also requires general information for the development of higher education pedagogics. The pedagogical problems of teacher education must thus be seen as part of the general problems of higher education pedagogics'.

(Institute for Educational Research, University of Jyvaskyla, 1975, p. 4).

The separation of educational studies into component 'foundations' disciplines, which in the United States and Great Britain has led to efforts to find principles of integration that will prevent excessive fragmentation and academic specialization, does not appear to have occurred at all in some European countries. In Belgium, for example, the Ecoles Normales, in which teachers for the kindergarten, primary schools and lower secondary schools follow two-year courses of training, offer an integrated education course, in which psychology, history of education and a certain amount of sociology is taught by the same member of staff (Ford, 1976). This education course contains nothing about statistics, psychometrics or reseach methods. The remainder of the curriculum comprises a study of Flemish or French, geography, mathematics and science, and art, plus periods of practical teaching in schools.

Secondary teachers, educated in the universities, are required to pursue education courses for a minimum of 12 per cent of the 1,200 hours in their third and fourth years.

There are few countries in which thought has not been given in recent years to ways in which those parts of the teacher's initial course that deal with the principles of educational provision, in terms of the ideas and concepts of psychology, sociology, philosophy, history and other humanistic and social science disciplines, can be related more closely to the experience that the student obtains through periods of school practice and other school-based study. In the words of a statement made on behalf of the Austrian authorities to the OECD Conference on Teacher Policies (OECD, 1974b) :

> '22. All efforts involved in producing a new teacher training model must serve to improve the relation between theory and practice. In this it is important that the content of the theoretical instruction be integrated with the practical education so that, by degrees, in the course of the training, certainty and reliability in the planning and execution of teaching may be achieved.'

As in other countries, those concerned with the reform of teacher education in Austria have felt the lack of empirical studies relating the content and effects of teacher education programmes to the actual work which teachers carry on in their classrooms (Thanhauser, 1970). Klingler (1975) and his associates at the Hochschule fur Bildungswissenschaften, Lehrkanzel Schulpadagogik, Klagenfurt, have surveyed some four thousand teachers in the compulsory schools, and two thousand college of education students in an attempt to relate the content of the college course and the practical requirements of teaching. Interviews were also conducted with a sample of both students and teachers with a view to seeing how the relationship of theory and practice is viewed by members of both groups.

Among other studies carried on at the Hochschule fur Bildungswissenschaften was an inquiry into the motivation of students preparing for teaching in relation to the organization of their studies and their success on the course. A variety of different techniques—straight lectures without discussion, lectures with questions and discussion, team work sessions between lecturers and students, lectures combined with smaller seminars and with small group work, etc.—were employed, in connection with systematically designed courses in psychology, sociology and education.

Most teachers in the Austrian compulsory lower secondary school have traditionally been trained as primary teachers in the 'normal school' and have upgraded their qualifications by means of in-service study (Wingert, 1971). In 1971-72 special training courses for teachers in the lower secondary schools were introduced to colleges of education, and the Federal Ministry of Education and Arts has been engaged in evaluating the success of this innovation.

The three-year (six terms) course includes 'Sciences of Education', including psychology, sociology, general theory, didactics and an introduction to the legal basis of the educational system, within which a student chooses one subject of concentration, and training in two curriculum subjects, chosen from two groups comprising, first, the mother tongue (German) a modern language (usually English) and mathematics and, second, all the other subjects taught in the compulsory lower secondary school.

Periods of practical teaching in both primary and secondary schools form an integral part of the course.

The training of secondary teachers is on a consecutive rather than concurrent basis, the course in the 'Science of Education' comprising 'psychology of education, learning psychology, introduction to the theory of cognition, pedagogics of today including a review of the historical development of the sciences of education, didactics, including media technology and an introduction into the organization of the Austrian Educational system' (OECD. 1974b). The introduction of courses in didactics and educational sciences is an innovation as far as the training of secondary teachers is concerned.

Research on teacher education curriculum in Europe has been piecemeal rather than comprehensive, and there is nothing comparable to the US Model Teacher Education projects, to which reference will be made in the sections that follow. Nonetheless, the need to construct curricula for new and reformed institutions, or, as in the United Kingdom, for the purpose of validation by universities or the Council for National Academic Awards, has given rise to a great deal more systematic development work than was common a decade ago. One of the themes that has run through such discussions is the relationship between 'Theory' and 'Practice' in teacher education. The importance of this issue justifies further consideration.

8

Problems of 'Theory' and 'Practice'

The relationship between theory and practice in teacher education is an issue with a long history. In the past year or two a number of factors have combined to give it central importance.

First, the introduction of new degrees, and the need for those who work in the colleges and departments in which teachers are trained to prepare new programmes and syllabuses have prompted a lot of new thinking about the purpose and organization of courses.

Second, faced with difficulties in responding to new kinds of secondary school organization, implementing new teaching methods, and coping with the problems of the inner city school, students and teachers have been seeking greater 'relevance' in their training, which often takes the form of a demand for less theory and more practice.

Third, the model of educational studies that has held away over the past dozen years or so, and which in its stress on the contributory disciplines owed a good deal to the recruitment in the Sixties to the colleges and departments of numbers of young staff qualified in sociology, philosophy and psychology, is beginning to show signs of wear. Assumptions about the nature of theory and practice alleged to be intrinsic to that model are criticized with increasing frequency and force, not least by those who adopt a Marxist standpoint.

At its lowest level, discussion of the theory-practice relationship takes the form of a series of crude assertions about the over-theoretical nature of the training that students receive, lack of contact with and understanding of the problems of the practising schoolmaster on the part of those who train the students, and the need for more time to be devoted to practical work in schools under the direct guidance and supervision of experienced serving teachers. Crude as they may be, such assertions appear from time to time in surprising places.

At a slightly higher level of sophistication, there is the view that whatever value theory may or may not have, it does not appear to interest students, who claim that they cannot see its application to the everyday problems of the classroom. Hence priority during the course should be given to those many other things that a student needs to learn if he is to survive in his first post. Theory can wait until later on, when he has learned to cope, and has a clearer notion of the importance of the problems on which educational theories might help to throw some light.

At about the same level is the argument from the other side that without a good dose of theory, students will be as conservative in their future practices as are many serving teachers, and that practices and procedures crystallize out from the kinds of understanding that a student achieves through the more or less intensive study of problems within one or more of the 'foundation disciplines.'

Whilst it would be convenient to put aside assertions of this kind, since they do nothing at all to explicate the relationship between theory and practice, the frequency of their occurrence in educational exchanges suggests that they represent deeply-help beliefs and reflect important vested interests.

As such, they cannot be ignored.

But even in statements that rise above the level of mere assertion, there is still a lack of clarity in the way in which the terms theory and practice are employed which vitiates the contribution that discussion of the issue might make to the design of new programmes and the better organization of educational studies. The worst confusions arise because of a failure to distinguish the use of theory and practice as descriptive terms for what tutors and lecturers in colleges and departments of education and teachers and students in classrooms spend their time doing, from the use of these words as epistemological concepts, referring to different modes of knowing about education.

Pedagogical usages predominate in much of what has been written on the subject recently. There are many who seek to criticize what Bartholomew (1975) has called the 'one-way transmission model between theory and practice'. Yet for many of these critics, both theory and practice remain unanalysed. Even on the part of authors willing to recognize the problematic character of both terms, the issue turns into one of institutional relationships, or the alleged status differences that separate those who teach from those who teach about teaching.

> 'My thesis is that theory, never itself explicated, is used to describe the activities (practices) of only certain people and not others, and that this, and the unexplicated relation of theory to practice in which the theorist "disappears" provides the mystified and ideological nature of educational theory' (Bartholomew, 1975, p. 68).

Now this says nothing about the nature of educational theory as such, but merely makes an assertion ('the mystified and ideological nature') about the activities of those who teach in colleges and departments of education. Few of those who write in this vein take the trouble to identify the kinds of concepts and ideas and statements which they see as constituting the theory that they wish to criticize, or to name the books and the authors who are guilty of peddling the kind of theory that they regard as ineffective, or distinguishing between the kinds of transmissions that are supposed to take place and which actually occur in the settings in which students interact with their tutors—lectures, seminars, discussions, through written work, in study practice, micro-teaching sessions, child observation periods, simulations, mini-courses and the whole gamut of contemporary techniques in use in colleges and departments. Yet without some attempt to make clear what theory is held to comprise, what kinds of activities and experiences are being described as being within the realm of the teaching of theory, and what is being transmitted as a result of these activities and experiences, such criticism has little point.

The nature of theory on the one hand and the justification or priority and timing of theoretical studies in education on the other are quite distinct kinds of questions, although the position that we take on the former is clearly relevant to any rational determination of the latter. All too frequently, those who comment on the theory/practice issue slip from the one question to the other without any apparent sense of contradiction.

A view of the relationship of theory and practice now becoming commonplace, yet one that still expresses the problem in pedagogic rather than epistemological terms, as a manner of approach rather than a philosophical issue, is that theory should 'arise' from the practice that it seeks to explain. The argument is presumably that by being made to think about the implications of what he is doing, the assumptions that lie benearth his practice, the teacher will achieve a higher level of reflective understanding, and be able to translate this into more successful (however defined) classroom activity.

As a piece of practical advice to those concerned with the design of programmes and courses for intending teachers, there is nothing wrong with the suggestion that students should be encouraged critically to examine their own practice, to ask questions about the curriculum, the pupils they teach, the factors that have led to their own self-perceived sense of success or failure. But if it is to be useful in guiding future action, such experience has to be conceptualized in terms that permit the communication and sharing of meanings, that encourage analysis and reference to the experience of others that is embodied in the language and literature of education.

Those who believe that practice as such will necessarily give rise to certain questions in the mind of the student which are capable without other intervention of being formulated into 'material' for training purposes are deluding themselves. Without acquiring some concepts by means of which his experience can be ordered, the student will have nothing to report. Such inability to suggest questions will all too likely be met by the tutor himself identifying for the student those issues which he (the tutor) feels to be important. In so doing, the tutor is of course to some extent imposing a definition of the situation that is not the student's own. More likely, however, is that the students will draw upon other principles to order their experience. They have been watching teachers at work for 13,000 hours or more before ever coming near the college or department of education. In doing so they will have acquired a host of preconceptions about the nature of the teaching transaction, how pupils and teachers should conduct themselves in classrooms, what constitutes a defensible curriculum content and so on. But if the influence of all this in shaping the experiences that they then have during periods of practice (whether simulated or direct) is to be handled in group teaching and tutorial sessions, then some categories for selection of topics and issues will have to be made, some priorities will need to be determined. As far as the individual is concerned, such a structure is still external, whether imposed by a tutor or within the framework of a public tradition.

(These points apply equally to other approaches that stress the importance of critical self-reflection by the teacher, e.g. Elliott and Labbett, 1975, p. 51; Elliott and Adelman, 1975, p. 29).

John Wilson (1975a) has some sensible things to say about the nature of classroom experience :

> 'The point is that the "experience" may be bad : that is, instead of making the person more aware, competent and so on, it may make him less so. Unless we are talking of a fairly tightly defined techne or craft, it seems to be generally true that the merits of "experience" are largely a function of the person "experiencing" age may bring wisdom, but may also bring folly. In some respects "being a teacher", or any educational job involving people and understanding, is like a techne, but in some respects it is not.'

If we pursued this line, we should need to go back to those who like Peters have argued that the main justification for theory in courses of teacher education is its capacity to transform the subjective experience of the teacher. There are clear gains for the student in being able to conceptualize his experience in terms of a language that is shared with contemporaries and with those who within the public traditions of organized knowledge that we label psychology, sociology; history, philosophy and so forth, have sought to explain to themselves and to others the nature of what is involved in the activities of teaching and learning. Some of those to whose work reference has been made would probably associate themselves with this position. But they would probably argue that the opportunity for experience to be transformed in this way is dependent upon the interactions between student, teacher and tutor that their pedagogy of the theory/practice relationship demands. Even so, the complexities of the psychological processes and situational constraints that govern the relationship between on the one hand the student's perceptions, memories, understandings, attitudes, dispositions and skills, and on the other, what happens in the classroom in the course of the teaching transaction, are either ignored or glossed over in many recent discussions of the theory/practice issue.

As we have seen, the thrust of much recent comment in

this area is to stress the problematic nature of theory, and doubts about the extent to which it contributes to more successful practice. But having abandoned the claims of theory to provide the bedrock of the course we cannot, as some authors would wish to do, substitute an unproblematic practice.

It is pity that after identifying the essential issue, namely that the integration of theory and practice depends upon understanding the processes by which we turn what we know into action, Bartholomew (1975) fails to recognize the consequences of his position by seeming to grant to practice the same keystone status as he would deny to theory. In doing so, he reflects a Marxist perspective which is relevant to an examination of the epistemological issues raised when we use terms such as theory and practice. And we cannot clarify the relationship between these terms without touching upon philosophical problems of some complexity.

Faced with these complexities, two extreme reactions have developed, both currently exercising considerable influence on thinking about teacher education. The first has its psychological roots in behaviourism, and is at one with what has been called the 'Technological-Benthamite' (Inglis, 1975) values of advanced societies. In its most systematic form as Performance-or Competency-Based Teacher Education (P/CBTE), it has enjoyed a considerable success in some universities and state systems in North America. Less comprehensively organized variants can be found in the micro-teaching units and skill-promoting courses that form part of teachers' preparation in the United Kingdom and a number of Luropean countries.

At the opposite pole emphases are being placed in some quarters on the contribution that Marxist analyses can make to the explication of the theory/practice relationship. It is argued that the anti-positivist trend that has characterized the rerent development of soeial theory has important implications for the work of the teacher and hence for teacher education itself. The separation of writing and talking and thinking about education into separate disciplines or 'forms of thought' is seen as fundamentlly elitist in its intentions and effects. Questions of knowledge and epistemology are seen as essentially political, because they arise in particular societies (Young, 1971). This position is consistent with those who argue that

> 'The sharp division between theory and practice, which contemporary positivists take to absured extremes, reflects a division, at a much more basic level, between mental and manual labour and this division lies at the heart of every exploiting society . . . ' (Hoffman, 1975, p. 11).

Writing from outside the Marxist tradition but from a standpoint highly critical of liberal-bourgeois values, Inglis (1975, p. 57) has argued that much of what is offered by these disciplines has the effect of justifying existing social and political arrangements—'The main charge against the philosophers is that they have cast themselves as quietist celebrators of the way-things-are'. In this Inglis agrees with M.F.D. Young, although the former's criticism is rooted not so much in Marxism as in that literary-romantic tradition that is endemic to the world of teacher education (Taylor, 1969c).

The unity of theory and practice is essential to the doctrine of dialectical materialism, and produces a powerful movement against pure intellectualism, seen as the product of idealist philosophy, and the allegedly contemplative character of philosophy in commodity society. As we have seen, in the second-hand form in which these ideas reach discussions of teacher education they can sometimes take on a crudely anti-intellectual character, elevating practice, downgrading the significance of theory. But in this context practice takes on a special meaning. In the familiar words of Marx's Eleventh Thesis on Feuerbach, 'the philosophers have only interpreted the world differently, the point is, to change it' (Fischer, 1973). Practice becomes praxis.

> ' . . . the champions of praxis insist that we are a part of the world we study and cannot possibly be expected to

theorize in some kind of detached, neutral manner. Where positivism preaches resignation and acceptance, praxis demands commitment and change; for conformity, it puts criticism; for passivity, it demands action, and hence instead of theorizing in the abrtract, it calls for concrete practice. It rejects therefore—in its manifesto of protest—all the self-defeating antitheses which are the hallmark of positivism, the supposed "gulf" between ideal and real, concrete and abstract, fact and value, the world of is and the world of ought. Thinking is a praxical activity, it insists, and its role is not to contemplate the universe, but to transform it' (Hoffman, 1975, p. 17).

The attraction of the 'wholeness' that these ideas promise, especially to students confused by the disputes between disciplinary specialisms and eager to take part in the reform of education are obvious enough. Equally obvious are the characteristics of the kind of society to which this revolutionary 'praxis' is supposed to lead—a classless society in which, in the contemporary cant, 'men have regained control over their lives'. It is also a society in which there is room for only one doctrine—that of dialectical materialism. In class societies Marxism is only a source of historical understanding and a theory for the practice of the class struggle. Once the stage of socialist construction is reached, however, and by a process of conscious transformation, class society has been transformed into classless society, Marxism must 'of necessity assume totality, and for this it requires a critical liquidation of idealism for its theoretical foundation . . . The critical liquidation of idealism has as its content the theory required for the practical liquidation of social classes divided on lines of intellectual and manual labour' (Sohn-Rethel, 1975, p. 50).

Not all Marxist thinkers are agreed on the significance of what one has called 'the challenge of praxis'. In particular, there is criticism of the formulations of Louis Althusser, who in his For Marx (1969) essays the following definitions :

'By practice in general I shall mean any process of transformation of a determinate given raw material into a determinate product, a transformation effected by a determinate human labour, using determinate means (of "production")... By theory, in this respect, I shall mean a specific form of practice, itself belonging to the complex unity of the "social practice" of a determinate human society. Theoretical practice falls within the general definition of practice. It works on a raw material (representations, concepts, facts) which it is given by other practices, whether "empirical", "technical" or "ideological" . . .' (p. 166).

Kolabrowski (1971) has suggested that this simply takes 'practice' to be anything that people are doing in whatever domain in which they are active, and that 'the traditional Marxist distinction and the opposition of "practice" and "theory" becomes obviously pointless if "practice" means simply any activity'. Hoffman (1975) has mounted a sustained criticism of what he calls 'praxis thinking' in favour of an orthodox Marxism.

These internal disputes, important as they may be to Marxist writers, rarely penetrate debates about teacher education. There is, however, considerable evidence of a somewhat derived, second-order influence of Marxist ideas, one or two examples of which have already been given in an earlier part of this chapter.

But it would be a mistake to believe that Marxist ideas exert their chief or only influence on educational thought or action at these programmatic levels. Such ideas have penetrated the realm of education in other more subtle but possibly more significant ways. One of these is the emphasis in recent years on studies in the sociology of knowledge and their implications for school organization, curriculum and classroom relations (Young, 1971; Keddie, 1973; Sharp and Green, 1975). The sociology of knowledge is not exclusively Marxist, and its development as a specialism within sociology owes most to the work of scholars such as Mannheim whose intellectual base is much broader. Nevertheless, in statements such as 'behind every theory there are collective forces expressive of group purposes, power and interests' Mannheim (1936, p. 110) displays an indebtedness to Marx, which does not prevent him from suggesting that Marxist ideas are themselves profoundly ideological.

Sociology of knowledge perspectives have received wide currency through, for example, the writings of Pierre Bordieu in France, empirical studies of classroom relations such as those of Keddie (1971) and analyses of the interest base of activities such as educational research and development (Taylor, 1973). In the work of these and other authors, there is a central concern with the way in which the organization and content of schooling serves to maintain a particular social order.

> 'The school may be seen as maintaing the social order through the taken-forgranted categories of its superordinates who process pupils and knowledge in mutually confirming ways. The ability to maintain these categories as consensual, when there are among the clients in school conflicting definitions of the situation, resides in the unequal distribution of power' (Keddie, 1971, p. 156).

Seen thus, theories are interest-based. The interests that underlie the organization and content of theories about education in capitalist societies are those of the ruling class. Those educational theories that stress individualization or aesthetic experience as the means whereby the development of consciousness may take place, free of the domination of the commodity society and of consumerism, serve the interests of a class society just as surely as theories that stress the importance of technological skill and vocational training. (A point also echood from a different standpoint by Inglis, 1975, p. 29ff.)

> 'Thus an adequate aesthetic education of man cannot be confined to an imaginary "inner world" of the isolated individual, nor indeed to some remote Utopian haven of aliented society. Its realization necessarily involves the

totality of social processes in their complex dialectical reciprocity with each other. This is why the separate programme of an "aesthetic education of man as an antidote to the spread of capitalist "rationality" is condemned to a hopeless utopianism under conditions when the uncontrollable second order mediations of the relified social relations of production determine—in a narrowly utilitarian framework—the educational processes just as much as all the other aspects of commodity society' (Meszaros, 1970, p. 292).

Thus the Marxist critique of 'theory' is total. The empirical question of the relationship between a student's attitudes, perceptions and exposure to ideas and his performance in the classroom fades into insignificance. The focus is entirely upon the extent to which the 'theories' that the student learns serve to prevent him from recognizing the exploitative and power-serving character of the educational regime in which he participates; how pedagogy, curriculum and evaluation are linked to the preservation of the political and social status quo; how the process of teacher education serves to develop an educational false consciousness and to block the possibility of radical change.

As critics have been quick to point out, this style of thought soon runs into a dead end. When one has said that all ideas are interest-based, what has one said ? It is the same criticism that can be levelled at that brand of crude and simplistic Freudianism, popular among undergraduates and in the press, which in exposing the bases of individual motives and actions, seeks also to disenchant, to demystify and ultimately to discredit. Furthermore, it is no great surprise that theories are interest-based. By definition, if what men say is to have meaning for themselves and for others, it must reflect some community of interest and understanding. Theoretical understanding, in common with most kinds of abstract thought, requires the seedbed of community if it is to develop. The development of language itself is dependent upon the existence of the community of shared assumptions. In Leavis' words

(1975, p. 44) :

> '. . . language is more than a means of expression; it is the heuristic conquest won out of representative experience, the upshot or precipitate of immemorial human living, and embodies values, distinctions, identifications, conclusions, promptings, cartographical hints and tested potentialities.'

The importance of such a community is equally well illustrated at the level of the Zeitgeist, that broad canvas of shared opinions and attitudes, which Boring (quoted Hudson, 1972, p. 158) suggests is that 'great prime mover of all intellectual activity, without whom no man would think as he does, nor have his thoughts make sense'. It is imortant also in the exact sciences, where Kuhn (1969) and others have drawn attention to the way in which the agenda of puzzles and problems and criteria for the identification of research priorities are defined in terms of a corpus of current scientific knowledge that is sociallv as well as empirically bounded. It is important in history, where as Levi-Strauss (quoted Leach, 1970, p. 130) has stated :

> 'Insofar as history aspires to meaning, it is doomed to select regions, periods, groups of men and individuals in these groups and to make them stand out as discontinuous figures, against a continuity barely good enough to be used as a backdrop. A truly total history would cancel itself out . . . a history of the French Revolution cannot simultaneously and under the same heading be that of the Jacobin and of the aristocrat'.

From different standpoints, the same position has been adopted by Richards (1938) and by Hirst (1974, pp. 139—140) :

> 'The notions of truth, reason and knowledge are the product of the relations established socially between words and the given form of life we have. Without that given element, and the existence of agreement in judgment as a given,

there could be no such things as truth, reason and knowledge.'

After the initial satisfaction of 'unmasking', of understanding that there is a situated or socially-constructed element to all knowledge, of recognizing that the very definition of what constitutes knowledge implies the existence of a set of social relationships, little else follows. Such limited empirical work as can be designed on this basis does little more than prove the same point over and over again, in greater and more stupefying detail. This has both weakened the value of a sociology of knowledge approach to an understanding of the nature and role of educational theroy and, perhaps more significantly, encouraged those committed to these approaches to take that necessary furtherstep into the adoption of that revolutionary praxis by means of which the process of unmasking takes on a new, programmatic relevance. At the same time, this step represents a means of escaping the need to analyse the empirical complexities of the theory/practice relationship—who teaches what to whom, with what effect by adopting a simple monistic viewpoint. In this context Marxism takes on some of the character of what Gellner (1974) has called 'oceanic monism', 'A unitary vision designed to give the beiiever a consoling, edifying or exhilarating sense of being merged with, sustained by, dissolved in the great One of which he and all else is a part'.

The adoption of a revolutionary programme avoids any necessity of subjecting the ideas and assertions of the doctrine to systematic critical analysis. Yet revolutionary praxis in no way removes the necessity for such analysis. As Runciman (1976, p. 46) has stated :

> 'How . . . is the superiority of the Marxist alternative to be made plain ? . . . We have still to ask whether Marxist sociology so defines its theoretical constructs as to immunize its hypotheses from disconfirming evidence; whether it implies the truth of counterfactual conditionals which there is reason to suppose would not in fact hold; whether it can

plausibly be applied to all capitalist societies, or only to some, or only in part; and whether its fundamental presuppositions are wholly incompatible with those of "bourgeois" sociology or whether differences in terminology may mask a broader area of agreement than either Marxist sociologists or their "conventional" critics are disposed to acknowledge.'

Nor does the adoption of the view that all theories are based upon interests remove the necessity of examining the substantive truth-claims of the theories themselves, of subjecting them to the kind of detailed evaluation that will sort out theories of some permanent value in helping us to understand what goes on in classrooms, in schools and in society from those that are trivial, ephemeral or spurious. There is in all this a dangerous reductionism, that also carries with it a 'knowingness', a tendency to believe that if the interest base can be exposed, then the theory is therefore invalid. But it may well be that one's understanding of a particular phenomenon gains from adopting a succession or concurrent set of possibly unrelated and perhaps even conflicting theories. As Chein (1972, p. 7) has stated :

> '. . . one who behave is utterly subject to behavioural law and . . . the latter is not incompatible with either physiological or physical law. It does not follow that behavioural law is reducible to physiological or physical law or that physiological law is reducible to physical law. A boiler system is subject to thermo-dynamic law, and it is also subject to mechanical law, but it does not follow that thermodynamic law is reducible to mechanical law. The concurrent relevance of two domains of law to one system does uot necessarily imply that the two sets of laws are necessarily reducible to one of them.'

A cynic might take the view that insofar as the doctrine of interests seems effectively to dispose of theory as an area of significant concern excepts, that is, for the one theory that is self-evidently true, and thus requires no analysis—it **would** have a built-in appeal to students, serving to justify their incomprehension, and legitimize their desire to 'get on with the job' and avoid the complexities of theoretical discussion.

The deeper sociological questions to which, properly conducted, this style of inquiry can give rise are seldom asked. For example, it would be worth while to relate the ideas of Durkheim and Mauss (1963) on the social basis of systems of classification to the assertions that are made by Marxists about the hierarchical nature of the concepts that describe theory and practice, and by sociologists of knowledge about status differentials implicit in most forms of social labelling (Hargreaves, Hestor and Mellor, 1976). Darkheim and Mauss' thesis ('we have no justification for supposing that our mind bears within it at birth, completely formed, the prototype of this elementary framework of all classification . . . every classification implies a hierarchical order for which neither the tangible world nor out mind gives us the model', p. 8) has been extensively criticized. Yet the idea that it embodies deserves serious critical consideration, particularly in relation to the more recent work of structuralists (see Douglas, 1976).

Insofar as community relalionships are attenulated by the consequences of the division of labour, by social and geographical mobility and by the speed of technological and social change, language tends to adapt to the performance of additianal functions. The implicit understandings and shared meanings that were once part of the unanalysed fabric of social interaction are eroded. As Gellner (1965, p. 155) has underlined, a larger proportion of ephemeral, non-repetitive and optional encounters puts a premium on message rather context. Paradoxically, however, this does not produce greater precision in language use. Because the relatiodships mediated by language include much that is unknown or speculative (What will this stranger think of my saying this ? Is this the right thing to say at this particular type of conference ? What do they expect me to do now ?), there is a tendency to play safe, to make frequent use of the conditional, to hedge statements about with protective verbal cotton wool, to eschew explicit commitment, to introduce totem words which indicate (frequently equivocal) adoption of some more or less temporary position on which the speaker or writer hopes he will be joined by others of a similar persuasion. It is this, rather than the use of technical terms as such, that leads to the accusation of 'jargon' in theoretical formulations relevant to education.

We have come a long way in this discussion from our initial claim that 'pedagogical' interptetations of the theory/practice relationship are of a different order from those which seek to analyse (a) the epistemological basis of the terms, and (b) the kinds of knowledge to which, on the one hand, theoretical discourse, and on the other, experience of classroom and school, give rise. Attempts in recent years to explicate the relationship in Marxist categories does not throw much light on the problem of how an intending teacher can acquire and develop the knowledge and competencies that will enable him better to satisfy whatever criteria may be employed for the designation of 'good teaching'. In much of the discussion of the theory/practice relationship, either one or the other, or sometimes both terms are treated essentially as unproblematical. There is almost no reference to tne psychology of the process, the means whereby an individual is exposed to and learns skills and types of competence that he can can then incorporate into his own classroom performance. There is a sense in which such learning must be learning on the job, in that the elements that constitute a classroom performance must at some stage be practised together rather than separately. Perhaps the most damaging comment that has been made about the usefulness of the kinds of practice that a students obtains during his course of initial is that 'most skills of teaching that we wish students to learn receive absurdly small amounts of practice, far underestimating even reasonable amounts to develop and fix skills at passable levels' (Hudgins, 1975, p. 12).

No discussion of theory and practice is likely to be adequate without sufficient attention being given to the now substantial body of evidence that exists concerning the learning of skills in both educational and non-reducational contexts. But if fifteen weeks or so of systematic school experience in the course of a typical programme of teacher education is grossly insufficient in terms of the development of classroom competency, it does not follow that an even larger slice of the limited period available should be devoted to such practical activity. Quite the contrary. If fifteen weeks is ludicrously inadequate, twenty weeks or thiry weeks are hardly likely tó be better. As every experienced teacher knows, the procees of skill acquisition is difficult to hurry. Some routinet are not mastered antil many years after qualifying. Nor is the need for more time to be given to practice an argument for discounting the place of theory, or believing that theoretical discourse will be without meaning unless it is rooted in experience that the student has had in an educational setting. I.A. Richads (1938, pp. viii—ix) stated the necessary balance many years ago.

'. . . a word's context is the words which surround it in the utterance and the other contemporaneous signs which govern its interpretation . . . . insufficient attention to the accompanying sign field (the setting and occasion) which controls the context (recurrent groups of events in the past) is a frequent cause of mistaken understanding. But equally, no care, however great, in observing the setting will secure good interpretation if past experience has not provided the required originative context. Here comes in the stress which teachers are so ofton forced to put upon the need for "actual experience" in the individual's past history if verbal representations are to be understood. The stressing is justified if it does not overlook the indirect ways in which words can analyse features of exprrience and recompound them into wholes which may never have occurred in the reader's history. It is these features of experience, not specific integral experiences as distinct of being, which enter into contexts with words. If words —to be understood—must reinstate such integral experiences, the services of language to us would be far less than they are . . .'

9

Trends and Innovations in the Pre-Service Curriculum

'Traditional instruction and its variants'

In a review of the state of the art of teacher education research at the beginning of the present decade, Peck and Tucker (1973) suggest that the available evidence on teacher education demonstrates the importance of seven main themes :

1. The effectiveness of what is done in colleges and universities is improved by a more systematic approach to the design of programmes, and by building in techniques such as interaction analysis, behaviour modification and micro-teaching.

2. Beneficial results flow from the attempt on the part of teacher educators to organize instruction in the college or department in accordance with the same principles as are advocated for the classroom practice of the inteding teacher.

3. The use of T-groups, sensitivity training, and classroom simulation, all of which involve greater direct involvement on the part of the student in the role that he is attempting to acquire, is more effective in producing

desired teacher behaviour than traditional modes of college instruction.

4. Teachers who through exposure to techniques such as those mentioned above have learned to be more self-initiatory and self-directed in their own learning, are better able to pass on these approaches to their own pupils.

5. Whilst conventional methods of teacher education do produce some sought-for results, they also have a number of unplanned consequences.

6. The virtually complete absence of any systematic attempt to train the teacher of teachers, and thus of research upon and evaluation of such training, is a serious drawback to further advance.

7. The employment of "pupil-gain" criteria for the evaluation of teacher effectiveness and of the teacher education process represents a substantial methodological advance.

Peck and Tucker go on to illustrate how a wealth of studies have illustrated the great significance of appropriate feedback mechanisms whereby the future teacher can develop criteria for the monitoring of his own performance. It is this which is at the henrt of techniques such as micro-teaching. Stress upon the self-monitoring character of human performance is also present in a good deal of contemporary philosophy and sociology, particularly where these disciplines focus on the reflexive and phenomenological aspects of perception and behaviour. Among a broad spectrum of theorists and investigators, from behaviourists on the one hand to contemporary psychoanalysts such as Jacques Lacan (1968) on the other, there is unanimity about the fundamental significance of man's reflexive capacities in relation to the development of his self-image and the ordering of his conduct.

Thus it is not suprising that more effort has recently bee devoted to the institutionalization of those techniques that aim to enhance the individual student's ability to observe and comment upon his own performances, whether this is by the use of CCTV and micro-teaching episodes, or in the study of works by phenomenological philosophers, or through the adoption of a research methodology that incorporates the importance of the so-called dramaturgical perspective (Harre and Secord, 1972; Goffman, 1962). The individualization that Durkheim saw as one of the consequences of the division of labour has taken on a new significance in the contemporary Zeitgeist in the form of the heightened self-consciousness characteristic of what Riesman has described as the 'other directed' society.

The current ideology of schooling requires that the teacher be sensitive to the finer nuances of behaviour and feeling on the part of both himself and his pupils. Evidence from psychiatric sources that, carried to excess, such sensitivity has a crippling effect on capacity for decision and action is seldom taken into account in the design of programmes, but may show itself in the tendency for many students to resist attempts to structure their perception of classroom realities in terms of increasingly differentiated sets of behavioural categories. Thus, whilst such devices as microteaching and simulations are intended to reduce the perceptual load that the student carries in the course of his training, they may, through the emphasis they place upon self-monitoring and reflexive categorization, produce a new and equally difficult set of problems for the neophyte teacher.

Much of the literature to do with the changing role of the teacher and of teacher educatien reflects a somewhat uncritical espousal of all forms of mechanical and audiovisual educational technology, with very little attention given to whether the use of such media alongside or instead of traditional instruction (TI) produces superior educational outcomes. Evaluation of this kind poses many difficulties, but a number of useful surveys have been made in recent years. The findings of some of these reflect the conclusions of Bruner and Olson (1973) on the relative effectiveness of learning through reinforcement, modelling or ordinary language. In Olson's words (1972) :

> 'The data we have examined permit us to discount the possibility that any one of the three paradigms of learning through reinforcement, modelling or ordinary language indicates the exclusive means of instructing a child on a cognitive motor task. The different experiments provided evidence that each of them could yield the required knowledge, some more economically than others, yet these experiments also showed that in cases where each of them was absent, the critical knowledge could still result. Given this equivalence there is no reason to believe that any one paradigm, be it reinforcement, modelling or ordinary language, is the basic paradigm to which the others may be reduced.'

A paper by Jamison et al. (1974) reporting a survey of evaluations of alternative instructional media (Instructional Radio (IR), Instructional Television (ITV), Programmed Instruction (PI), and Computer Assisted Instruction (CAI), showed (p. 55) that 'students learn effectivively from all these media, and relatively few studies indicate a significant difference in one medium over another or of one variant of a medium over another'.

Jamison and his colleagues make some important points about the implications of such findings for policy. First, they reject the view that the use of more educational technology in the instructional 'mix' would produce substantial economies, even in a labour-intensive occupation such as teaching. They argue that the purpose of technology must be not to replace teachers, but to make them more productive. So far, most alternative instructional media have been applied regardless of cost, with a view to improving quality rather than productivity. There are significant exceptions. The British Open University, the Japanese Secondary School of the Air, and the German Telekolleg all produce 'graduates' at a much lower per capita cost than their traditional equivalents. Jamison maintains that if the goal in employing more educational technology was to introduce productivity improvement instead of the enrichment of quality, there might be a greater possibility of significant goal achievement. It is concluded that research beyond that surveyed is needed in the following areas :

> 'First we must examine if the savings in time exhibited in some of the studies using PI or CAI can be shown to be significant over longer periods and for a higher percentage of the total instructional programme of students.
>
> Second, we do not yet have an appropriate detailed evaluation of the impact of the various technologies on the long-term motivation of students.
>
> Third, the long-term effects of individualization and the privacy of learning characteristic of some technologies also need more extensive evaluation. We do not know, for example, whether students who are given highly individualized programmes in the elementary school for most of their instruction will strongly prefer the continuation of such methods in secondary school and college or whether they will desire to return as they grow older to more traditional forms of instruction.
>
> Fourth, it has been indicated at a number of points in this review that most evaluations, particularly those considered well controlled, compare TI to a form of IR, ITV or CAI that closely emulates TI. It is at least plausible that many of the conclusions of this survey would be overturned were more imaginative uses of the media explored, which still permit comparative evaluation' (p. 59).

One version of PI that has found favour in many institutions in the United States and in the United Kingdom is the 'personalized system of instruction', or PSI for short, associated with the work of F.S. Keller (Keller and Sherman, 1974; Matthews, 1975; Keller, 1968). In Matthews' words (p. 57). 'The Keller plan is based on Skinnerian reinforcement theory and the main principles are mastery, individual pacing, and repeated instant feedback'. Within the framework of PSI, 'learning situations' are rigidly defined :

> 'From the point of view of reinforcement theory, the task of changing behaviour, including that which we desire in the field of education, is one of making appropriate reinforcements dependent upon specific instances of human conduct in clearly denoted environmental circumstances. From this it follows that any "learning situation" in which the task is not identified or is unclear, in which the critical behaviour is our can be absent, and in which the rewards are not assured, is not a learning situation in the proper meaning of the term,
>
> This climinates from serious consideration as a teaching method the usual lecture, the usual classroom demonstration, the usual discussion group, and the usual assignment of paper to be written. In none of these is the behaviour guaranteed or optimal reinforcement provided, even when the tasks are well defined. Learning may occur in all these situations; therapy may occur in some (for example, in discussion); but each one is deficient in one or more of the requirements for effective teaching' (Keller, 1974, p. 53).

There are very few institutions or departments, if any, which pursue a consistent approach based on one or other of these varieties of learning theory. Indeed, it is all too possible that students working under Professor X in subject A are exposed to a completely different set of assumptions about the nature of teaching and learning from those which characterize the lectures and tutorials of Professor Y on subject B. This is not to argue that the pluralism this represents is a bad thing. It is to suggest that where it arises fortuitously, and members of the faculty are unaware of the range of views represented among them, the result for the student can often be confusion and lack of direction.

In this, what goes on in lecture and seminar room is little

different from aspects of the research scene. As Travers (1971, p. 33) has noted 'Our basic difficulty in utilizing the knowledge derived from classroom reasearch is to put together the finding from different studies. Each investigator tends to use his own favourite language in naming variables, and no synthesis of different studies is possible without engaging in a guess-what-this-means game. At present there seems to be no end to the creative task of invenling new names for vague some-thing or others that happen to intrigue a particular investi-gator; but the result is not organized knowledge, only 'chaos'.

It can be argued that teacher education would be more effective if there were in each country a number of institutions that systematically committed themselves to the design and implementation of programmes that reflected a coherent theory of instruction. A comparison of the educational outcome of such inter-institutional diversity (as compared with the intra-institutional variety, that exists today) might necessarily be impressionistic, but could yield insights of greater value than those obtained on the present unplanned diversity. All this is inevitably more difficult as institutions for the education and training of teachers become larger, or are incorporated into and form departments of universities and polytechnics.

A report of an experiment in a single school (the CES, or lower secondary school intended for the 11 to 16 age group in-Marly-le-Roi) which was based upon a thorough institutionali-zation of educational technology, has been reported by Poins sac (1974). The experiment had a strongly technological bias :

> 'Technology involves the rationalisation of tasks in a school just as in a business firm. Thus the traditional separation between education for adolescents in a cloistered world, and working life for adults comes to an end. In every case, the teacher becomes a specialist in certain jobs which are entirly comparable to those performed in business life (p. 57).

The basis of learning activity in the school is programmed, with follow-up sessions in medium size and, subsequently, small groups. A complex resource centre has been established, and study is fully individualized.

> 'The functional architecture, modular down to the individual booth, has allowed information transmitted by any medium to be made available to the pupil. . .At whatever time he chooses over a fairly long period, the pupil can work at whatever discipline he perfers. He can call upon teacher supervisors to advise him about the actual information or about the management of his time, untill the utiliza tion of self guiding programmes confers the status of independent work on the experiment' (p. 60).

Poinssac reports that the individualized, modular basis of instruction had the effect of overriding the traditional distinctics between teachers with different forms of training. The teachers working in the school needed to be retrained for their fresh tasks, which included the production of audiovisual and programmed material for information purposes, supervision of small and large group learning and team teaching, and the design of docimology and evaluation. Cooperation between teachers was an essential aspect of the scheme, the various teams operating according to a pattern that was agreed at a weekly meeting under group supervisor with a reduced timetable. On a subject basis, syllabuses were organized by means of local seminars 'meeting under the authority of a high-level specialist outside the CES'. Teachers took part in fortnightly seminars at which research work relevant to their own teaching was reported upon and 'specific directives' issued for the next two weeks' work.

In reviewing current teacher education provision in a number of European countries, it is impossible to avoid the impression that what is offered is unsufficiently systematic, sometimes lacking in coherence, poorly focused upon the kinds of tasks that students will later have to undertake in schools, and without adequate intellectual substance. To urge a more systematic approach is not to espouse the principles of behaviourism, programmed instruction, or performance-based teacher educatian.

The intellectual and professional rationale for a course based upon traditional instructional principles need be no less precise and carefully worked out than that for a programme based on PI and PSI. Nor need it imply any greater certainty about the outcome of teacher preparation than is justified by our existing knowledge and the problematic character of teaching today. But it seems doubtful if, without greater clarity of aim and of organization, the institutions responsible for producing the next generation of teachers will be able to take full advantage of the growth of our knowledge about how children learn, about the social environment of a classroom, and about the ways in which learning and teaching can be made more effective.

As noted in an earlier chapter, teacher educators, faced with information overload and a plethora of competing opinions, respond favourable to the apparently carefully articulated instructional system; however shaky its philosophical and psychological foundations. Complex bodies of ideas become reduced to a relatively small number of assertions or empirically-based conclusions. But the ability to parrot a few slogans is no substitute for understanding or for the ability to translate ideas into classroom practice. The intellectual content of many teacher education programmes, because it lacks internal coherence and fails to win student commitment, becomes little more than a cosmetic gloss on a largely prescriptive offering.

Research on micro-teaching and mini-courses

Of all the techniques currently in use in colleges and departments of education, none has attracted as much attention from researchers as micro-teaching. Developed by Allen and others early in the nineteen-sixties, and intended as a means whereby students might practise particular teaching skills with groups of students and peers, reviewing their performance with the aid of videotape feedback and tutorial advice, there are now few centres of professional teacher education that do not make some use of the micro-teaching concept. Allen has emphasized that micro-teaching is an idea rather than a technique :

> '. . . at the core of which lie five essential propositions : ....Micro-teaching is real teaching that lessens the complexities of normal classroom teaching for you by focusing on training you to accomplish specific tasks, thus allowing for increased control of your practice which, in turn, gives a focus to your feedback that allows it to be greatly expanded beyond the usual knowledge-of-results dimension you would normally experience in teaching' (quoted Gregory, 1972).

Micro-teaching is a form of 'laboratory' training, and as such has played an important part in the development of performance and competency-based teacher education and in the more systematic approach to the development of classroom skills that characterizes an increasing number of 'eclectic' training programmes. Evaluation of its effects on, for example, student confidence, the performance of discrete skills and on classroom work generally has been complicated by the large number of variations that have emerged on the original 'teach—review and analysis—reteach' sequence, and by the attempts of some of those concerned with such variations to find a broader conceptual basis for their work than that which they see as characterizing the original model. (Brown and Armstrong, 1975, p. 51, for example, claim that their 'Ulster skills teaching programme' is 'derived from the work of philosophers such as Othaniel Smith, Israel Scheffler and Paul Hirst, and from the social skills model of Michael Argyle'.) Some of the difficulties of evaluation are brought out in an extensive review of the literature by Brusling (1974), whose bibliography lists some 250 studies and sources. Brusling suggests that there are at least three classes of questions to which answers need to be sought. First, is micro-teaching an effective method of teacher education? This will depend upon what competing alternatives are available, the cost of the technique in terms of time, resources and curriculum opportunities foregone, the criteria that are employed in evaluation and the part that micro-teaching plays within the teacher education programme as a whole. Second, since there are almost as many variants of micro-teaching as there are qusestion of efficiency become one of identifying behavioural changes in students and relating these to specific components of the micro-teaching sequence. Third, the value to be attached to micro-teaching sequence. Third, the value to be attached to micro-teaching depends finally on the validity of the skills it is intended to enhance, and it has to be asked if such skills affect student behaviour in the classroom as predicted.

Given the onerous conditions that much be met, it is not surprising that much of the research that has been done on this topic producers results which are easily challenged, not readily generalizable to different or less well-controlled settings, and frequently ambiguous. Nonethelees, the substantial body of work now available has shown, for example, that many students value micro-teaching experience and feel that it adds to their subsequent or parallel classroom teaching skill (Perrott et al. 1975), although there are variations according to personality type (Baker, 1970); that micro-teaching can improve the ability of students and teachers to use specific techniques such as questioning (the nature of which has generated its own theoretical and empirical literature); that the mode of feedback adopted—videotape with or without expert commentary, sound tape, verbal analysis, etc.—may be less critical than has cometimes been claimed (Borg et al., 1969; Doty and Cotrell, 1971; Leonard, 1971; Rutherford 1973) and that, as might be expected, the relationship between improvements in teaching skills in the laboratory setting and subsequent performance as an employed teacher remains problematic.

Much of the development and evaluation research undertaken to date is American in origin. Perlberg (1972) refers to a number of European centres where active research efforts are going on—the Centre for New Learning Methods of the University of Tubingen, Osnabruck, Reutlingen, Schwabisch

Gmund, Malmo, Goteborg, Stirling, Liverpool and the New University of Ulster. Extensive studies of the use of CCTV in teacher education have been undertaken by Naeslund and his associates at the Stockholm School of Education (Naesland, 1969; Ljung and Naeslund, 1970; National Board of Education, 1972b).

The OECD facilitated a study in which American-designed materials were tested in a number of European countries, the UK group at the University of Lancaster being specially concerned with the development of qutstioning skills. It was not simply micro-teaching that was under test, however, but an example of one of the 'mini-courses' developed by the Far West Laboratory for Educational Research and Development in San Francisco, in which micro-teaching is one of the component elements, others being verbal instruction, modelling techniques, focus, feedback, and self-instruction (Applebee, 1976; Borg et al., 1969).

For purposes of illustration, we can refer to Atkin and Raths' (1974, pp. 42-43) description of the Far West Laboratory's Mini-course I', designed to improve the questioning techniques of teachers :

> 'The first sequence instructs teachers to ask a question, to pause at least five seconds, and then to call upon a student for a response. Teachers are urged to be accepting of student responses and to call upon both volunteers and non-volunteers to keep students alert. The second sequence in the minicourse demonstrates how teachers can ask questions that require longer pupil responses. Teachers are shown how to ask questions that require students to use higher cognitive processes, and how to redirect the same question to a number of different students to decrease the amount of teacher participation and increase pupil involvement in the discussion. A third sequence in this mini-course is designed to improve the 'probing' techniques of teachers. Teachers are shown how to prompt students, how to clarify students' views, and how to refocus student

responses. The final sequence demonstrates teacher behaviors that might impede the flow of discussion in a class. Such behaviors as repeating the questions and/or repeating students' answers are demonstrated to illustrate the deleterious effects they have on the pattern of discussion in the classroom.

A number of other mini-courses have been developed, e.g. Higher Cognitive Questioning (No. 9), Divergent Thinking (No. 20), Classroom Management through Positive Leinforcement (No. 23; Teaching Reading as Dicoding (No. 18)—all based upon a common training model, as described by Ward (1974).

STEPS IN THE MINI-COURSE INSTRUCTIONAL MODEL

Step 1	Step 2	Step 3	Step 4
Study Skills	Observe Skills	Practice Skills	Refine Skills
Read about teaching skills	View brief illustrations of skills	Plan and conduct microteach lesson to apply skills	Replan and conduct lesson
	View model lesson in which teacher uses skills	Evaluate use of skills in microteach lesson	Evaluate use of skills in reteach lesson

The mini-courses that are available fail into a number of what Ward (1974) has called 'competency clusters' viz., Questioning/Discussion, Responding, Management of Independent Individualized Learning, Teaching Reading and Teaching Social Studies. This stress on competency and individualization has earned such courses a place within programmes of training that are based on performance principles, but as Brusling (1974) has pointed out, there is more involved than straightforward behavioural assumptions such as underlie a good deal of performance-based teacher education. In particulor, the inclusion in these methods of an importent element of self-reinforcement is more readily accommodated within a social learning theory such as that of Bandura (1969, 1971) than within the terms of classical operant conditioning.

The Lancaster study produced the following results of instruction in the questioning skills included in Mini-course I (Appleber, 1976) :

Questioning Skills	*Pooled results*
A. Increasing pupils' readiness to respond	
1. Pausing	Improvement; not retained
2. Dealing with incorrect responses in an accepting manner	No improvement but satisfactory initial levels
3. Calling on non-volunteers	No change
B. Increasing the amount and quality of pupils' participation	
4. Redirection	Improvement; retained
5. Asking questions that call for longer responses	Inconsistent results
6. Asking questions that call for higher order responses	Mixed results : some increase in lower levels of 'higher order'
C. Improving pupils' initial responses	
7. Prompting	Improvement; retained
8. Seeking further clarification	Improvement; retained
9. Refocusing	No change

Questioning Skills	*Pooled results*
D. Eliminating habits that interfere with discussion	
10. Avoiding repetitions of own questions	Improvement; retained
11. Avoiding repetitions of pupils' answers	Improvement; retained
12. Avoiding answering own questions	Inconsistent change, but satisfactory initial levels

Results for the questioning skills:

Demonstrated improvement which is retained	5
Satisfactory inital levels	2
Mixed results	3
No improvement	2

Although eclectic instructional models of this kind are customarily built from elements that have each been validated in some context or another, they are exposed to criticism concerning the indispensability of certain of these elements to the achievement of the overall objective. Quoting the relevant sources on each of his points, Applebee has this to say about Mini-course I (1976, p. 39) :

> 'The Mini-course Model has never been submitted to the rigorous R and D cycle which is insisted upon for the specific course materials, but a research literature has gradually built up to suggest that in this case the whole is considerably less than the sum of its parts. Various investigators have concluded that discrimination training may be as effective as micro-teaching in developing teaching skills . . . ; that videotaped models can be replaced with a script without reducing subsequent learning . . .; that audiotape is as effective as video-tape as a feedback device . . .; that the effectiveness of Mini-course I is not increased by

adding nucro-teaching, micro-teaching and feedback, to the instructional films and handbooks . . .; and that adding modelling and feedback adds nothing to the performance of teachers who have heard a lecture, studied written materials, and done micro-teaching without feedback . . .'

It will be apparent from the examples that have been given that the research trend is far as such techniques as mini-courses and micro-teaching are concerned is towards more sophisticated evaluation, the careful identification of the element or elements in the training sequence that contribute most to the development of the skills concerned, and a desire to get behind the surface technology to a closer engagement with the developmental and classroom implications of particular training methods. There are risks in making general points about a field of inquiry that has attracted, and continues to attract, large numbers of well-qualified research workers, and which is characterized by highly specific and tightly designed investigations involving an often forbidding technical and statistical apparatus. Nonetheless, it does appear that in this, as in so many other fields of human activity, most innovations in techniques of teacher education are rated as reasonably successful in the short term, and that many contribute something to the long-term improvement to teacher education .

The two chief factors involved are probably motivation and organization. Staff concerned with a new development are usually highly motivated to see it succeed. They work harder and with greater enthusiasm, especially if they see themselves as leaders (within the intellectual or professional commudity, or within a single institution) in a direction that others have yet to follow. Some of this rubs off on their students, who are likely to be more involved, to participate more actively, and to be themselves committed to the success of the innovation. Furthermore, the task of planning and implementing requires that much more systematic thought be given to what is involved, categories be more clearly defined, objectives discussed, and that some provision be made for formal or infoemal evaluation. Micro-teaching, mini-courses, simulations, computer-aided instruction and so forth all require that more attention be given to what it is that we are trying to achieve in teacher education, to the careful selection and comparison of means to achieve our ends, and to systematic implementation of projects and plans and schemes that have often had to be argued for against the implicit or explicit opposition of those who prefer the status quo or have claims on resources for alternative purposes.

Teachers and administrators easily become impatient with the research worker's concern with the minutiae of a particular comparison, with his stubborn insistence on the importance of small differences in student gain or teacher satisfaction, with his apparent unwillingness to recognize that these tender plants readily shrivel when exposed to the strong and uncontrolled winds that blow outside the laboratory or the boundaries of an experiment. Such impatience reflects the very differing imperatives of the research and the practitioner role, but it would be wrong to believe that the researcher's fastidiousness is unnecessary, or fails to serve the purposes of education. Sometimes it does of course, and there is no lack of examples upon which to draw for the person who wants to prove the futility of what goes on in the 'ivory towers' of university departments and schools of education. Yet it is only by a concern with detail, by seeking to refine the questions that need to be asked, by trying to learn from the ideas and the findings of workers in related fields of inquiry, that the slow process of sifting out what is valuable from what is merely new can proceed, and the numbers of those in the education profession who are capable of functioning critically and scientifically in the real world of schools and students can be increased.

Simulations and games

Within the past decade a great deal of interest has been shown in using a wide variety of simulation and game techniques in both pre-service and in-service teacher education (Tansey, 1969a, 1969b; McCormick, 1972; Selmes; 1974; Brace,

1973; Taylor, 1972a, 1972b). The approach to learning implied by simulation and case study is of a piece with the adoption of a systems approach to the study of organizational structure andprocess (McLeish, 1970) and with attempts to bridge the widening gap between what we are capable of knowing about individual and social behaviour and our capacity to alter that behaviour in the light of this knowledge. It is consistent with the task of reconciling the absence of a generally accepted set of implicit cultural and social assumptions, the 'common culture' of the sociological literati, with the growing complexity of what has to be learnt if we are to work successfully together in the pursuit of particular short-term and long-term goals. In Oakeshott's words (1967, p. 168) :

> 'Facts, rules, all that may come to us as information, itemized and explicit, never themselves endow us with an ability to do, or to make, or to understand and explain anything . . . What is required in addition to information is knowledge which enables us to interpret it, to decide upon its relevance, to recognize what rule to apply and to discover what action permitted by the rule, should, in the cirumstances, be performed; knowledge (in short) capable of carrying us across those wide open spaces, to be found in every ability, where no rule runs.'

In a traditional, stable society, or in one in which at least the élite groups had shared a common pattern of education and upbringing, much of the 'knowledge' to which Oakeshott refers was acquired through socialization, absorbed through the social pores rather than incorporated in specific educational experiences. In circumstances of social mobility, rapid change and organizational complexity, this integrative, evaluative and interpretative context for facts and figures has to be made explicit; judgment has to be taught as well as caught. Such teaching cannot be accomplished simply by refining our techniques of organization and task analysis, exposing the assumption and implications of individual behaviour, and presenting all this to the practitioner in the hope that it will lead to changes in his practice. Homans (1950, p. 15) makes a useful distinction between analytical and clinical sciences :

> 'An analytical science is for understanding but not for action, at least not directly. It picks out a few of the factors at work in particular situations and describes systematically the relations between these factors. Only by cutting down the number of factors considered can it achieve this systematic description. It is general, but it is abstract . . . A description of particular cases of anaemia is clinical science, whereas a theory of blood chemistry is analytical. When progress is rapid, clinical and analytical science help one another. The clinicians tell the analysts what the latter have left out. The analysts need the most brutal reminders because they are always so charmed with their pictures they mistake them for the real thing. On the other hand, the analysts' generalizations often suggest where the clinicians should look more closely . . .'

Jamieson (1973) has drawn attention to research findings that throw light on the relationship of simulation to the development of skill, Identifying basic skill components as

(a) timing,

(b) cues,

(c) feedback,

(d) anticipation,

(e) decision making, and

(f) transfer of learning, he shows how these have significance for the design and use of simulation. Jamieson argues (pp. 245—246) that :

> ' . . .research into simulation might profit equally well from the adoption of some of the methodological techniques which have evolved from research into skill. For instance, simulation experiments could be planned in such a way that cues are given in specified forms and at specified times; "feedback" could be systematically controlled to suit the

decision-making capacities of the participants; conversely, excessive information could be generated to produce "overload" when it is desired to create stressful situations and concomitant anxiety states. Moreover, various aids to communication and information flow could be called upon, e.g. CCTV for the purpose of (a) increasing the availability of information, and (b) ensuring greater fidelity of replication. These are just some of the possibilities, with a little more thought, wider opportunities for research would only out.'

The importance of feedback has already been referred to in discussing techniques such as micro-teaching, which can itself be seen as a form of simulation. Numerous experiments have shown the important place that feedback occupies in the development of skill, the psychological and physiological processes involved have been studied in depth in a variety of learning and there is even one branch of research which seeks, by providing the subject with information about his own bodily processes through electroencephalographs and other instruments, to train the control of, e.g. alpha-wave activity, heart-beat rates, and the function of other internal organs (Collier, 1973; Ornstein, 1975).

Simulations and games permit the control of the perceptual load and conceptual vocabulary with which the student has to deal, whilst at the same time retaining contact with the multi-layered, non-linear, perceptually-dense reality of the world of decision and action. If the simulation or case is not rooted in the reality of this world it fails to carry conviction; if it does not respect the integrity of the analysis of the psychologist, sociologist, philosopher and historian, incorporating these in its teaching on their own terms, then it is unlikely to be useful as a means of advancing the student's understanding and effectiveness.

It would clearly be a mistake to claim too much for case and simulation techniques. Some of their advantages, such as realistic simultaneity, motivation capability, controlled perceptual and conceptual vocabulary, and sensitizing capacity, have been referred to in the preceding paragraphs, but courses of teacher education are seldom based solely upon such techniques. They are generally employed alongside more conventional methods, such as lectures and group discussions. This is in contrast to the approach in some other educational settings, which have a more explicit reliance upon such materials. The catalogue of the Harvard Business School included the following statement :

> 'Instruction in all the educational programs at the Business School is by the case method. Lectures are kept to a minimum, and if assignments of collateral reading are given, they are primarily for purposes of technical background. In the business world, where every decision must be appropriate to the specific situation and no two situations are identical, it is the ability to analyse, to judge trends, to weigh diverse influences, that leads to sound judgments; and that ability can be developed only through practice. Therefore, from the outset students at the Business School discuss cases, i.e., real business situations in which executives take action and are responsible for their results . . . The students study the case individually. Then they meet in small groups for further exploration, sharing their varied backgrounds of experience and sharpening their ideas in argument. Individually, again, they arrive at a decision which they must be prepared to defend. Then, in class, under the questioning and guidance of an instructor, they weigh the factors, probe the underlying issues, compare the advantages and disadvantages of different moves, and work out a course of action in the light of the company's objectives' (quoted Orth, 1963).

Similarity between the resolution of cases and the work that the business executive does at his own desk or in committee room is greater than that between the teacher's discussions of a case or simulation item and the way in which he interviews a parent or handles a classroom problem. Few of the teacher's activities and decisions are expressed in written form, and his direct verbal instructions have a somewhat different character from those of the executive. In a review of Administrative Performance and Personality (Hemphill, Fredericksen and Griffiths; a book that reports the research on which the well-known Whitman school materials, published and distributed by the Universities Council for Educational administration in the United States were originally designed), Erickson (1963) has drawn attention to the fact that '. . . (1) all responses were required not only to be verbal, but to be in writing; (2) the responses occurred under stressful conditions, including severe time limitations; (3) the in-basket items did not reflect the continuous interaction of a normal environment . . .; (4) the subjects knew that they would not be held responsible, in the usual workaday sense, for their actions . . .'

These last two points are of particular importance. Critics sometimes invoke them as adequate reasons for dismissing the value of simulation techniques. In fact, of course, many of ways in which simulations are used to provide for the provision of feedback, e.g. in the follow-up sessions of a micro-teaching sequence, or through the electronic computer that is used as the base of some man/computer and all-computer simulations that have been developed in business (Zuckerman and Horn, 1974; Gibbs, 1974).

The second problem to which Erickson refers is the absence of responsibility in the simulated situation. To some extent, this is the essence of the technique. The aircraft in the wind tunnel can crash without killing anyone; the student in the Link trainer can make mistakes that would be fatal in real life; the businessman can suggest courses of action that later analysis shows would have brought down his firm in ruins, without a penny being lost. Through the syndicate and plenary discussions of a tricky parent/teacher problem, the head can come to see the weakness of his own solution and ways in which it might be improved. But not all these situations are of the same order. Personality dispositions and other variables enter into the businessman's and the head's skills to a considerable extent, and it is more difficult to categorize their answers as right or wrong. As yet, there have been few attempts to trace links between an individual's behaviour in a simulation or game, and his behaviour on the job, although research on evaluation in this field is now beginning to attract attention (Gunn, 1971). Walford (1972) has drawn attention to the fact that :

> 'Many existing evaluation procedures are unsuited to evaluating simulation, the pre-test and post-test set of questions, for example, defines most easily matters of factual (or at least cognitive) learning. The intention of simulations . . . . is complex and may resist simple evaluation style (i.e., to test simulations only for their transmission of factual knowledge is to give only a partial test).
>
> In addition, some procedures may test the management skills of the teacher handling the game successfully, rather than the game itself.'

Erickson's criticism also relates to the lack of reality in simulation. For all its frequency, this is one of the less cogent and important criticism which the technique has to face, for it misunderstands the purpose of devising a model of a real life situation in the form of games or other materials. As has been pointed out, such a model 'involves abstracting from reality those components and relationships which are hypothesized as crucial to what is being modelled' (Guetzkow, 1962). Different aspects of reality will be seen as crucial according to the perspective of the simulation designer and the use to which the material is to be put. One of the basic justifications for the technique is that the perceptual load of reality is often too heavy to cope with, and that, in order to make sense of the situation, we impose upon it stereotyped model of attributes and relationships that has been derived from unreflective experience.

By suggesting a new model, the case draws attention to features of the situation that might otherwise have been ignored; this can be done only by reducing the perceptual load, omitting a great variety of things that form part of the familiar environment. Resistance to simulation sometimes spring from the way in which it is seen as requiring a new perspective, which it may be painful to acquire. Max Black (1967, p. 101) has referred to the phenomenological compression that is characteristic of the action of the experienced performer :

> 'In such cases, the agent's resistance to a proposed articulation . . . may arise from his use of a private symbolism of visual cues; that have ousted the public and official terminology of the original instructions . . . Rule-guided action, that is appropriately articulated by non-verbal symbolism, and the intuitive transformation or "condensation" that makes it possible, ... is connected in the most intimate way with the learner's necessary effort to impose a memorable order upon what looks initially like a chaos of unrelated items.'

One final criticism remains to be dealt with. If simulation is to help teachers and heads fully to realize what it is they are about, to benefit from their experience in terms of increased knowledge and skill, and to assist in relating the minutiae of day-to-day activity to the wider purposes of school and society, then it must take place in the context of enhancing their intellectual range, cognitive grasp and capacity for fruitful generalization. Bruner (1966) has suggested that this kind of cognitive learning depends partly upon a 'denaturing' process :

> 'It involves at least three things. There must first develop a system of cognitive organization that detaches concepts from the modes of action that they evoke. A hole is to dig but it is also a hole. Secondly, it requires the development of a capacity to detach concepts from their affective contexts. A hole is not just a reminder of a hidden orifice. Finally, it demands a capacity to delay gratification so that the outcomes of acts can be treated as information rather than as simply punishing or rewarding.'

It can be argued that to place too much reliance upon simulation and related techniques is to hinder a process whereby the student builds an adequate cognitive map of his world; this criticism certainly seems to have some validity when applied to the way in which some other methods, such as role playing, group study and discovery methods have been used in the past. If it is to be effective, simulation needs to be associated with a variety of other kinds of learning. At its present stage of development, it is too unsystematized to yield the kind of knowledge that can effectively be integrated into an adequate cognitive system. Zetterberg (1962, pp. 27—28) has drawn attention to some weaknesses in this respect :

> 'Case studies provide vicarious experience. When faced with problems similar to those reported in the case studies, practitioners might consider the solutions that were reported as effective in the case study. The facts of the case history through a process of induction become generalisations, and these generalisations through a process of deduction are applied to the new case in hand. This, of course, can be very useful. The trouble is that the whole procedure is usually "intuitative"; that is, the inductions are never formulated, no limiting conditions are stated for the generalisations, and no deduction to the new problem is made explicit. Thus the possibilities of error multiply.'

Much of the simulation material available for use in teacher education today works on the buckshot principle. There is a broad scatter of explicit and implicit concepts and skills, but little attempt to systematize these in terms of a coherent theory of educational organization or of teaching. Most tutors concerned with initial training have sufficient understanding of what is involved in teaching and learning to be able to select those materials most relevant to the needs of their students. Written cases and printed simulation materials are cheaper and easier to prepare than those which make use of videotape, sound-tape, film and other audiovisual techniques, and even if their scope is limited, they do appear to have a considerable range of usefulness in initial training. One example of such use is provided by Cameron Valley School : A Casebook for students Preparing for Work in Secondary Schools, prepared for use by postgraduate students in the University of Bristol Department of Education. Students working for the Postgraduate Certificate in Education spent the whole of the spring term, a period of approximately twelve weeks, practising teaching in schools under the supervision and guidance of teachers and tutors from the University Department. The students themselves attached a great deal of importance of this period of guided practice; there was considerable keenness during the autumn term to acquire the kind of knowledge and skill that look like being useful during the practice period.

It was decided to produce a book of case and simulation items based on the experience of one year's group of students that could be used to acquaint those of the following year with some of the difficulties and problems they might encounter. Both to preserve anonymity and to make the material usable with the minimum of editing, students were asked to write certain of their experiences within the context of an imaginary comprehensive school, details of which were supplied. Each student was asked to provide one or more short cases, which could either be open-ended ('issue cases') or with details of outcome and discussion of the issues involved ('descriptive cases') (Horvat et al., 1965). In addition, where problems lent themselves to such treatment, items of correspondence between the head, staff, parents and the local education office were requested. The cases and items provided by students were then edited, mimeographed and used on a trial basis with tutorial groups in the Department.

The cases and items were grouped according to the chief focus of interest and concern, and pairs of students asked to prepare two or three related cases or items for discussion by tutorial groups, endeavouring where possible to link the problems involved with their other work in the basic disciplines and their experience during the pre-course observation period. Experience confirmed the motivating capacity of the approach and suggested that the method was very popular with the students themselves. No attempt was made to systematize the material in terms of other learning activities that formed part of the course, or to make explicit particular uses to which various parts of the casebook might be put and the background reading that might be relevant to the issues raised.

In a number of American centres experiments are currently being conducted with printed simulation devices as part of programmes of initial training. A project at the University of Indiana included the preparation of simulated exercises in pupil evaluation, on reporting to parents, lesson planning, the preparation of examinations, the diagnosis of learning difficulties in pupils, and conferences between parents and teachers. Background data included printed records and film of classroom work (Cunningham, 1968). Elsewhere, simulated materials have been prepared to help teachers assess reading difficulties and requirements and in connection with a variety of other school and classroom skills (Utsey et al., 1966; Cruickshank, 1966).

In addition to the use of CCTV for micro-teaching, which is discussed elsewhere, teaching machine simulators have been employed in courses of initial training. An interesting example of these is the Professional Decision Simulator, developed by the Learning Systems Institute at Michigan State University (Ward, 1966). An audiotape cartridge and a film cartridge are loaded into a machine, which then provides the student with a sound and film presentation of the circumstances leading up to a decision-making problem and some suggestions as to alternative plans of action.

The student then selects what appears to constitute the most appropriate decision. If this coincides with the preferred decision that has been programmed into the tape and film, positive feedback is provided by the reinforcing continuation of the sound and film, which shows the chosen decision being acted out. If, however, an incorrect choice is made, one of seven aural instruction tracks provides information about the likely outcomes of the decision made and a number of sensitizing cues to restructure the student's perception of the problems. Part or all of the problem sequence of the original film is then repeated.

In addition to motion picture simulators, experiments are being tried with what is called Variable Interval Sequence Action Camera which produces a series of still photographs, spaced at a pre-selected time interval, synchronized with the continuous sound recording. A major advantage of this technique is that the raw film cost is only one twenty-fifth of what is required for motion picture coverage of the same amount of classroom time. This type of presentation has been used in the production of a Selective Observation Simulator, which, as its name suggests, teachers students how to attend selectively to what is going on in their classroom (Learning Systems Institute, 1966).

As yet there appeer to have been few attempts to develop game simulations for use in connection with programmes of initial training. Definitions of game, like those of the simulation, vary. Dorson (1962) quotes the view of E.W. Martin that a game is 'a simulation in which the results for one group depend on the action of their competitors'. The elements of competition and win/lose seem essential to the game simdlation and are largely absent from some of the approaches so far discussed in this chapter. Several existing teaching games appear to be potentially useful in courses of initial training, such as the parent/child game described by Schild (1966) :

> 'The structure of the game gives both players in a pair a great power to damage the other player. The child can, by consistently being "delinquent" (i.e. by always choosing the behavior alternative favourable to himself) keep the parent's score down to a minimum. At the same time the parent can keep the child's score down by issuing strict orders and by being punitive. Such a situation is fertile ground for "strategic moves" of commitments and counter-commitments with the attendant risk of mutual destruction.

Against a weak player who can be intimidated, it may be good strategy for the child to be delinquent or for the parent to be strict and punitive. But for two reasonably good players, the only way to success is to establish some kind of modus vivendi. Such a modus vivendi must be based on mutual yielding: the parent must agree to some behavior alternatives desired by the child, in return for the child's obedience on some issue when the outcome is in the parent's favour.'

This passage immediately evokes a series of concepts and theories from other fields that seem to have some relationship with simulated situations, e.g. the exchange theory of authority outlined by Blau (1964), Homans and others, accounts of teacher—pupil relationships in secondary schools (e.g. Hargreaves, 1967) and even more directly, the conflict theory of Schelling (1960) and Boulding (1963).

Behaviour modification and teacher education

Behaviour modification is now a subject with a large and growing literature, and one which generates a substantial volume of research as well as strong sentiments of support and condemnation. There does not appear to be a college or department of education in a European country that bases its methods of training entirely on operant conditioning, but a number of schools have developed 'token economies' and many teachers now employ reinforcement techniques when dealing with behaviour problems and as aids to instruction. A number of 'self-help' manuals for teachers have been published, one of which begins in the following manner :

> 'This book was not written to be quickly skimmed in a few hours. It was written for the purpose of guiding you, a teacher, through a process of changing the behaviour of one or more of the students in your classroom. To achieve this purpose, chances are that you, too, will have to modify your own behaviour so that it will "fit in" to the approach you will use.

This book was written for you to read, re-read and at appropriate times in the future, to read again. As your behaviour gradually accommodates to the ground rules expressed in this book, you will find that you are more positive in your outlook on teaching, you seem more patient, and you experience fewer problems in individual and clossroom management. Sounds good, doesn't it? Let's begin this adventure . . . ' (Potect, 1974, p. 1).

The basic principle of behaviour modification can be stated quite simply, in the form of a stimulus—behaviour—reinforcement sequence, within within any reinforcement that increases the probability of a given behaviour being emitted is known as a 'positive reinforcer'. The timing and contingency of such PRs are the keys to a behaviour modification strategy. Large claims are made on behalf of such strategies. Platt (1973) cites evidence to show that animal learning can be accelerated by factors of between 10 and 100, that the rate of school and college learning can be doubled, behaviour in psychiatric wards improved, conditions that have defied psychiatric treatment (such as enuerisis and speech defects) cured, unwanted habits controlled and even voluntary control achieved over functions of the autonomic system (on this last claim, see DiCara, 1970 and Ornstein, 1975).

The potential implications of operant conditioning for teaching and the education of teachers are clearly considerable, and as yet largely unexplored within European institutions. That this is so is in part due to the rejection by many educationists of what they see as the mechanistic assumptions and manipulative consequences of Skinnerian doctrine, and which outweigh any advantages that operant conditioning may have in terms of efficiency and economy. In the words of Argyris (1971, p. 551) :

'I concede that many of Skinner's claims about the validity of his technology are substantiated or eventually will be substantiated by him and his colleagues. But the important question about a technology that is science-based and works, is, do we waut, it around? What kind of world would we have if its potentialities were fully realised? What would be the quality of life after years of using an experimentally-based, empirically-validated technology for behavioral change?'

To which the reply comes that it is only by replacing the contemporaay Promethean imperatives of industrial society by alternatives that will guarantee happiness without constituting such a high charge on the environment that man has any hope of survival at all (Pirages, 1973). (For an argument from a biological perspective that reaches similar conclusions see Martin (1975). Wheeler (1973) has brought together a useful collection of papers that argues the case for and against operant conditioning.)

Behaviour modification now has its own journals and a number of established applications in fields such as mental disorder and deviance. There are signs of increasing interest in such techniques for more general educational purposes (Haring and Phillips, 1972; O'Leary and O'Leary, 1972; Ackerman, 1972) which if stimulated by new and well-publicized research may eventually have an impact on programmes of teacher education. Already, of course, behavioural concepts and Skinnerian ideas have influenced the development of approaches such as performance-based teacher education, but usually in less direct ways than would be the case if operant conditioning was applied, and without many of the philosophical and social overtones that the latter has come to possess.

The development of protocol materials

Discussions of the use of micro-teaching, mini-courses, behaviour modification techniques, simulations and games, field-based experiences and skill training units are often found in the same places. If the distinctions between their contents are sometimes unclear, those between their conceptual and theoretical origins are even more so. Protocol is a term generally reserved for those materials designed to illustrate in a 'lifelike' situation key concepts drawn from the disciplines that underlie the study of education and the development of educational theory (Burdin and Cruickshank, 1974). In traditional English terms, they contribute to the 'Education' rather than the methods courses, at least insofar as the former have developed since the early Sixties. Such a distinction between education and methods is a good deal harder to make for some European countries, where countries, where courses in pedagogics still embrace both theoretical and applied aspects. Part of the support for the protocols movement in the United States has come from those who feared that heavily field-based courses, planned to satisfy performance and competence criteria laid down by state legislatures, would squeeze out theory and leave no place for the exploration of psychological, philosophical, sociological and historical issues—to name but four of the disciplines that can claim to contribute to an understanding of educational processes and institutions.

The movement has also gained from the press towards relevance among faculty and student bodies, the need to devise methods of instruction, even in fields such as the philosophy of education, that appenr to satisfy some at least of the competency criteria, and the popularity of organizing content into smaller and smaller units of instruction, the student's understanding of which can be rapidly evaluated and reinforced on an individualized basis. But it has to be admitted that distinctions between these protocol materials and those that are developed for the training of skills are by no means as clear cut as some statements (e.g. Howey, 1975, p. 28) suggest.

Protocol materials are currently being developed and tested in a number of United States centres, with financial and other help from the US Office of Education, and in accordance with complex guidelines embodied in a 'Master Coordinate System' of concepts relevant to teacher education (Cruickshank, 1974). Hudgins et al. (1974) have since produced a catalogue of concepts in the pedagogical domain of teacher education which has two functions—first, to 'begin the conceptual mapping of the pedagogical domain by identifying appropriate concepts that appear in the literature of teacher education, estimating the overlap or redundancy among such concepts and identifying ostensible gaps within the domain, and the kinds of concepts needed to fill those gaps' (Hudgins, 1974, p. 2). The second function of the catalogue is to produce information helpful to those who wish to develop materials that illustrate the concept. Two examples are given below of items taken from the Catalogue, one ('Response Range Focusing') from the section headed 'Process Regulating', the other ('Learning by Inquiry') from the 'Divergent Productivity' section :

Kesponse Range Focusing

Definition : An aspect of content control whereby the potential range of pupil responses is either expanded or restricted as a consequence of teacher questions and directives.

Indicators : This concept is relatively independent of the cognitive levei of responses at the same or at verying cognitive levels.

Illustrations

1. (Narrow) Teacher: Was Adams a strong president?
   (Broad) Teacher: In what ways would you say Adams was either a strong or a weak president?
2. (Narrow) Teacher: What's the right way to solve that problem?
   (Broad) Teacher: How many ways can you get that answer?
3. (Narrow) Teacher: Do you like to watch a sunset?
   (Broad) Teacher: How does a sunset make you feel? (p. 70)

Learning by Inquiry

Definition : Established when a pupil or group of pupils are confronted with a phenomenon or outcome for which they have no immediate explanation, and for which neither the teacher nor instructional materials offer an explanation. In learning by inquiry the pupils must apply rules of logic and/or scientific method to obtain and to organize information that will contribute to an explanation of the phenomenon or consequence. As a practical matter, learning by inquiry in schools must usually be carefully programmed by the teacher to avoid aimless manipulation of data or variables by pupils.

Indicators :

1. Inquiry learning necessitates that the learner (s) be confronted with an event they are unable to explain.
2. Inquiry learning also necessitates that a methodology or set of procedures be available that can channel the pupils' intellectual efforts in productive ways.
3. Divergent thinking, asking questions, offering hypotheses and suggestions that would lead in numerous different directions, if followed, is characteristic of inquiry learning.
4. Inquiry learning may proceed individually or in groups.
5. Inquiry learning can be conducted in a variety of curricular areas; certainly in arithmetic and mathematics, science and the social studies.

Illustration: 5th graders view a brief film in which a large container with three holes in it spaced from top to bottom is filled with water. Water spurts from the three holes in arcs of different magnitude. The film ends with the question, "Why does the water go farther from A than from B and C?" (These holes are labelled on the film.) The children then engage in systematic question asking designed to give them information about conditions and events.

> The teacher will only answer questions "yes" or "no" which constrains pupils to formulate their questions in answerable form. Finally the children employ the knowledge gleaned from their answers to propose that the different streams from the container (pp. 134--135).

The number of concepts suggested within the pedagogical domain is very large. When those from other theoretical domains are added, the total begins to astume formidable proportions, suggesting what Cruickshank (1974) has called 'concept overkill'. It is also argued that the original idea for a protocol, which began with a typical situation that might be encountered by a teacher, and then by means of careful inspection and analysis yielded the key concepts required to understand and interpret the event, has now been reversed--'situations first' has become 'concepts first', with a consequent loss of theoretical relevance and usefulness.

Everything that has been said so far about protocols is taken from United States experience, and there are few examples in Europe of attempts to develop materials or to systematize concepts on the scale undertaken by the Americans. There are, however, many examples of efforts being made to devise teaching materials for the theory of education based on topics and situations rather than courses in the psychology, sociology and philosophy of education, especially when the programme of professional training is short (typically for university graduates one year or less) (University of Nottingham School of Education, 1975; University of London Institute of Education, 1977). Few such attempts are as analytical as the American work, partly because of a lack of reseach and development resources for this purpose, partly because there are fewer teacher educators in the United Kingdom and European countries than in the United States who are convinced of the feasibility of constructing an understanding of educational theory from the consideration of often highly discrete situations and concepts, and in the possibility of systematizing such work on a quasi-scientific basis.

Performance and competency-based teacher education

Performance-based or competency-based—the terms are for all practical purposes interchangeable—teacher education developed in the United States towards the end of the Nineteen-Sixties as a response to an interlocking set of political, social, educational, technological and intellectual pressures, and has for the past few years been the dominant theme of discussions about the content, organization and control of the professional aspects of teacher preparation in that country. The movement has had remarkably little impact upon Europe. There are signs, however, of a developing interest among European teacher educators in some elements of performance-based programmes, and, subject to the general provisos made elsewhere in this book about the future of teacher education research, it can be expected that as the knowledge base of teacher education practice is enlarged, so there will be attempts to incorporate the outcomes of this work into the planning and execution of programmes. This possibility is strengthened by the likelihood that the research best able to obtain project funding will be that which promises usable results, of a kind that lead to the improvement of teacher education.

The literature of PBTE is already enormous. Houston (1974) in a book of 452 pages on the subject lists in excess of 700 references. A great deal of what has been published consists of exhortatory and descriptive statements, records of the experience of particular institutions and authorities in the design and implementation of programmes, lists of performance objectives and criteria, instruments for the purpose of evaluation and, finally, criticisms (sometimes fiercely expressed) of the PBTE concept as a whole or of particular aspects of it. There is a trend towards more systematic research on PBTE, particularly in respect of the means of evaluation employed, A search of the ERIC files for such evaluation research, undertaken in the course of writing this book, produced one hundred and forty four items from 1973 to mid-1976. It can be expected that this trend will continue as performance-based programmes become established and as, no doubt, the high hopes that were held out for their success come to be revised.

The intellectual roots of PBTE are to be found in Skinnerian behaviourism, in systems theory, in a body of research on teacher effectiveness, and in an interpretation of humanistic psychology that stresses the value of individualized and personalized learning on the basis of modularized programmes. Its political roots are in accountability, the importance of meeting—and being seen to meet—minority needs, the shift of power in teacher education from the professors to practitioners and the public (evident in several European countries as well as in the United States), the press towards participation (Taylor, 1976), student demands for relevance and administrators' and legislators' concern about the impact of left-wing ideas on college youth. Other predisposing and supporting conditions for PBTE have included dissatisfaction with the outcomes of 'traditional' teacher preparation, a desire to link pre-service, induction and in-service training in a continuous sequence, the introduction of a more sophisticated technology of instruction, including CCTV, video recording and computers, and the development of a stronger research base for the discussion of procedures intrinsic to performance assessment, such as feedback.

The proximate stimulus for the PBTE movement included the funding by the US Office of Education of a number of major research and development projects, in particular the Teacher Education Models Programs at a number of major universities, by means of which the teaching skills that formed the basis of performance objectives came to be identified. By the beginning of the Seventies the main dimensions of performance-based preparation had been spelled out, and state authorities began to mandate colleges and universities to produce teachers trained in accordance with these specifications. The following diagram, adapted from Elam (1971), indicates the main elements of the PBTE Model :

Essential Elements	*Implied Characteristics*	*Related, Desirable Characteristics*
1. Teacher competencies to demonstrated are role-derived, specified in behavioral terms and made public.	1. Individualization	1. Field setting
2. Assessment criteria are competency-based, specify mastery level, and made public.	2. Feedback	2. Broad base for decision making
3. Assessment requires performance as prime evidence, takes student knowledge into account.	3. Systematic program	3. Protocol and training materials
4. Student's progress rate depends on demonstrated competency.	4. Exit requirement emphasis	4. Student participation in decision makking
5. Instructional program facilitates develoment and evaluation of specific competencies.	5. Student and program accountability	5. Research-oriented and regenerative
		6. Career-continuous
		7. Role integration

PBTE depends heavily on the use of instructional modules, which have been defined by Elam (1971, p. 9) as follows :

'A module is a set of learning activities (with objectives, prerequisites, preassessment, instructional activities post-assessment and remediation) intended to facilitate the student's acquisition and demonstration of a particular competency. Modularization increases possibilities for self-pacing, individualization, personalization, independent study, and alternative means of instruction. It also permits accurate targeting on the development of specific competencies.'

Modules are designed to achieve specific behavioural objectives, such as the following (Burke, 1972, p. 25) :

'On completion of the materials and learning experiences in this WILKIT (module) you will be able to :

1. Demonstrate your comprehension of structural analysis skills by scoring eighty or more points on the Structural Analysis Test (W—31 Structural Analysis skills) . . .

3. Demonstrate a knowledge of the three levels of comprehension by defining the three levels in writing and giving examples of each (W—34 Reading Comprehension) . . .

6. Respond to the group interation of a classroom meeting in which you will assume the leader role, as measured by a 75 per cent agreement with the faculty adviser on a teacher-designed summary of group interaction (W—21 Classroom Group Meetings).'

As Haberman and Stinnet (1973, p. 96) put the matter :

'*Wherever possible* the competency behaviors taught to teachers are attitudes, skills, understandings and behaviours that research evidence suggest leads to intellectual, emotional and physical growth in children' (italics mine).

Leaving aside the question of how attitudes and understandings can be said to constitute 'competency behaviours', the facts are that very few teacher behaviours have up to the present been validated against pupil learning outcomes. Given the complexity of the variables involved, and the context-bound nature of the teaching transaction, it seems doubtful if it will ever be possible to identify competencies that have a specific relationship to particular forms of pupil learning. So there has been something of a retreat from the earlier pupil outcome criterion :

> 'Recognizing the difficulty of making a large number of specific connections between teachers' behavior and pupil growth, the CBTE approach also requires clear statements of the teachers' role . . . Behaviors to be taught to students are actually the functions students must perform in order to fulfil the role of teacher that has been conceptualized as the progıam goal. Frequently, behaviors taught to students can be substantiated by the research literature as correlates of various forms of pupil growth; other competency behaviors are supported as having logical, theoretic connections to pupil growth' (Haberman and Stinnett, 1973, pp. 96—97).

There has been no lack of criticism of the PBTE movement particularly of its psychological and philosophical assumptions and its political consequences. Travers (1975, p. 418) suggests that 'the titles of works on the subject have become progressively more extravagant and more like toothpaste commercials', and argues that the claim that PBTE is research-based is specious, the very term 'competence' having its origins in the discourse of politics rather than that of research. Broudy (1972) has challenged the logic of PBTE, the possibility of assembling discrete teaching skills into whole teaching acts, and its political naivety (p. 5). Nash (1973), from the standpoint of humanistic psychology, has underlined some of the threats that PBTE might pose to such values as freedom, uniqueness, creativity, productivity, wholeness, responsibility and interdependence.

There is also the question of the feasibility of a full-blown PBTE-based professional education, not just in terms of relating teacher performances to teacher effectiveness and pupil outcomes, which is likely to pose problems for a long time to come, but even in respect of the types of programme at present being developed and implemented. These are very costly in time and resources. Darcy (1974, p. 326) comments that 'It took almost a year of working together on a weekly if not daily basis for the seven experienced teachers and the university professors involved in the (State University of New York at Albany—Schenectady Teacher Corps) project to come to a point where they could begin to write out the list of competencies . . . After the group was ready to begin writing competencies for the beginning teacher, it took more than two months of daily work, collectively and individually, for the group to prepare a document . . . of 25 closely typed pages'. It is easy in a conference address or statement to an education authority to make such dedication and concern seem valuable and commendable, but it has to be asked what cost those concerned are incurring in time that might otherwise be spent on equally valuable activities, in developing their own professional skill and subject knowledge.

Another point, of considerable relevance to the position in a number of European countries, is the political feasibility and effects on programme contents of having to obtain agreement amongst bodies as diverse as University Senates and Faculties, Ministries of Education, Teachers'Unions, Governors of institutions, and sometimes representatives of parents and local communities. Lindsey (1976) has shown just how serious these problems can be, especially when the complexity of the processes involved makes exceptional demands on the time and ability of even the most experienced and best informed of those involved. Anyone who has taken part in the attempts made in European countries to base teacher education practices on a broader basis of agreement than the college or department faculty will recognize the force of Lindsey's point (1976, p. 513) that 'In some instances, building agreements about membership, meetings, voting rights, minutes and tasks consumes so much time that program development gets short notice'.

Finally, it has to be said that although there are those who believe that the kinds of emphasis encouraged by PBTE and its variants will encourage support for more research relevant to the improvement of teacher education, this is by no means certain. There is a danger that the tests applied for research support will be too narrow and programmatic, that 'results' will be looked for to the exclusion of gains in understanding, theoretical development and conceptual clarity, and that the time that staff might otherwise give to research will be taken up in coping with the consequences of participatory decision-making and field-centred courses. (It is interesting in this connection to note the findings of a study by Seldin, 1975, on how the deans of US liberal arts colleges rate their professors. Apparently there has been a significant decline between 1966 and 1973 in the importance attached to publication and research, whereas campus committee work and student advising increased sharply as 'major factors' in faculty evaluation. The dangers of such trends for the research role of the university are plan.)

Studies of the field-based element in initial preparation

From their earliest days, programmes of initial teacher preparation have included periods of practical work in classrooms and schools, and there is clear evidence that students have for a long time attached considerable importance to 'school experience', 'teaching practice', 'practicum', or whatever other name such parts of the course have borne. Hakansson and Wikander (1974) report that Swedish teacher candidates 'judge their training term to be "the most important part" of their education'. They go on to say that 'the positive evaluation of the training-term expressed by the candidates is partially connected to their low expectations as well as generally negative experiences from the remainder of the teacher-training program'. (See also Poole and Gaudry, 1975).

The purpose of school experience has been to give students opportunities to practise their skills, to achieve familiarity and understanding of the needs of children and the institutional environment of schools, and to relate the kinds of learning in which they engage in the college or department to the realities of the classroom. The possibility of these objectives being fulfilled has in many countries been reduced because the relationship—timing, sequence, preparation—of school experience to college work has not been carefully thought through, because the links between school-based and college-based experience have been left to chance, because supervision has been inadequate and feedback insufficient in quantity and quality to promote positive learning. Much of the recent work that has been done on this aspect of teacher preparation has been designed to identify and to document these weaknesses, and to devise means whereby a better 'fit' can be achieved between the various parts of the initial programme.

Such work has also been stimulated by the desire of experienced teachers to play a more active part in the preparation of new members of the profession, and the shift towards field-based training that has been a feature of recent teacher education reforms. Whilst in some countries the preparation of some grades of teachers has traditionally been 'school-based', e.g. in Italy, for Danish secondary teachers in the pedagogicum and for those in the Federal Republic of Germany in Studienseminars, this is less a reflection of current thought about the links between theoretical and practical studies than a survival from earlier arrangements, in which the provision of professional study opportunities for such teachers was in any case minimal. This does not mean, however, that some of these traditional patterns cannot be adapted to hew needs, and this is in fact being attempted in the Federal Republic.

The kinds of knowledge and theory that bear upon the study and analysis of what we have here called 'school experience' are legion. Many years ago, John Dewey drew attention to the effects of strong teacher models on student behaviour (quoted Barnett, 1975, p. 47) :

'The student adjusts his actual methods of teaching, not to

the principles which he is acquiring, but to what he sees succeed and fail in an empirical way from moment to moment; what he sees other teachers doing who are more experienced and successful keeping order than he is; and to the injunctions and directions given him by others. In this way the controlling habits of the teacher get fixed with comparatively little reference to principles in the pedagogy, logic and history of education.'

Lortie (1965) has emphasized how significant and such strong models can be, given that future teachers have been exposed to many thousands of hours of teacher behaviour before they ever reach college. Unless efforts are made to create systematic linkages between college-based and school-based study, the supervising teacher may simply become one more teacher-model, and little new learning may occur. It has also to be recognised that the opportunities for practice that the usual periods of school experience offer are very limited in scope and in time.

Much of the research that has been done on modelling behaviours in connection with the development of micro-teaching is relevant to the evaluation of school experience (Brusling, 1974; Bandura, 1969), as is the work of Bruner and Olson (1973) on modelling as a form of learning. It appears, however, that little of this work has yet been taken into account in planning school experience, partly no doubt because of the greater difficulty of controlling variables in a real classroom as compared with a micro-teaching laboratory.

The learning curves characteristic of micro-teaching skill practice plus expert feedback have been shown by Brown and Armstrong (1975) to approximate those for the learning of psycho-motor skills.

Against this background, there are very great difficulties in implementing programmes that satisfy criteria such as the following (quoted Smith and Sagan, 1975, p. 91) :

'The effectiveness of clinical experiences is largely determined by the extent to which they are an integral part of a comprehensive teacher education program. If the analytical experience is to illustrate an educational principle, the relationship must be clear. If theory is to be tested and applied, the clinical experience must be fashioned to that end. It is not enough that elements of the program are scheduled during the same semester or that course work occurs concurrently with direct and simulated experiences. The programme must be planned to clarify relationships and provide opportunities to consider the implications of varied experiences within the context of a total program.'

If these difficulties are to be faced and as far as possible overcome, attention has to be given, inter alia to matters such as the following :

1. The timing, sequence and organization of periods of school experience, in relationship to the various elements of initial training.

2. The establishment of liaison between the training institutions and the schools of a kind that facilitates the achievement of school experience objectives.

3. Planning and preparing school experience for the individual student, including the identification of the skills that are to be practised, the knowledge that will require to be employed and the understandings to be achieved.

4. Devising appropriate supervisory arrangements, including means for the evaluation of the experience gained and, if necessary, its assessment against agreed criteria of performance.

There is work going on in a number of countries in each of these areas, most of it in Sweden, the United Kingdom and the United States. The general trend is towards an increase in the proportion of time devoted to school experience, and for a more graduated distribution over the course as a whole. Efforts are also being made to conceptualize the whole course—school-based and college-based elements alike—as a single whole (Webster, 1975) within which decisions would be made as to the most appropriate settings for various kinds of learning experience.

The establishment of close relations between colleges, schools, national and local authorities, teachers' and students' organizations and the community is part of the rhetoric of teacher education reform in most countries at the present time. The difficulties to which such arrangements may give rise have already been discussed, but the forging of closer links between teacher educators and classroom practitioners in respect of school experience has stronger possibilities of success than some of the other forms of cooperation proposed, if only because there is a defined task, a limited remit and, in some places, an existing record of mutual assistance.

The possibilities of giving a larger measure of supervisory responsibility to the school has been explored by Cope (1971) and the implementation of 'teacher tutor' schemes and school partnership' arrangements reported by Bell (1966), Baker (1970), Lacey and Lamont (1976) and Martin et al. (1976).

The preparation of the individual student in a way that ensures maximum benefit from school experience has implications for the whole course of initial preparation, and has been extensively discussed by Stones and Morris (1972). There may be much that can be done to encourage explicit connections between skills acquired in the college and teaching performances in the classroom—certainly more than has been attempted so far—but such systematization is essentially limited by the unpredictable nature of many classroom events, a fact that has led Travers (1974) to argue for an emphasis, not on the development of skills ('The idea that there are specific classroom situations to be handled by specific skills learned in specific modules of teacher training is a bureaucrat's dream quite divorced from the realities of the modern classroom', p. 419), but on the characteristics of teachers, such as clarity, variability, enthusiasm and task orientation, and of teacher roles that have been shown to be related to the academic achievement of pupils, which help the teacher engage in productive, as distinct from reproductive problem-solving.

Effective supervision, the fourth of our list of desiderata, has generated a large literature and a good deal of research, again much of it American in origin and focus (Fuller and Manning, 1973; Cope, 1971). The literature includes much on on the training and preparation of supervisory teachers, reflecting the trend towards giving greater responsibility to practitioners as distinct from professors (Tom, 1974). Cope defines supervision as a way of intensifying student learning, over against the stress upon grading and assessment with which it has traditionally been associated; and there is a clear movement away from the assessment function of the supervising teacher and college tutor (Goldhammer, 1969).

The reconceptualization of 'teaching practice' called for by Stones and Morris (1972) does not yet appear to have made a great deal of progress in the programmes of European teacher education institutions, although there are indications of interest in the concept of 'field-based' experience that is now in use in the United States, defined by Sinclair (1975, p. 6) as 'the most recent in a long history of similar terms used to denote practice teaching, student teaching, professional laboratory experiences, pre-student teaching, or some other aspect of that part of teacher education that takes place in a setting other than the college lecture hall'.

Such settings need not be restricted to classrooms and schools. Students are being encouraged to spend more time working with community groups, assisting with youth clubs, sharing experiences with ethnic and cultural groups other than their own. Course credit is sometimes given for such work.

The Danish Ministry of Education provides funds in support of an experimental teacher training programme that takes students all over the world in old buses which they have helped to prepare and equip themselves—but requires that such students should satisfy normal examination requirements before they are given qualified status!

10

Basic Techniques

Educational research not a mechanized routine

Although relatively definite techniques will be described in this and several of the following chapters, the reader should not infer that educational research can be reduced to a mechanized routine. A problem, whose study is worthy of designation as educational research, represents a "new" situation. In meeting this situation the research worker must define the problem and then determine what technique, or techniques, are appropriate for collecting the necessary data. In making this decision he must consider not only the nature of the problem but also the conditions which he will likely encounter in collecting his data. For example, he may have to choose between two techniques on the basis of their relative feasibility with respect to the conditions current at the time of the investigation. After a technique has been determined upon, it is frequently necessary to make adaptations to the problem and to the conditions under which the research is conducted. Sometimes considerable ingenuity is required to obtain the needed data. The handling of the data collected may be a relatively routine activity but the interpretation of the derived statistics is likely to require critical reflective thinking of a high order. Hence, the reader of this text should, at all times, bear in mind that educational research cannot be conducted in a routine fashion.

Types of data

When reference is made to the data of educational research, one is likely to think of test scores, school marks, chronological ages, teachers' salaries, counts of things such as pupils or language errors, and the like. The term, however, is used with a broader meaning. In dealing with some educational problems it is necessary to secure statements of beliefs or opinions, statements descriptive of schools or events, conclusions reached by previous investigators, or historical information. Hence, data should be thought of as including all facts, concepts, and principles useful in deriving answers to the questions listed in the definition of a problem.

Data that represent measures or counts of things are expressed in numerical terms and are commonly referred to as quantitative. Statements of beliefs or opinions, descriptions of schools or events, and the like are referred to as non-quantitative data.

Objective data versus subjective data

The data of educational research are often regarded as subjective when they consist of expressions of judgment made by subjects participating in the investigation as sources of data. From this point of view, responses to many questionnaries would be labeled "subjective data." It is more desirable to regard as subjective, data obtained in such a manner that they may be influenced by the person collecting them. For example, observations of the behavior of small children made by a research worker would be subjective because, in collecting the data, he gives meaning to his sensations in perceiving over acts. To the extent that another research worker making the same observations would be likely to give different meanings to the "sense data," we are justified in regarding the recorded observations as subjective.

The converse of this statement gives the definition of objectivity which will be used in this book. When data are such that there has been very little or no opportunity for them to be affected by the prejudices, opinions, and judgment of the person collecting them, they are to be regarded as objective.

It should be noted that the subjectivity of data is a matter of degree. Certain types of data are regarded as "highly subjective" because experience has shown that in general two persons working independently will obtain significantly different data. This is true in the case of marks assigned to examination papers of the essay type. Other types of data are known to be only slightly influenced by the person who collects them and may be described as "slightly subjective." Sometimes such data are designated as "objective" but it is wise to reserve this term for data whose degree of subjectivity approaches zero. In other words, "subjective" has a somewhat broad and relative meaning while "objective" has a more restricted meaning.

The Problem a guide in collecting data

The problem, when adequately defined, specifies the data to be collected, and usually the items collected should be limited to the requirements of the problem. Collecting unnecessary data consumes time and may distract the attention of the investigator from the issues of his problem. Occasionally it may appear desirable to redefine the problem so as to extend its scope, or the investigator may find that it is feasible to collect data for one or more related problems without adding greately to the time required for this phase of the work. It is unwise, however, to collect data merely because they are thought to be interesting. Data which are not used represent wasted effort.

The basic techniques for collecting data

Although the details of the procedure followed in a given problem are determined by its nature and the availability of sources and instruments, there appear to be only a few basic techniques. In the following exposition, seven are recognized.

1. Copying data from records and published sources.
2. Analyzing texts, records of activities, etc.
3. Interviewing.
4. Constructing and using questionnaires.
5. Securing a current record of activities, etc.
6. Making estimates and ratings.
7. Selecting and administering tests.

1. *Copying data from records and published sources*

When data are to be copied from records or published sources, the principal considerations are accuracy and economy of time. Accuracy in copying is attained when the entries made are identical with those in the source. The number of errors can be reduced to a minimum by employing certain techniques and devices, but checking is necessary to insure accuracy.

The details of the process of copying and the form in which the copied items should be arranged vary with the nature of the source and the use that is to be made of the data. A resourceful person will usually think of devices that will facilitate the work as well as reduce the errors of copying to a minimum. When data are being copied from several columns of a table, a strip of cardboard may be used to assist in following a line across the table. Alexander has suggested a helpful device when data are to be copied from only certain columns of a table. It consists of a strip of paper, or cardboard, one edge of which is notched so that when it is placed horizontally on the table, the items to be copied are exposed and the irrelevant items are masked.

In copying numerical data from records and published sources it is important to label accurately each item or each group of similar items. What this means may be illustrated by reference to numerical data recorded in a publication of the

United States Office of Education. For example, Table 10 of this publication gives data pertaining to students in state normal schools. Any item copied from this table should be accompanied by the words, or phrases, which give meaning to the datum. For example, one figure given in the table may be copied "2805 women resident state normal school students enrolled in regular session in New Jersey, 1927-28." The fact that this figure includes both white and colored women students should probably be recorded also.' The figure 7291 when copied should be given the label : "resident men students in all courses, excluding duplicates, enrolled in state normal schools of continental United States, 1927-28; including both white and colored men students." If the precise meaning of the label is not apparent, it should be ascertained and recorded. Such labels as "per pupil in average daily attendance," "per cent," and even "enrollment" may vary in meaning.

Economy of time in copying is attained by devising an appropriate plan of work and by employing special devices such as the one described by Alexander. Contributions are made to economy in the total time of the research by copying the data in a form that will facilitate their tabulation and by making certain that all of the needed data are copied when the source is at hand. Frequently much time can be saved by anticipating the tabulations to be made from the copied data. Items copied from several sources which pertain to the same topic can be copied on the same card, or page. Items can be grouped so that calculation of measures of central tendency, such as means is greatly facilitated. Occasionally, it may be desirable to plan the tables which are to appear in the reported research and to organize the copying of numerical data so that blanks in the prepared tables may easily be filled in. Careful planning reduces the probability of omitting needed items in copying. Furthermore, careful planning will tend to restrict the tendency to copy interesting but irrelevant data.

Although it is not a part of the process of copying, the investigator should inquire concerning the accuracy of the sources. Sometimes one source may be checked against another. An illustration of this is found in the work of Rugg in the St. Louis Survey. In this investigation Rugg checked the statistics of the United States Bureau of Education against the statistics of the United States Bureau of Census and showed, for example, that "the per pupil cost for salaries and expenses of supervisors, principals, salaries of teachers, repairs, textbooks, salaries of janitors, obtained from the two sources. . . show a very satisfactory agreement. . . ." The investigator who utilizes numerical data from records and published sources should regard his data in somewhat the same manner as the historical research worker. He should seek to establish the validity and accuracy of his data by attempting to secure "affirmations of independent witnesses."

Finally, when copying data from records and published sources, it is important to make a complete record of the exact source from which the data are being taken. Such a record serves three purposes : First, the source may be more easily located again if further data are needed. Second the source may be more easily located for checking the accuracy of the data copied. Third, it is very desirable to present in the report of the investigation adequate and accurate citations of the sources of the numerical data. It is not scholarly to do otherwise.

2. *Analyzing textbooks, courses of study, records of activities, and the like.*

In analyzing textbooks, the investigator may wish to determine what topics are treated, what words are used, what types of learning exercises are given, and so on, or his purpose may be that of determining the amount of space given to topics, the frequeney and order of appearance of words, the frequency of different types of learning exercises, and the like. In analyzing courses of study he may wish to determine what courses are offered and the characteristics of these courses. Pupil writing may be analyzed with respect to language errors.

The identification of words, language errors, topics, and other characteristics requires the recognition of certain criteria. The problem, when adequately defined, specifies or at least implies the criteria to be observed. For example, if the problem calls for the determination of the arithmetical processes needed in solving problems given in commonly used chemistry texts, the meaning of the term "arithmetical processes" furnishes a criterion. More precise definition may specify the identification of particular number combinations.

The analysis usually requires careful reading of the texts, courses of study, or other materials during which the items that satisfy one or more of the criteria are identified and copied on data sheets or cards. Occasionally the reading may be completed before the work of recording is begun. In such cases the investigator may check with suitable symbols the items that are to be copied later. This is an excellent procedure when a trained analyst is needed in the identification of the items, but the work of copying may be left to clerks.

The criteria to be observed may be simple, For example, if pupil compositions are being analyzed for misspelled words. the spellings given by a dictionary furnish they criterion. When the problem is to determine the "vocabulary load" of textbooks, the Thorndike Work Book is often used as the criterion. This list contains Thorndike's determination of the ten thousand most commonly used worbs in the English language and when used as a criterion the analysis becomes the identification of the words not found in this list. The analysis may be made more detailed by identifying the words in the first three thousand, those in the next two thousand, and so on. Thorndike's list is not entirely satisfactory as a criterion because no attention is given to the particular meaning with which a word is used. Precise identification of technical terms in a particular field would require a more complex criterion.

The more common analyses of records of activities are those of pupil writings for language errors or misspelled words and of arithmetical work for calculation errors. Charters has reported an attempt to ascertain the arithmetical operations used by salespeople. He selected at random 7337 charge cheeks (records of purchase transactions in which the goods are charged to customer accounts) and analyzed them for the addition and multiplication combinations involved. Another illustration is the analysis made of the Reader's Guide to Periodical Literature for the three-year period of 1919-21. A card was made for each of the eleven thousand topics appearing in the Index. The number of articles relating to each topic was noted. The cards were then sorted into piles, "one pile for each general field of human action or interest that seemed to be indicated or called for by the cards themselves." The sorting was carried on in this way until an apparently satisfactory grouping was attained. This work of classification resulted in a list of 46 topics with a range of from 9920 articles on the topic of government down to 89 for mathematics. The research of Finley and Caldwell illustrates another type of analysis. They sought to determine the extent to which biological material appears in the public press.

Sometimes the formulation of criteria creates an important subordinate problem because the investigator is exploring a new field. For example, in a study of arithmetic texts by Monroe and Clark it was necessary to determine the elemental types of problems before the analysis could be begun and a list of 333 problem types was evolved only after several weeks of labor. In this case the task was unusually difficult because little attention had been given to the determination of problem types.

Many of the simpler types of analysis tend to be objective and a careful worker will secure highly accurate data, but not infrequently the process of analysis is rather highly subjective. In such cases steps should be taken to reduce the effect of subjectivity to a minimum. The first few hours devoted to the analysis should be considered a period of training and the work should be done over, preferably toward the close of the total period of analysis. A memorandum should be kept of all decisions made, so that consistency may be attained. All of the materials should be analyzed by the same person rather than be divided among two or more worers. If the materials can be analyzed independently by two or more persons, their results may be averaged.

3. *Interviewing*

The interview and the questionnaire are used for securing unrecorded data in the possession of other persons. Both of these techniques involve subjective elements, but when appropriate precautions are taken, the data obtained will usually be at least reasonably satisfactory.

In order to be successful the interviewer must be prepared for his task. An important phase of this preparation is determining the questions to be asked. An essential characteristic of the questions formulated is their relevance to the problem. The words and phrases used in asking the questions should be such as are likely to be understood by the individuals interviewed. It is desirable to avoid "leading" questions, since they tend to bias the responses. A question beginning "Do you—" will secure information of one type while a question commencing "How do you—" will secure a different type of information. Questions beginning "Do you—" and "How do you—" are instrumental in securing factual information, while questions beginning "Do you favor—" "How do you feel about—," "Do you recommend—" function in the collection of opinions, judgments, and the like. A question beginning "Why do you—" may secure either facts, or opinions, or both.

General questions are not likely to be very effective. For example, consider a typical group of elementary school teachers being asked, "What difficulties do you encounter in teaching silent reading?" Many of those interviewed will be able to recall only a few difficulties and probably none of them will mention all of their difficulties. More satisfactory results will be obtained if the interviewer asks specific questions: "Are you able to interest all pupils in silent reading?" "Are you able to determine the reading difficulties of pupils?" "Are you able to stimulate reading for enjoyment?"

The persons to be interviewed should be representative of the population or conditions for which conclusions are desired. Some steps should be taken to enlist the cooperation of these individuals. It is helpful in this connection to secure the sponsorship of some institution or association which those interviewed are likely to respect. If one wishes to interview the teachers in a given school system, the approach should be through their superintendent. The investigator should arrange appointments that will be convenient to the persons interviewed, and which are for a sufficient duration of time. It is desirable to stimuiate an appropriate frame of mind on the part of the person to be interviewed.

This may often be done through an appeal to pride, some reference being made to the competence of the person to give the information desired. It is frequently effective to point out that the person interviewed is being given an opportunity to aid in the study of an important problem and that the information requested may not be obtained in any other way. The interest of the person interviewed can be stimulated by the interest exhibited by the research worker in his problem.

An interview should not degenerate into a quiz in which the person being questioned is caused embarrassment because he is unable to give the information desired. Personal or confidential matters should not be inquired into unless the interviewee indicates a willingness to be questioned about them. Whenever publication of the solicited information might cause embarrassment to the interviewee, assurance should be given that he will not be quoted and that information given in confidence will not be revealed.

It may not be wise to have a list of questions in evidence during the interview. It will sometimes be desirable for the investigator to memorize his list of questions. Usually, however, in collecting facts or opinions from mature individuals the presence of a question list should not result unfavorably; rather, it should aid in maintaining the control of the interview needed if all questions are to be answered. When it is evident that a question is not fully understood, the investigator should explain the terms used, or restate the question. If the investigator does not fully understand the response he should ask further questions. The investigator should be careful at all times to keep to the subject.

It is desirable to record in detail the responses of the subjects interviewed, but sometimes it may not be wise to do this in the presence of the subject. The time required for making the record may interfere with the interview, or it may be that the subject will be intimidated or that a hostile attitude will be engendered. When it appears that either of these conditions will prevail the interview should be writien up as soon as possible after it has been made. The writers are of thc opinion that most adults are not likely to be embarrassed by the open recording of their responses to questions. A superintendent, principal, or teacher is likely to respect the interviewer for his evident system. It is probable that the presence of a list of questions and the open recording of answers is most likely to have unfavorable effects when children are being interviewed.

The use of the interview is illustrated by the studies of Rufi and Sharman. In addition to securing data by the administration of tests, examination of records, and observation, Rufi collected many facts by interviewing principals and teachers in five small high schools. It is possible that some of these data could have been collected by questionnaire rather than by interview, but it is likely that this procedure would not have been as satisfactory. Some of the facts obtained by interview appear to be of the type which individuals would be hesitant to record on a questionnaire, but would be less hesitant to reveal in the course of a conversation. It is probable that in many cases the principals and teachers elaborated their replies so that they were clearly understood, which is not always true in the case of responses to a questionnaire. It is also probable that much information was volunteered relative to conditions, which the investigator would not have had the forethought to ask for if he had restricted his technique to the use of a questionnaire.

Data were obtained in the investigation of Sharman by interviewing principals, athletic coaches, physical education teachers, and other members of the faculties of a random sample of 38 per cent of the 275 public accredited high schools of Alabama. The investigator spent from one and one-half to two and one-half hours in each of the schools. Data were obtained relative to the distribution of full-time and part-time physical education teachers, physical examiners, requirements relative to health education, credit for physical education, types of activities in physical education programs, and facilities for physical education.

4. *Constructing and using questionnaires*

The questionnaire has long been subjected to criticism as a means of collecting data. The following comment was made in 1839.

> It is impossible to expect accuracy in returns obtained by circulars, various constructions being put upon the same question by different individuals who consequently classify their replies upon various principles.

Thorndike made the following statement in 1911.

One vice of statistical studies in education today is the indiscriminate use of lists of questions as a means of collecting data by correspondence.

Since 1911, numerous writers have criticized the questionnaire as a means of collecting data. Examination of the various criticisms reveals three general claims.

1. The questionnaire is not an effective means of collecting data, The reasons given include (a) construction of questionnaire unsatisfactory, (b) responses carelessly made or mere opinions, (c) per cent of returns too low or the returns are not from a representative sample of the population.

2. The problem studied is unimportant, or the investigation is so limited in scope that the findings have little significance.

3. The questionnaire is an unjustifiable nuisance to superintendents, high school principals, and other recipients. Too many questionnaires are mailed out; many of them are unreasonably long; in many cases some of the information asked for is too personal or could be obtained from published sources; in some cases the recipient is asked to make time-consuming calculations.

When these claims are examined critically it is apparent that competent and courteous use of the questionnaire in the study of worth while problems is not condemned. The questionnaire is an important labor-saving device and it is obvious that its use as an instrument for collecting data cannot be completely dispensed with. The United States Office of Education, state departments of education, and other administrative units must use it as a means of collecting information that is generally recognized as valuable. The cost of collecting this information by actual visitation and interview would be prohibitive. It would also be prohibitive in many survey investigations which cover a large area.

Although it is apparent that unqualified condemnation of the questionnaire is not justified the present writers are fully aware that even in the hands of a competent investigator, this instrument may yield faulty data. Wyile has reported a personal first-hand investigation of the data secured by a questionnaire administered to eleven-and twelve-year-old pupils. Although the questions called for simple factual information, many answers involved a significant error. Self-interest of the respondents is sometimes a cause of a systematic error Mathews has shown that the order of the printed response words to be underlined on an interest questionnaire may introduce a systematic error. Frequently it is not possible to give precise and accurate answers to questions calling for factual statements descriptive of practices or conditions without adding much explanation.

It is well known that failure of many of the recipients to respond to a questionnaire is a frequent cause of systematic errors in questinnaire data. Possibly the most adverse criticism that may be made of this technique, as it is most usually employed, is that lhe degree of reliability, validity, and representativeness of the data is uncertain.

The use of the questionnaire should be limited to worth while inquiries for which the needed data cannot be conveniently obtained by other means. Even in such cases the study should not be attempted unless the resources at the command of the investigator are such that success may reasonably be anticipated. These statements may seem platitudinous, but a surprising number of questionnaire investigations deserve to be classified as of minor, if not trivial importance.

A questionnaire will be most successful when it is limited to requests for simple factual information in the possession of the recipients or easily accessible to them. A questionnaire that requires the recipient to spend much time in collecting computing the requested information is not likely to be very successful and should be used only when the problem is one of considerable importance, A questionnaire asking for expressions of opinion should be employed only when the problem is important and the correspondents, in addition to being persons whose opinions will be significant, may be expected to be sufficiently interested so that they will give the questions thoughtful consideration.

The questions should be stated so clearly that they cannot be misinterpreted, Technical words and other unusual terms should be explained. The questions should be formulated so that they will not suggest or bias the answers. They should call for responses involving as little writing ae possible. Questions calling for numerical data or for responses of "yes" or "no," underlining, or cheeking are most desirable. In some cases, questions should be inserted which will serve as checks to other questions. When this precaution is observed, the investigator is able to make an estimate of the reliability of his questionnaire data on the basis of "internal evidence."

The respondent should not be asked to do work which the investigator can do himself such as computing totals, averages, or per cents. The questionnaire should be just long enough to secure the necessary data. Data irrelevant to the problem should never be requested. The investigator, however should make certain that he has anticipated all of his needs. If the data required for the problem are not thus anticipated, the investigator may find it necessary to do without important information, or to impose a second questionnaire on his respondents.

In preparing a questionnaire considerable attention should be given to its appearance. An attractive looking blank is more likely to secure a good response than an unattractive one. If possible, the questionnaire should be printed. When it is more than two or three typewritten pages in length and several hundred copies are required printing is usually less expensive than mimeographing.

The questionnaire should have a heading which includes an institutional or associational designation, and possibly a title. Spaces should be provided for the name, address, and position of the respondent. The questions should be spaced with care, ample room being allowed for responses. Respondents are less likely to overlook Items when they are spaced effectively. The size of the questionnaire should be one that is convenient for handling and filing. Letter size (8—1/2 by 11) is recommended. Legal size sheets are frequently inconvenient.

The first draft of the questionnaire should be submitted to competent and disinterested persons for criticism. If possible it should be given a preliminary trial by submitting it to persons typical of the proposed mailing list. Criticism and trial often reveal inadequacies not apparent to the author of the questionnaire. For example, it may be found that certain questions are easily misinterpreted. Analysis of these questions may disclose that the terms used are more technical than necessary or are in need of definition Attempts to tabulate the data secured in a trial may suggest changes which will make for greater ease in tabulating.

The questionnaire should be accompanied by a tactfull letter of explanation. The recipient should be informed of the nature of the problem and of its importance. It should be indicated that the responses wiil be help in confidence if their nature makes this action desirable. In this connection it should be mentioned that the questions should not be unduly personal in nature. Before sending out an elaborate questionnaire the willingness of the prospective recipients to respond should be determined by a preliminary inquiry. When this precaution is taken, greater interest is likely to be stimulated. Furthermore some of the expense of sending elaborate questionnaire to individuals disinclined to respond will be avoided. The recipient should be told that a summary of the data collected will be mailed to him. It is an excellent procedure in cases where the summary refers specifically to institutions or school systems, to accompany the summary with requests for criticism by its recipients. When these criticisms have been obtained, they may be used to improve the report of the study.

The questionnaire should be mailed at an opportune time. Seasons of vacation or period of excessive activity should be avoided. For example, it is unwise to mail out a questionnaire just prior to the Christmas holidays or at the beginning or close of a semester. The questionnaire should be accompanied by a self-addressed stamped envelope for its return. A follow-up letter may be sent, under certain conditions, to those who fail to respond. Frequently, a tactful follow-up later will greatly increase the per cent of responses.

It is desirable to keep a record of the responses. In some cases it may be worth while to graph the number of questionnaires returned daily and to mail the follow-up letters when the curve falls unduly. Toops has reported two studies which reveal that the per cent of response may be increased to an acceptable figure by means of follow-up letters. A similar conclusion has been reported by Lindsay.

In connection with emphasizing what an investigator who employes a questionnaire should do, it may be pointed out that a recipient should recognize his responsibility. Many problems cannot be studied except by employing a questionnaire and when the problem is a worthy one and the investigator has exhibited competence and good judgment in preparing the questionnaire, the recipient should make an effort to respond. It is not courteous to throw it in the waste-basket. If there are valid reasons why the information should not be given, the questionnaire should be returned with a note of explanation. In answering the questions asked, an effort should be made to give correct information. If a question is not understood or if the recipient is unable to give an answer that he believes to be corret, the question should be omitted. When there is some doubt in regard to the meaning of the question asked, a notation indicating the interpretation given it may be made.

In concluding this discussion of the details of the questionnaire procedure, it may be reiterated that the problem should be worth while. The use of a questionnaire is not justified if it is feasible to collect the data by other means. The questionnair should be carefully prepared and mailed to a wisely selected list, of persons who are in a position to provide the desired information.

The graduate student about to collect data by means of a questionnaire should secure the sponsorship of his institution. In many cases the sponsorship of an accrediting agency, or educational association, will secure an excellent response. Freqently, the letter accompanying the questionnaire should be signed by the sponsor rather than by the student. Many persons are unwilling to respond to a questionnaire from an unknown person, but are glad to respond to one authorized by an institution or organization that they respect. It should be mentioned in this connections that institutions and organizations should not violate this trust. The sponsor should accept the responsibility for making certain that the problem is worth while, a questionnaire necessary, and that the blank is well constructed. Furthermore, the sponsor should see that the respondents receive a summary of the results without under lapse of time.

5. *Securing a current record of activity*

When an activity does not normally result in an observable record, the various devices and techniques employed to secure a current record may be classified uuder three heads :

(1) mechanical,

(2) stenographic, and

(3) observational.

The moving picture camera, dictaphone, and other recording instruments are included under the first head. Usually the operation of the instrument requires little technical skill, but infrequently considerable ingenuity is required to devise an instrument adapted to the conditions under which the record must be secured. The apparatus now used at the University of Chicago to secure a photographic record of the eye-movements of a reader is a good illustration.

When a competent stenographer or stenotypist is not available, a satisfactory record may be obtained by a person who takes a few notes and then soon afterwarde expands them into a partial verbatim account. This method is generally employed by competent newspaper reporters, especially when interviewing persons whose times is limited. In an investigation reported by Helseth a record of recitations was obtained by having two or more observers take such notes as they could. These notes were turned over to the teacher who expanded them into an approximately verbatim account of the recitation. Other cases have been reported by Horn, and Knudsen, and Stevens.

The record securcd by an experienced and competent stenographer may be expected to be highly accurate, at least so for as the meaning of the record is concerned, but if detail of diction are considered, a stenographic record will usually involve errors. Obviously, a larger number of errors is to be expected when the record is an elaboration of notes taken by an observer. For some purposes, however, accuracy in the details of a record is not essential.

In descriptive recording, the human element is even more important. An observer tends to interpret what he observes. For example, an observer may see that certain symbols appear on the blackboard. He perceives, or observes, that these symbols are addition examples. His perception or observation has an inferential element since he has given meaning to his sensations. Further inference may be made before the observation is recorded. He may infer that the class present in the classroom has been engaged in drill in addition, and further, he may formulate and record some inferences with respect to the quality of this drill. It is evident, therefore, that the skill of the observer and his experience are important factors in descriptive recording.

The observer must identify what he should record. Checklists, score cards, and other devices of this type are useful aids since they focus the attention of the observer on the items which are to be observed. Rating scales are an aid since they serve to control in some measure inferences of the evaluative type. Without the aid of some device to focus his attention, an observer, especially an untrained one, is not likely to report a satisfactory description.

The record is likely to be a mixture of statements descriptive of action or conditions observed, inferences relative to mental activity, and evaluations of aspects of the scene observed. Given a checklist or other suitable device, the record of a trained observer is likely to be rather highly reliable. An untrained observer working without a checklist or other aid is not likely to secure a reliable record unless the items to be recorded are obvious.

When the presence of one or more observers is likely to affect the activity of which a record or description is desired, a technique should be devised which will eliminate this difficulty. This is especially important in the observation of young children. Gesell and his associates at Yale University have perfected a one-way vision screen for their study of the behavior of infants.

A number of devices have been prepared for the purpose of securing records of the amount and character of pupil participation in classroom activity. Usually these devices are seating charts of the class in which the squares representing the individual pupils are used as the spaces within which to record the symbols showing the extent and character of the pupil participation. Puckett devised symbols to indicate that a pupil asked a question, raised his hand once without being called on, raised his hand another time, was called on and made a good recitation, was called on once when he didno't have his hand raised and made a single word response.

In the device reported by Twitchell the symbols are recorded along lines drawn from pupils' names spaced about the chart. Some of the symbols refer to such items as: "called on and responded-verbally or otherwise (without hand raised)," "called on and gave no response or said, 'I don't know,' " "called on (without hand raised) for board work and responded with board work," "volunteered to participate by raising hand and was called on." Horn prepared a device which is somewhat simpler than those of Puckett and Twitchell, and which does not provide for recording so many details.

Morrison describes a technique for measuring group attention. The observer takes a position where he can observe easily all of the pupils in a class. The position recommended is the front of the room, but to one side so as to be out of the line of vision between the teacher and the pupils. The observer runs his eyes up and down each row of pupils and at minute intervals records the number of pupils who appear inattentive.

The group attention score is obtained by dividing the number of actual minutes of pupil attention by the number of possible minutes of pupil attention. For example, if there are 30 pupils in a class and the class-period is forty-five minutes long, the number of possible minutes of pupil attention is $30 \times 45 = 1350$. If the sum of the numbers of pupils inattentive for all of the minute intervals of the forty-five minute period is 86, then the actual minutes of pupil attention are 1350 — 86 = 1264. The group attention score is 1264 ÷ 1350 = .936 or 94 per cent.

The reader interested in collecting data with respect to individual attention, group attention, or individual-group attention should consult an article by Blume in which he gives an excellent discussion of the techniques and three facsimiles of data sheets used. The reader will also find it profitable to study the discussions by Kundsen and Gray and the investigations reported by Bjarnason and Bridges. In the writings by Blume and by Knudsen evidence is presented to show that when the techniques are used with skill rather highly valid and reliable data are secured with respect to group attention.

When the activity of which a descriptive record is desired extends over a considerable period of time, observation is seldom feasible. In such cases the persons involved may be asked to keep diaries. For example, Flowers sent a request to 170 principals of elementary schools to keep diaries of their daily work for a period of two weeks. Sixty-seven of the principals complied with the request. In using this technique it is well to restrict the record to activities that individuals are capable of observing with respect to themselves.

A principal may easily note in a diary the amount of time given to a conference with a parent. He should be able to record, at least so far as the broader aspects are concerned, the nature of the conference. It is doubtful, however, whether the technique will secure dependable data when much introspection, or retrospection, is involved. It is also probable that highly dependable records should not be expected from pupils when they are requested to keep diaries of their activities.

6. *Making estimates and ratings*

Since estimates and ratings are subjective, a scale or score card is usually employed as a means of minimizing the effect of the subjectivity of the process. A scale consists of a series of samples or descriptions of the thing to be rated arranged in order of ascending quality or merit. Usually a numerical value is assigned to each sample. This instrument is illustrated by the scales used for measuring compositions, handwriting drawings, and the like. A score card consists of a list of the characteristics with respect to which estimates are to be made. Usually the scale of points on which each characteristic is to be rated is given so that when the several ratings are combined they will be appropriately weighted.

The "man-to-man" rating scale, devised in a seminar conducted at the Carnegie Institute of Technology by W. D. Scott now president of Northwestern University, is a useful device when no better technique is feasible. The rater selects, for example, the best teacher he ever knew and writes the name at the top of a sheet of paper. He next selects the poorest teacher he ever knew and writes his name at the bottom.

In between he writes the name of an average teacher, the name of a better-than-average teacher and the name of a poorer-than-average teacher. Numerical ratings such as 15, 12, 9, 6, and 3 may then be assigned to the five names listed. Descriptive statements may be added as a means of assisting the rater to keep in mind the significant characteristics of the teachers of the scale. Freyd has developed a "graphic" rating individuals with respect to twenty traits such as neatness, physique, flexibility, and talkativeness.

When employing a rating scale it is desirable to have several independent ratings made. The average of the several ratings will be more reliable than a single rating. Symonds has suggested that in general eight is the minimum number of ratings that should be obtained when the resulting measures are to be considered diagnostic of individuals.

Score cards are useful instruments in making estimates

since they tend to maintain the same basis of evaluation from one observation to another. A significant limitation lies in the fact that an essential element may be lacking in the thing observed, and yet the total score may be high. For example, in the Strayer-Engelhardt Score Card for City School Buildings, 65 points are to be deducted from the perfect score of 1000 points if there are no provisions for fire protection. Hence, a building without fire protection but otherwise well planned and constructed would receive a relatively high score that would tend to be misleading with reference to the actual status of the building for school purposes. While this limitation should be remembered it is not usually a serious one.

In addition to score cards for the rating of school buildings and equipment, and of janitorial and engineering serveice, a number have been prepared for rating such things as health habits, textbooks, teacher characteristics, and supervisory progress. Recently a unique score card has been prepared by Hall for the purpose of rating schools with respect to provisions for gifted children. The Chapman-Sims Socio-Economic Scale has been proposed as an instrument for measuring home environment. Heilman used a modification of this scale in his study of "Factors Determining Achievement and Grade Location."

7. *Selecting and administering tests*

When adequately defined, the problem specifies the particular abilities or traits to be measured, and these specifications constitute criteria to be used in judging the validity of the test or tests being considered. Determinations of validity have been made for some of the available tests, but a test that is highly valid for one purpose may be unsatisfactory when considered with reference to a different purpose. When no available test appears satisfactory for securing the data specified by the problem, the investigator should, if he is able to do so, construct his own tests. Curtis and Irion are examples of research workers who have devised measuring instruments for dealing with their problems.

The investigator should also consider the cost of the test materials and the time required for administration and for scoring the test papers. In some types of studies, the availability of norms and of duplicate forms must also be considered.

The test or tests selected should be carefully administered. If comparisons are to be made with established norms, the published directions for administering must be followed carefully. When such comparisons are not to be made, the directions may be modified, but any changes should be made intelligently, and it is usually important that the directions be the same for all groups of pupils tested.

Application of basic techniques

The preceding exposition of the basic techniques does not adequately reveal the difficulties encountered in collecting data in educational research. In addition to overcoming those inherent in the basic techniques, there are other problems. In experimental studies, an important phase of the process of collecting data is setting up and conducting the experiment. Sometimes an investigator cannot obtain the data called for by the problem or it is not feasible for him to secure them and he must resort to indirect measurement. For example, certain problems relating to silent reading call for measures of the mental processes involved. A substitute for this information is secured by measuring the eye-movements of the reader.

In studies of the supply and demand for teachers, the number of teachers available within a specified area cannot be determined directly. Frequently it is not possible, or at least not feasible, to collect data for the entire population specified by the problem. For example, in a study to determine the value of certain measures for predicting teaching success, the problem may call for measures of teaching success for all students who enter teacher training institutions. Of course, such data can be obtained for only those who actually become teachers and even in the case of this population, measures of teaching success may be difficult or impossible to obtain for all members because the persons involved are scattered over a wide area. When data for only a portion of the population are secured, the dependability of the findings is a function of the representativeness of the sample studied. Hence, the investigator is controned with the problem of obtaining a sample that is representative or one whose degree of representativeness is known.

When a universe is stratified, that is, consists of relatively homogeneous units or groups, a carefully selected sample from each of the several strata is likely to be highly representative of the total universe. For example, if it is desired to sample pupil achievement in the schools of a large city or of a state, the first step would be to classify the schools on the basis of size or other appropriate criteria.

The administration of the test to a few wisely selected classes within each group will be likely to result in a highly representative sample of the total population. When an investigator does not have an opportunity to select a stratified sample, he may be able to present evidence to show that his sample is highly representative. For example, if data have been obtained from the fifth-grade pupils in a given city, he may be able to show that this group of pupils is highly representative of fifth-grade pupils in general by presenting evidence of their general intelligence, chronological age, and other factors which may be expected to influence school achievement.

Occasionally a more mechanical system of sampling may be employed. For example, the students enrolled in a large school may be sampled by taking every fiftieth record from an alphabetical file. The defined words in a dictionary may be sampled by taking the first defined word on the odd numbered pages. The vocabulary of a textbook may be sampled by taking the words in certain lines on every fifth page. Lively and Pressey have proposed a method of obtaining a thousand-word sample of the vocabulary of textbooks. The procedure of sampling is based upon an estimate of the number of pages which must be sampled, taking one line per page in order to cover one thousand words. For example, a book of five hundred pages with an average of ten words per line would be sampled by taking a specified line on every fifth page throughout the book. Patty and Painter recommend samples that are proportional to the length of the books analyzed.

If the procedure of selection is such that the sample is determined merely by chance, it is called random. A random sample is not necessarily representative but any non-representativeness is due to the operation of chance. Frequently in educational research it is difficult to demonstrate that the conditions of random sampling have been satisfied. They are likely to be approximated when an alphabetical file is sampled by taking records at regular intervals. Critical inquiry has revealed that in a number of cases procedures presumed to result in a random sample have failed to do so. For example, if the defined words in a dictionary are sampled by taking the last defined word on each page, Williams has shown that the sample thus obtained is not random when judged with respect to children's vocabularies.

The more commonly used words, whose definitions in general occupy more space than those of unusual words, are more likely to be selected. Hence, a sample obtained by taking the last defined word on pages of a dictionary is biased in favor of the more commonly used words. Ward has criticized the method of sampling proposed by Lively and Pressey when used as a means of measuring the vocabulary burden of textbooks. Dolch contends that any process of sampling fails to reveal the repetition of words and hence operates to make the book appear more difficult than it really is, because the repetition of words in a text tends to reduce its vocabulary difficulty. Walker describes a number of sampling procedures in which the conditions of random sampling are not satisfied. The sampling that usually occurs when a questionnaire is employed in collecting data is likely not to be random. It appears, therefore, that random rampling is not often possible in educational research. A sample should not be treated as random unless convincing evidence can be cited in support of this characteristic.

A practical question in sampling concerns the size of the sample that may be considered satisfactory. When the sampling is random, the probable error formulae provide a means for determining the number of cases necessary to reduce the probable error of the statistics due to random sampling to any specified limit. In certain types of situations the representativeness of the sample may be estimated by noting the effect of the addition of sub-samples, Suppose a large number of pupil compositions have been accumulated and it is desired to ascertain the types of language errors and their relative frequencies.

The investigator may select a series of relatively small random samples and note the changes in his tabulations as additional samples are analyzed. When he finds that no new types of error are being added and the relative frequencies are approximately constant, he is justified in assuming that the total sample is large enough to be highly representative. Johnson and Eurich have reported a study in which they show that a random sample including 30 per cent of the cases yielded satisfactory results in a certain situation. Although one should not generalize from a single investigation, it is likely that a random sample of this size will usually be satisfactory. In some cases, a smaller random sample may be satisfactory.

This discussion of the application of the basic techniques suggests only a few of the difficulties that investigators actually encounter in collecting data, The particular difficulties are so varied that a complete treatment is not feasible in this volume. A person, especially one inexperienced in educational research, who contemplates the study of a problem, should consult reports of similar researches with respect to the techniques employed in collecting data. The bibliography of survey investigations at the end of Chapter VIII and that of experimental studies at the end of Chapter IX are recommended to readers who are interested in extending their study of collecting data in educational research.

11

Constructing Measuring Instruments

A. GENERAL PRINCIPLES

The scope of measurement in education

When measurement in the field of education is mentioned, we commonly think merely of the administration of a test designed to measure either general intelligence or some segment of school achievement. This is an unfortunate restriction. For years a fundamental credo of research workers has been: Whatever exists at all exists in some amount and can be measured. Although this ideal has not been fully realized, many ingenious measuring instruments have been devised and today we are able to measure, at least crudely, many things other than general intelligence and school achievement. These include personality traits, interests, attitudes, socio-economic status of homes, school buildings, quality of supervision, educational need, and the like.

A basic assumption

It may seen platitudinous to point out that in attempting the measurement of human abilities and traits, their existence is assumed, but this assumption means more than is commonly realized. Existence implies stability. Human performance varies even when conditions are considered to be unchanged and forgetting is a characteristic phenomenon. Hence, it may be inferred that human abilities and traits are not perfectly stable. To the extent that they fluctuate, the basic assumption of stability is not satisfied and their measurement is subject to a significant limitation.

The meaning of measurement as applied to human abilities and traits

In measuring distance, weight, and the like, the procedure may be described as "direct," meaning that the measurer deals "directly" with the magnitude whose measurement is desired. The most direct measurement of human abilities or traits is accomplished by securing the performance that the ability or trait makes possible or insures and then describing this performance in quantitative terms. In this sense the measurement of calculation skill in arithmetic or of ability in handwriting may be described as direct. Measurement, however, may be indirect. Temperature is measured by measuring the height of a column of liquid. In this case, indirect measures are valid because the correlation between temperature and the height of the column of liquid is approximately 1.00.

The weight of children may be measured indirectly by measuring their height but obviously the measures obtained in this way will not be highly valid. Many of our measures of human abilities and traits are indirect. For example, when measuring the silent reading ability of sixth-grade children, we usually desire an index of their performance when they read assignments in history, literary selections, and the like. In a particular case, we may desire an index of their performance when they read a particular type of material in response to certain directions and under certain conditions such as reading an article in an encyclopedia to secure information relative to certain questions and doing this in a library where there are distracting influences. In such cases, scores on a typical silent reading test are indirect measures of the designated ability. In many cases the difference between the obtained performance and the one we are interested in is even more obvious. We use the performances given in response to true-false exercises or some other type of objective test as a means of securing measures of the ability to do something very different. Such indirect measures may be useful but frequently they involve relatively large variable errors of validity.

A test score should be thought of as a measure of ability to do, capacity to do, or tendency to do under certain conditions and at a certain time. Achievement is commonly thought of as having some degree of permanency. Usually the ability whose measurement is desired is that which will function at some date after the administration of the test. Hence, the complete label of test scores as measures would include specifications in regard to the conditions under which the ability to do, capacity to do, or tendency to do is to function and the date on which the functioning is to occur. For example, spelling achievement might be defined as the ability to spell under the conditions of actual writing a week after the testing, assuming normal forgetting and only incidental learning. Hence, if the meaning implicitly associated with the scores yielded by a test were explicitly stated, the attached label would be of the following type : "numerical index of ability to .... under .... conditions at .... date the intervening learning and forgetting being ...."

A measure of an ability or trait is a numerical index of a designated performance to be given under prescribed conditions, and hence the only essential requirement is that the obtained measures correctly discriminate between individuals whose future performances differ even when these differences are small. In other words, the scores made by pupils are to be considered satisfactory measures if the difference between them corresponds to the difference between the future performances of these pupils under the prescribed conditions.

Direct measurement is not essential but it should be noted that indirect measurement depends upon the stability of the relationship between what the test measures directly and the ability or trait whose measurement is desired. This relationship is not necessarily a fixed one. It depends upon the objectives towards which the instruction has been directed and it likely to be changed by the repeated administration of a test of a given type. Hence, indirect measurement is based upon a relationship that is subject to change. This means that the validity of a given instrument is not necessarily a stable characteristic.

In other words, a test that is highly valid in one situation is not necessarily equally valid in another. This point is especially important in connection with true-false, multiple-choice, and other types of tests constructed by teachers. Such instruments may yield highly valid indirect measures of achievement when first administered to a group of students but the validity is likely to decrease as the students direct their efforts to becoming able to respond to them unless the ability to respond to such exercises is recognized as a desirable educational objective.

General types of instruments for measuring human abilities and traits

The most common types of instrument for measuring human abilities and traits is the performance test, which requires the person, whose capacity or achievement is being measured, to give a performance, usually a written one, which represents the functioning of that capacity or achievement or which is considered to be indicative of this capacity or achievement. Psychological questionnaires, which are used to obtain measures of general patterns of conduct, represent a second type of measuring instrument.

The performance required consists of answers to questions concerning practices, beliefs, preferences, judgments, and the like. A third type of measurement procedure is rating or estimating with or without a formal scale on the basis of general acquaintance or systematic observation. To these three types of instruments there may be added observation (noting the frequency of performance of certain acts), interviewing, and laboratory and clinical techniques.

Basic problems in the construction of measuring instruments

Before the construction of a test is begun, it is necessary to determine what is to be measured. Ability in spelling, ability in silent reading, ability in arithmetic, and the like are commonly used as if such phrased designated defined achievements. Usually they do not. In fact, we know relatively little about the nature of the abilities we claim to measure. Within a given subject-matter field, achievement usually represents a combination of two or more types of controls of conduct. There is also considerable overlapping between achievements in different fields, due in part to the presence of general intelligence as a common factor. Beyond such general items, our information is limited.

The analysis of human abilities and traits and the identification of their elements are basic problems & logically their solution should precede the construction of measuring instruments. These problems are engaging the attention of a number of workers, but it will be some time before we have the basic information that we need in test construction. Meanwhile, a testmaker should attempt to specify as definitely as possible the nature of the ability or trait he desires to measure. It is especially important that he recognize and distinguish between the different types of achievement. In the measurement volume of the report of the Commission on the Social Studies, seven rubrics are indicated for this field :

(1) exact information (memorized facts).

(2) technical vocabulary.

(3) ability to apply ideas and information to new situations,

(4) skills ,

(5) interests,
(6) attitudes,
(7) ability to express.

The learnings included vary with the subject-matter field but an analysis of this type indicates the general character of the achievement. A testmaker may not wish to measure all phases but he should explicity recognize the restriction.

The general problems involved in constructing a performance test.

Given the specifications of the abilities to be measured, the next problem is to determine the type of test to be constructed. With reference to the difficulty of the exercises of a test, their arrangement may be irregular, uniform, or scaled. In the first type, the arrangement of the exercises is not related to their relative difficulty. Tests of this type are illustrated by those prepared informally by teachers. In the second type the exercises are of equal difficulty, or approximately so. In the last type the exercises vary from easy to very difficult and are arranged in ascending order of difficulty. Frequently, in such tests the increase in difficulty from exercise to exercise is approximately uniform. Variations of these types include spiral and cycle tests. In the former, different sub-tests may be arranged in order of increasing difficulty, the exercises within each sub-test being uniform in difficulty. In cycle tests, different types of exercises recur at regular intervals. In determining the type of test to be constructed, the testmaker should be guided by the nature of the measurement desired. If it is desired to secure a measure of the rate of the functioning of a group of skills, the test should be uniform in difficulty. When "power" is to be measured, a scaled test is generally employed.

The second problem is that of devising and selecting test exercises that will secure pupil performances satisfactory for the measurement of the specified ability or trait. It is necessary that the performance given in response to an exercise be observable. A second requirement is that the exercises be valid. It is desirable that the responses to the exercises be objectively scorable.

The third general problem relates to the determination of the length of the test (number of test items), organization of the test items, administration time, and formulation of an explanation of the nature of the exercises to the subjects taking test and of instructions for administering it.

The fourth problem relates to the quantitative description of the obtained test performance. Several questions are involved—rules for scoring, weighting of the exercises, units of the scale of description, and its zero point. In the case of handwriting, written composition, and other performances for which a general quality description is desired, there are the problems of devising an appropriate quality scale and determining the best technique for using it.

Testing the completed instrument forms the final problem. Two questions require consideration :

(1) How accurately does the test measure what it actually measures ?

(2) How accurately does it measure the specified ability or trait ? These two questions are commonly designated as those of reliability and validity.

In view of the large number of tests and other measuring instruments that have been constructed, it may appear that these problems should have been solved for many abilities and traits. It is true that for measuring general intelligence, general educational status below the senior high school level, and achievement in certain subject-matter fields, a number of tests are available whose scores are highly reliable and exhibit fairly close agreement with the criterion measures used to determine their validity. Critical study of available tests, however, reveals a number of unsolved problems and the research worker who has occasion to select a measuring instrument for a particular purpose, especially when conducting an experimental investigation, seldom is able to find one that exactly meets his requirements. Hence, the field of measurement still offers challenges to the research worker. In fact, there are a number of important problems that have scarcely been touched.

B. DETAILS OF TEST CONSTRUCTION

Devising and selecting test exercises

The criteria to be observed in devising and selecting test exercises are :

(1) observability of performance,

(2) convenience in administering the test and in scoring the test papers.

(3) objectivity in scoring,

(4) difficulty of the test items, and

(5) validity,

The second and third criteria are important requirements when the test is designed for general use, but when it is being devised as a means of securing measures needed in an experimental study or some other investigation, convenience in administering and in scoring the test papers and objectivity are desirable but not necessary. Having determined upon the type or types of exercises to be employed, the testmaker proceeds to devise a number of such exercises being guided by his estimates of validity and difficulty. These exercises are then administered to a typical population for an experimental determination of validity and difficulty.

Criteria of validity to be observed in devising test exercises.

Although indirect measurement is possible and the only dependable determination of validity is by ascertaining the degree to which the exercise contributes to the identification of individual differences in the ability or trait whose measurement is desired, the testmaker should give attention to the content of the exercises. It is desirable to make the measurement as direct as possible. If specific habits are to be measured, it is sometimes possible to devise exercises that will call for the normal functioning of them.

In the case of the calculation skills of arithmetic, there is the obvious suggestion that the test exercises consist of typical examples. In many cases, however, normal functioning is not feasible. When spelling ability is to be measured, the dictation of word lists does not provide for normal functioning. The act of silent reading does not eventuate in an observable performance. Hence, it is necessary to devise a type of exercise that will call for silent reading plus an observable performance indicative of the ability to read. When an exercise calling for normal functioning is not feasible, the testmaker should be guided by the experimental evidence pertaining to the relative validity of the possible types of exercises.

When the achievement to be measured consists of the ability to respond to arithmetical problems or to other types of thought questions, an obvious suggestion is that the test exercises should present typical problematic situations in the field of knowledge achievement being considered. In complying with this suggestion, it is necessary to bear in mind the requirement of convenience and objectivity in scoring. If the test is designed as an instrument for general use, there is the further requirement that the time necessary for responding to an exercise be reasonably short. In order to satisfy these requirements, testmakers have proposed various types of objective exercises—true-false, multiple-choice, completion, and the like.

The use of such exercises raises the question of the extent to which they measure the achievement that functions in responding to questions that ask the student to discuss, explain, compare, and the like. They cannot measure such achievement directly, but indirect measurement is possible. On the basis of rather crude data, some testmakers have concluded that tests consisting of objective exercises do measure such achievement to a sufficient extent to justify their use. More carefully planned inquiries indicate that an objective test measures about 60 per cent of what is measured by an essay tpye of examination when the latter is carefully prepared and scored. A community of function of this degree does not make the measurement of knowledge achievement by means of objective tests very satisfactory. When a short testing time and convenience and objectivity in scoring are not imperative requirements, the use of exercises that will yield more direct measures of knowledge achievement is to be recommended.

When the achievement to be measured consists of general patterns of conduct, the nature of this rubric of controls of conduct suggests that the criterion of the acquisition of an attitude, interest, ideal, or other generalized control is the conformity to the pattern in responding to a variety of situations. This seems to be implied in the concept of a generalized control of conduct. There is the further implication of conformity to the pattern spite of temptation to do otherwise, or at least of conformity in situation in which there is no expressed or implied requirement of conformity. Hence, a formal test administered within a typical time limit does not provide for the normal functioning of a general pattern of conduct. This means that the construction of a formal test to measure an attitude, interest, ideal, or other generalized control must be based upon the principle of indirect measurement, at least in part.

Criteria relating to the difficulty of test exercises

In the case of speed tests, especially when the function is narrow, the nature of the exercises is determined by the purpose of the measuring instrument. This would be true of a test designed to measure skill in the fundamental addition combinations or skill in doing arithmetical examples of a given type. In many cases, however, the difficulty of the exercises requires consideration.

Although a testmaker's estimates of difficulty will not be very dependable, he should endiavor to devise exercises whose difficulty is that desired in the completed test. In a scaled test, the exercises vary in difficulty from very easy to very difficult. Hence, when this type of test is being constructed, the test-maker should endeavor to devise exercises that represent a wide range of difficulty. If a uniform test is being constructed, he should endeavor to have the exercises approximately equivalent in difficulty and the degree of estimated difficulty should be that for which the test will yield the most valid measures.

It is obvious that an exercise so easy that all subjects give the correct response or so difficult that none respond correctly is worthless for testing purposes, because its discriminating value would be zero. This condition suggests the inference that the maximum discriminating value is attained when an exercise is done correctly by about fifty per cent of the subjects. This inference is supported by some experimental evidence, but it appears that the discriminative value only slightly between thirty and seventy per cent of correct responses. Hence, when devising exercises for a uniform test, an effort should be made to have the difficulty fall within these limits.

Experimental determination of the relative validity of individual test exercises

A valid test reveals differences in ability that exist and one that fails to reveal a difference which is at all marked is distinctly lacking in this quality. This concept of validity may be applied also to individual test items. When so applied, it means that in general the responses to a single exercise will be different for groups of pupils known to differ with respect to axerage status of the ability whose measurement is being attempted. For example, if two groups of pupils differ with respect to silent reading ability, a valid exercise will yield a higher per cent of currect responses by the group whose average status in the higher. If the per cent of currect responses is appoximately the same for the two groups, the validity of the exercise approaches zero. Another way of thinking of the validity or discriminating power of a test item is in terms of the accuracy with which subjects responding to the exercise are correctly placed on the scale of ability by their responses. Perfect placement is attained when all subjects who fail the item occupy positions on the scale below any subject who gives the correct response.

The first of the above expositions of the meaning of validity as applied to individual test items suggests a method of determining the relative validity of the exercises of the preliminary form of a test. The essential requirement is two or more groups of subjects differing in average status with respect to the specified ability. For precise determinations it is necessary to have a series of groups whose average standings are evenly spaced over the range of the ability within measurement is desired. For example, suppose ability to spell in normal writing is specified.

The first step would be to secure a number of groups of pupils differing in average status with respect to this ability and evenly spaced on the scale of the ability. Suppose that ten such groups have been indentified. Then the validity of a single test item would be indicated by the corresponding series of per cents of correct responses. A high degree of discriminating power would be indicated by a series of per cents exhibiting fairly uniform positive increments.

A criterion is essential for the determination of groups that differ with respect to the specified ability. In the case of general intelligence and achievement abilities that obviously increase from year to year or from grade to grade, sequential age or grade groups of typical pupils have been used. Binet, who in collaboration with Simon in 1905 devised and published the first general intelligence test, employed age groups and selected those exercises that were responded to correctly by a larger per cent of the pupils of the older groups. Otis in 1923 employed one group of retarded pupils and one of accelerated pupils. Thurstone selected groups on the basis of scholarship records.

In validating exercises for trade tests, groups classified on the basis of training and experience as novices, apprentices, journeymen, and experts have been used. Groups selected in such ways are not likely to be very evenly spaced with reference to average status and there will be considerable overlapping. Hence, the determination of the validity of the test items will not be entirely satisfactory. A more precise criterion is needed for selecting spaced groups. If a test is available which experience has proven to yield reasonably valid measures of the ability or trait, it may be used for selecting the members of the several groups. The Stanford Revision of the Binet test is frequently used for this purpose in constructing a group intelligence test. Usually, however, such an instrument is not available.

After the test items have been administered to a series of spaced groups, there remains the task of calculating an index of the discriminating power of each item. Vincent has reported a study in which an index of discriminating power of test items was obtained by calculating the per cent of pupils making a wrong response to the exercise who had criterion scores equal to or greater than the median of the criterion scores of the pupils doing the exercise correctly. Other techniques have been described by Paterson, Symonds, Wilson, Welsh, and Gulliksen, Lentz, Hirshstein, and Finch, and Zubin. Cook has reported a study in which he evaluated five methods applicable to test items whose scoring is dichotomous. He claims that the biserial *r* technique is probably more reliable than the other methods he investigated experimentally and should be used where the items approach uniformity in difficulty or represent high levels of ability. When the scoring of the exercises of a test is not dichotomous, i.e., when the responses may be classified into more than two categories, three methods have been proposed—correlation ratio or eta, McCall method, and Long method.

Although the techniques proposed for determining the validity of test items have not been described, it has perhaps occurred to the reader that the amount of labor involved is so enormous that precise test construction is not possible except for one who has a large and trained clerical staff at his command. This is true, but is should be noted that the number of hours of labor may be greatly reduced when calculating and tabulating machines are available. Lindquist and Cook state that for bi-serial *r* they devised a procedure by means of which a single operator using Hollerith tabulating equipment can compute this index for from 50 to 75 items per hour, not including the time required to punch the cards.

The obtained index of the discriminating power of a test exercise is a function of the criterion and the experience of the subjects to which it was administered as well as of the content of the item. If the criterion measures are lacking validity, the obtained indices will be in error. If the exercise is unknown to the subjects and they merely guess in responding to it, the validity of the item will be zero. If the subjects have been taught the wrong response, a negative validity will be obtained.

In general, the discriminating power of a test exercise at a particular grade level depends upon the curriculum and the quality of the instruction. Hence, experimental determinations of validity should not be thought of as characteristics of the test items alone. They are subject to change. Determinations for one school population may not be correct for another.

Experimental determination of the difficulty of test items

The relative difficulty of test items for a given population of subjects is indicated by the per cents of correct responses but when it is considered desirable to have the items of a test evenly spaced with reference to difficulty, it is necessary to secure the translation of these per cents into measures of difficulty expressed in terms of an ability unit. The procedure commonly employed is based on the assumption that in a large unselected group the distribution of the ability for which a test is being constructed is approximately that of the normal probability curve. In other words, if the members of a large unselected group were classified on the basis of measures of the ability, the frequencies thus obtained would form a normal distribution. A point on the scale of this distribution designates a degree or level of ability and its location may be specified in terms of the per cent of the group to the left of the point. For example, if 35 per cent are to the left of the point, it is located a distance of $.385\sigma$ to the left of the mean of the distribution.

If a test exercise has been administered to a large unselected population, the subjects responding correctly are assumed to be the ones whose ability is greater than those who fail to give the correct response. Hence, the per cent of correct responses defines a point on the scale of ability. Tables have been constructed which give the points on the scale of ability corresponding to various per cents of correct responses. This scale is usually expressed from an arbitrary zero point instead of the mean. McCall has proposed a point at 5.0σ to the left of the mean, but 2.5σ and 3.0σ have been used.

Stability of determinations of validity and difficulty of test items

On page 174, it was noted that changes in the curriculum or instruction may change the validity of an item. The difficulty value obtained for a test exercise depends upon the general status of the population to which it has been administered and upon the training the subjects have received relative to the exercise. Hence, determinations of the validity and difficulty of test items should not be thought of as stable characteristics. This principle that a test item which is "good" for one population may be "poor" for another and that an item which is "good" at the time of the construction of a test may be "poor" at a later date.

It is also possible that "poor" items may become "good" items. It is probably true that the quality of test items does not often change very rapidly, but determinations of validity and difficulty should not be thought of as highly stable. Furthermore, the validity index obtained for an item is probably influenced by the context in which it appears. Hence, the validity of an item in the final form of the test may not be the same as in the preliminary form.

Validity of items versus validity of test

The calculation of a validity index for a large number of items and the selection of those having the highest indexes for the test makes the process of test construction impressive, and many testmakers appear to have assumed that the procedure insures the best test that can be assembled from the items. The prime consideration in test construction is that the resulting instrument yield highly valid and reliable measures and it does not necessarily follow that the items with the highest validity indexes will make the most valid test. Investigation indicates that a test consisting of the "best" items may not be more valid than one consisting of "mediocre" items. These findings raise the question of the value of elaborate difficulty and validity analyses of test items. It is likely that selection of items on the basis of simple procedures will usually result in a test validity little lower than that attained by the elaborate procedures described.

C. DESCRIPTION OF TEST PERFORMANCES

Quantitative description of objectively scorable test performances

In formulating directions for scoring the responses to the exercises of a test and for combining the credits into a point score, attention should be given to :

1. dimensions of ability,
2. rate units versus work units,
3. weighting, or relative credit for correct responses to the various exercises,
4. correction for guessing.

1. *Recognition of dimensions of ability*

A complete description of a test performance requires determination of its quality or accuracy, the difficulty of the exercises, and the rate at which the performance was given. In other words, a performance may be thought of as three dimensional. Little attention has been given to the dimensions of test performances, but precise measurement seems to require it. The number of exercises right is generally taken as the score. This score represents an unknown combination of two or all three of the dimensions. Under the caption of the Law of the Single Variable, Burgess suggested that the form of the test and its plan of administration be such that the difficulty and rate of work will be constant in all pupil performances. This condition is approximated in a timed sentence dictation spelling test.

The Courtis Silent Reading Test provides for measuring rate and quality of comprehension independently. A few other testmakers have provided for separate scores to describe different aspects of the performance. It seems reasonable that recognition of the Law of the Single Variable might lead to significant refinements in measuring human abilities and traits. At least this detail of test construction offers a challenge to the critical student of educational measurement.

2. *Rate units versus work units*

In the case of a speed test, the performance may be described in terms of the number of units of work done (usually the number of exercises done correcly) within the allowed period of time, or in terms of the mean number of seconds per unit of work. The two methods of description yield different results and, hence, may lead to conflicting conclusions, particularly in research on the effect of practice on individual differences. In such cases, it is advisable to express the measures in terms of both units of work and units of time.

3. *Weighting or relative credit for correct responses to the various exercises*

If the exercises of the test are approximately equal in difficulty, the usual practice is to assign the value of one unit to each. When they vary materially in difficulty, a number of test-makers have devised a plan of weighting, usually based upon a measure of the relative difficulty of the several exercises. In the case of tests of the scaled type, a pupil will not ordinarily do all of the exercises up to a given point of the scale and then fail in all beyond this point.

The typical performance is one in which there is a scattering of correct responses beyond the point of the first incorrect one. This situation has caused some testmakers to devise a technique for computing a difficulty score which involves weighting. It appears, however, that a system of weighting does not affect the reliability of test scores to a marked degree and the usual practice is to take the number of exercises done correctly as the pupil's score even though there may be marked variations in difficulty.

Most of those who studied the effect of weighting have employed reliability as the criterion. The effect of weighting upon the validity of the measures has received relatively little attention. Furthermore, it appears that the social value of an exercise should receive consideration as well as its difficulty. Frequently these criteria are incompatible as may be shown by considering two exercises, the first, calling for the data of the signing of the Declaration of Independence, and the second, calling for the date of a minor battle of the Civil War.

The first exercise calls for information of much greater social value than the second. One would be considered ignorant indeed if he did not know the significance of the data, 1776. On the other hand, frequent contact with the data its significance makes the first exercise a very easy one for most eighth-grade pupils. The second data is of much less social value, but it would probably be known by very few pupils.

On the basis of the criterion of social value, the first exercise merits the greater weight, but on the basis of difficulty, the second exercise would be given the greater weight.

4. *Correction for quessing*

When the number of possible responses to an exercise is limited, it is possible to make the correct response merely by guessing. Hence, if the subjects to whom the test is administered guess when they do not know the response to make, the "number right" will tend to be too large as a score. The formula usually used to secure a corrected score is.

$$\text{Score} = \text{Number right} - \frac{\text{Number wrong}}{(n-1)}$$

The symbol, n, stands for the number of possible responses to an exercise. In the case of true-false and other alternative test exercises, the formula becomes :

$$\text{Score} = \text{Number right} - \text{Number wrong.}$$

For exercises requiring a choice from three possible answers, the formula becomes :

$$\text{Score} = \text{Number right} - \frac{\text{Number wrong}}{2}$$

When the number of possible responses is increased to five or more, the correction is probably not essential. After reviewing the research relating to correcting for guesing. Such concluded that the question of the effect upon reliability is still debatable, but that correction for guessing appears to increase the validity of the scores. It is likely that the effect of correction for guessing is conditioned by the character of the exercise and the instructions relative to guessing.

Quantitative description of recorded performances by means of quality scales

Performances such as samples of handwriting or written compositions cannot be scored as "right" or "wrong." They must be described in terms of degrees of quality. This description may be accomplished by constructing a quality scale and then matching the performances with a step of this scale. The essential steps in the construction of a quality scale are as follows :

1. Collecting sample performances which represent as wide a range of quality as possible;
2. Selecting from this collection a limited number of samples (10 to 20) which represent the entire range of quality, and which differ from each other by approximately equal increments of quality;
3. Determining the quantitative description of the quality of each sample with reference to an established zero point, and arranging the samples in the form of a scale.

The procedures for the second and third of these steps have been described in several texts on educational measurement and need not be considered here. The merit of the resulting quality scale depends upon the original collection of sample performances. Insofar as possible they should differ only with respect to the quality to be measured. For example, if the scale is to measure handwriting, the children should write the same text and employ the same style of writing. If the scale it to measure composition, the pupils should write on the same topic. Another consideration is that all degrees of excellence should be represented. For example, in the case of drawing, one sample should approximate zero drawing ability. It should be characterized as an attempt to draw, but an attempt which represents no accomplishment. The number of samples collected should be large so that one can be reasonably sure that all degrees of ability are represented.

The matching of the test performances with the steps of the scale is a subjective process which contributes to the unreliability of the measures secured. Several investigators have compared ratings by means of a scale with estimates of quality made without the use of a scale. The evidence is conflicting and hence disappointing. Odell, after summarizing investigations of the reliability of ratings made by means of composition scales and considering data with respect to the reliability of a set of scales for rating pupils' answers to thought questions, concluded that "if the scales themselves possess high merit and if those who employ them do so after the best possible preparation and in the best possible manner," the reliability of the resulting measures of quality will be higher than that of estimates made without the use of a scale.

Derived scales of measnrement

The scale of measurement on which the point scores are expressed is determined by the structure of the test and the manner of computing the score. Usually the zero point is arbitrary and does not represent "not any of the thing measured." McCall has proposed a scale of measurement having the zero point at 5.0σ below the mean score of a large and unselected population of 12-year-old children. The unit of measurement is $.1\ \sigma$ and the measures expressed on this scale are known as T-scores. Test scores can be converted into a number of other types of derived measures. Transmutation into age scores is a common procedure. Familiar examples are mental age, educational age, achievement age, arithmetic age, and reading age. A given reading age of 115 months means that the pupil who obtained this score did as well on the test as the median pupil whose chronological age is 115 months or 9 years 7 months. When the median scores for a series of grades and for each month of the school year have been determined, point scores may be transmuted into grade scores. A grade score of 5.6 obtained by a pupil would indicate that his achievement on the test was equivalent to the median pupil in the sixth month of the fifth grade. The use of age scores and grade scores rests on the assumption that the groups whose scores are compared have been subjected to comparable educational experience. That is to say, the pupils have been subjected to the same curriculum and school organization.

The computation of the percentile points of a distribution of scores makes possible the transmutation of scores into percentile measures. For example, if a score of 83 falls within the interval between the 47 and 48 percentile, it may be expressed as a percentile score of 47. The pupil's ability may be described as of the 47 percentile. Although percentile scores are expressed in terms that can be easily understood, they do not possess the qualities which are possessed by derived scores expressed in terms of the variability of a chronological age group. The unit is not constant.

The distribution is divided so that equal areas are obtained in calculating percentile scores. The divisions do not mark equal distances on the base line of the distribution. The result is that the difference between the degrees of ability represented by a 45 percentile score and a 50 percentile score is not at all equal to the difference between the degrees of ability represented by a 90 percentile score and a 95 percentile score. The latter is much larger. Percentile scores are useful, however, when precise comparison is not attempted, and at the high school level where age and grade scores are not applicable.

Composite score of a battery of tests

When the measuring instrument consists of several subtests and a single composite score is desired, it is necessary to derive a procedure for computing it. If it is desired to give equal weight to the measures resulting from the several subtests, the scores may be reduced to a common basis and then added. If criterion measures are available, the weights for the maximum validity may be obtained by calculating the multiple regression equation.

The psychological questionaire

The psychological questionnaire is used to measure human traits (attitudes, interests, ideals, and other general patterns of conduct) by asking the pupil questions relative to what he has done, how he is accustomed to do certain things, his likes, beliefs, choices, wishes, preferences, interests, and the like. The distinction between it and a performance test is that the latter attempts to secure the functioning of the ability whose measurement is desired or the functioning of a closely correlated ability. In the psychological questionnaire there is no such attempt. It merely asks questions whose answers experience has shown to be indicative of the status of the trait whose measurement is desired. Some of the questions call for deliceration and the expression of a judgment. Others ask for immediate expression of choices or other reactions. Usually the questions are expressed in a form such that the scoring of the answers is objective.

The only essential criterion for devising and selecting the items of a psychological questionnaire is their effectiveness in indicating individual differences in the trait whose measurement is desired. A question may appear to be inconsequential or even ridiculous, but if experience shows that it is effective, its appropriateness has been demonstrared. In general, however, a superior initial selection of questions will be secured by analyzing the behavior associated with the trait and attempting to formulate pertinent questions.

A psychological questionnaire may be used as a means of securring a controlled interview for the purpose of diagnosing children individually. When used for this purpose by a competent person, a definite plan of scoring may not be advisable, but when groups of subjects are being studied, a numerical score is usually desired. The criterion of the validity of a method of scoring is the effectiveness of the resulting measures in revealing individual differences in the trait whose measurement is desired. In general no answer can be considered as wrong. The questions do not call for facts as in the case of performance tests. Any response to an item of a psychological questionnaire may be significant and in the present stage of the development of this field of measurement a person constructing a measuring instrument of this type should try out several methods of scoring, at least all promising ones, and calculate the correlation between the resulting sets of scores and the criterion.

A number of psychological questionnaires were used in the comprehensive investigation of Terman and his co-workers, "Mental and Physical Traits of a Thousand Gifted Children." In Chapters XIII, XIV, and XV are described instruments for the measurement of scholastic, occupational, play, and reading interests. In Chapters XVII and XVIII are described questionnaires for the measurement of character and personality traits. Voelker's ten tests of trustworthiness, Cady's measures of incorrigibility, and the Woodworth-Cady Questionnaire for the measurement of emotional stability are also described. The Woodworth-Cady Questionnaire is reproduced in full on pages 501 to 505. An illustration of the efforts to measure the less tangible and definite controls of conduct is afforded by an attempt to measure "faith in God."

D. ESTIMATING THE EXCELLENCE OF MEASURING INSTRUMENTS

The reliability and validity of a measuring instrument

After a measuring instrument has been constructed including the formulation of directions for administering it and for obtaining the score, it remains to determine how accurately the instrument measures the ability or trait specified by its expressed or implied function. In Chapter V four types of errors were noted :

(1) variable errors of measurement,
(2) variable errors of validity,
(3) systematic errors of measurement,
(4) systematic errors of validity.

Since the systematic error in the scores yielded by a test fluctuates with the manner of its administration and other conditions not connected with its structure, indices of only variable errors of measurement and variable errors of validity can be associated with a measuring instrument. The reliability of a test has reference to the variable errors of measurement and the validity of a test to the variable errors of validity. When used in a technical sense, these terms have no connection with systematic errors.

The association of an index of variable errors of measurement or of the variable errors of validity with a test implies that the "average" magnitude of the errors to be expected in the case of a given test is a fixed characteristic of the measuring instrument. This implication is not necessarily true. In the case of a particular administration of a given test, the actual variable errors of measurement or the actual variable errors of validity may be materially greater than the index indicates. It is also possible that they may be less. Hence, the indices dealt with in the following pages should be thought of as representing estimates of the magnitude of the variable errors to be expected rather than as fixed characteristics of a test or other measuring instrument.

Determining an index of the magnitude of the variable errors of measurement to be expected in the scores yielded by a given instrument

The determination of an index of the magnitude of the variable errors of measurement to be expected in the measures obtained by means of a given instrument is based upon two independent sets of scores for a group of subjects representative of the population for which the test is designed. Three methods are used for securing these :

(1) repeating the administration of the test,

(2) administering two forms of the test, and

(3) securing two series of scores by dividing the test into two equivalent parts, usually by using the odd num-

bered items as the basis of one score and the even numbered ones as the basis of the other.

None of these methods is entirely satisfactory. Both sets of scores should be typical of testing conditions that may be expected to prevail when the test is administered to a group of subjects. When a test is readministered, the conditions are likely not to be typical because the subjects may remember some of the exercises and their responses. Their attitude may also be affected. When two forms of a test are used, there is likely to be some "transfer" from the first to the second testing. Furthermore, unless very carefully constructed, the two forms are likely not to be entirely equivalent. When the two sets of scores are obtained by dividing a test into halves, the testing conditions are identical and hence the effect of typical variations in testing conditions is eliminated. Furthermore, this procedure introduces other difficulties that will be noted later.

1. *Coefficients of reliability*

The term "reliability coefficient" appears to have been used first by Spearman in 1910. Reliability coefficients, however, appeared in his writings as early as 1904 and were defined as "the average correlation between one and another of these several independently obtained series of values." In other words, the basis of a reliability coefficient was to be two independently obtained sets of measures of the same thing. This is equivalent to saying that the basis should be two sets of measures the pairs of which differ only because of the presence of variable errors of measurement. A reliability coefficient does not measure any systematic error that may be present. When a coeffieient of reliability is calculated from IQ's or other quotient scores, "spurious correlation" is introduced. For example, if an intelligence test with zero reliability is administered to a population heterogeneous with reference to chronological age, the reliability of the IQ's will be .50. For references dealing with "spurious correlation" see Chapter XI, page 388.

The coefficient of correlation between the two sets of paired scores obtained by either of the first two of the above procedures is commonly called the coefficient of reliability ($r_{1}I$). As pointed out above, the paired measures obtained either by repeating a test or by using two forms of a test do not completely qualify as "two independently obtained sets of measures of the same thing." In general, the coefficient calculated from scores obtained by repeating the test is likely to be slightly too large and one calculated from scores obtained from duplicate forms slightly too small.

The Spearman-Brown formula is employed as a means of calculating a coefficient of reliability from the coefficient of correlation between the two sets of scores obtained by the third procedure. Using the symbol,

$$r_{\frac{1}{2}\frac{I}{II}},$$

to designate the coefficient of correlation between the two halves of the test, the formula is

$$r_{1}I = \frac{2r_{\frac{1}{2}\frac{I}{II}}}{1+r_{\frac{1}{2}\frac{I}{II}}}$$

The use of this formula has been questioned. Shen has shown that the standard error of the estimated coefficient is greater than that of an equivalent reliability coefficient calculated directly. In practice, however, this condition is likely to be less significant than failure to satisfy completely the assumptions on which the Spearman-Brown formula is based. The formula is a special case of the one for the correlation of sums which simplifies to the above form only when certain conditions are satisfied. The reliability coefficient $r_{1}I$ may be written

$$r_{\left(\frac{1}{2}+\frac{1}{2}\right)\left(\frac{I}{II}+\frac{I}{II}\right)}.$$

When expressed in this form, four, sets of measures are apparent, those from the two halves of Test 1 and those from the two halves of Test I. Two assumptions are made :

(1) the standard deviations of these four sets of measures are equal;

(2) the various intercorrelations are equal.

In applying the Spearman-Brown formula, one has only two sets of measures, one designated as

$$X_{\frac{1}{2}}$$

and the other as

$$X_{\frac{I}{II}}$$

If the standard deviations of these two sets of measures are equal, the r_1I obtained is the boefficient of correlation between two hypothetical tests, one formed by doubling the half designated as ½ and the other formed by doubling the half designated as

$$\frac{I.}{II}$$

The obtained r_1I is the correct r_1I provided the measures resulting from the added portions have the same standard deviations as the measures yielded by the original halves and provided further the various intercorrelations are equivalent. Brownell has shown that in the case of objective tests constructed by an instructor for measuring the achievement of his students, different methods of forming the halves result in a wide range of values for

$$r_{\frac{1}{2}\frac{I}{II}}.$$

This condition is probably due, at least in part, to failure to satisfy the assumptions just noted. It is likely that they are not fully satisfied in more carefully constructed tests.

A reliability coefficient obtained from halves of a test and the application of the Spearman-Brown formula does not represent the same thing as one obtained from two applications of the test or the application of two forms of the test. Variations in the scores of individual pupils are due in part to differences in mind-set, effort, and the like. Such differences are probably eliminated in the case of two halves of the same test, but they are likely to be significant when there are two separate testings, especially when there is an interval of a day or more between them. Hence, the coefficient derived from the two halves of a test and the Spearman-Brown formula may be expected to be somewhat larger than would be obtained from a second administratton of the test after an interval of at least a few hours.

The reliability of psychological questionaires has been determined by the teachniques used in determining the reliability of ordinary tests. Some investigators have administered their questionaires twice to the same group of subjects and correlated the results. The weakness of this method is that the subjects may remember some of their initial responses, deliberately change them, thus reducing the reliability coefficient obtained. The use of equivalent forms is most desirable but it is often exceedingly difficult to construct equivalent forms of a psychological questionnaire. Symonds, after summarizing the reliability coefficients of a number of psychological questionnaires, concludes that these instruments compare favorably in reliability with ordinary tests of the recall, multiple-response, and true-false types.

The reliability of a battery of tests may be computed from the reliabilities and intercorrelations of the sub-tests by means of the formula for the correlation of sums. If the sub-tests are approximately equivalent in reliability and the intercorrelations are high, the general form of the Spearman-Brown formula will give nearly the same result. When these conditions, are not satisfied, the result obtained will be spuriously high.

2. *Index of reliability*

The coefficient of reliability, r_1I, is an index of $X_1—X_1$ rather than of $X_1—X_\infty$. A measure of the latter may be obtained by calculating the inder of reliability as indicated by the formula

$$r_{1\infty} = \sqrt{r_1I}$$

in which $r_{1\infty}$ represents the coeffieient of correlation between a set of obtained scores and the corresponding set of theoretical true scores.

3. *Probable error of measurement*

The variable errors of measurement are the differences between the obtained scores (X_1) and the corresponding theoretical true scores (X_∞). The media a deviation of these differences, which is called the probable error of measurement, is given by the formula

$$PE_{1.\infty} = .6745\sigma_1 \sqrt{1—r_1I}$$

The $PE_{1\infty}$ may be interpreted with respect to the group to which the test was administered or with respect to any member of that group. In the first case, the calculated $PE_{1.\infty}$ is the median deviation of the variable errors in the obtained test scores. When the interpretation of the calculated $PE_{1.\infty}$ is with reference to the score of a given pupil, it is to be thought of as specifying the limit for which the chances are just fifty-fifty that the variable error will not be greater. For example, suppose $PE_{1.\infty} = 4.0$. Then for a given pupil the chances are fifty-fifty that his score involves a variable error not greater than 4.0. It is also possible to interpret the coefficient of reability in terms of the per cent of pupils whose scores involve a varialiable error greater than a specified amount.

The formula for the probable error of measurement affords a means for an interpretation of coefficients of reliability in terms of the corresponding median deviations of the variable errors of measurement. Unless the value of σ_1 is known, it will appear as a factor in this median deviation. It should be noted that unless σ_1 is relatively small, a reliability coefficient must approach 1.00 in order to indicate small variable errors of measurement.

Generalizing a measure of reliability

When a calculated coefficient of reliability, index of reliability, or probable error of measurement is associated with a test as an index of the variable errors of measurement to be expected when it is administered to a group of pupils, generalization is implied. Representativeness of the group from which determination of the index is made is a requirement for such generalization. As pointed out on page 110, a coefficient of correlation is affected by the variability or range of talent of the group. For a given measuring instrument, the coefficient of reliability calculated from a single grade group will be smaller than one calculated from a population including a sequence of grades. A coefficient of .60 calculated from a single grade group may be indicative of smaller variable errors of measurement than a coefficient of .90 calculated from a population including grades III to VIII. Hence, generalization of a coefficient of reliability must be restricted to populations of the same range of talent. Even in such cases, consideration of the causes of variable errors of measurement suggests that their magnitude may not be entirely stable. Hence, the generalization should not be considered highly dependable.

The probable error of measurement is assumed to be independent of the population from which the determination is made. On the basis of this assumption, a calculated probable error of measurement is commonly associated with a test as a measure of the magnitude of the variable errors of measurement to be expected in the scores yielded by it. This assumption is probably only approximated and hence a calculated probable error of measurement may not be a highly dependable index. Furthermore, when comparing tests with reference to their probable errors of measurement, it should be remembered that the significance of a probable error of measurement depends upon the range and magnitude of the scores yielded by by the test. If the scores range from 125 to 200, a probable error of measurement of 5.0 has less practical significance than when the scores range only from 25 to 75.

Determining an index of the variable errors of validity to be expected in the scores yielded by a given test

Although we speak of determining the validity of a test, it should be remembered, as pointed out on page 174, that this characteristic of an instrument for measuring human abilities and traits is not stable. Hence, generalization from a determination for a given test is hazardous. Furthermore, it should be noted that the phrase, "validity of a test" has no reference to the systematic error of validity.

The determination of an index of the variable errors of validity requirse criterion measures of the ability or trait specified by the function of the test. In the case of a prognostic test, certain criterion measures are obtainable. For example, if the function of a test is to predict future scholastic success, which is defined as the school mark received in the field specified, the criterion measures are the school marks received by the pupils to whom the test is administered. If the test is designed to measure the same abilities or traits that are measured by an available test, the scores yielded by this instrument may be used as the criterion measures. For example, the Stanford Revision of the Binet Test is believed to yield highly valid measures. Hence, mental ages obtained from its use are used as criteria for determining the validity of new intelligence tests. The more common case, however, is one in which the ability or trait to be measured is defined by a phrase such as "ability to read silently," "ability to solve arithmetical problems," "achievement in history," "language ability," "study habits," or "success in teaching, and no instrument is available for securing measures of it that ase known to be highly valied. In such cases, testmakers have used school marks, teachers' estimates, and composite scores from a selected group of tests. Obviously such measures, or combinations of them, are subject to criticism as criterion measures and hence determination of an index of the variable errors of validity to be expected in the scores yielded by a test is usually not very satisfactory. When criterion measures are available, the coefficient of correlation between them and the scores yielded by it, r_{1c} is called the coefficient of validity.

E. IMPROVEMENT OF TESTS

Revising a test to increase its reliability and validity

After a testmaker has determined the reliability and validity of his instrument, he may desire to investigate the possibilities of improving it in these respects. An obvious procedure is that of lengthening the test. The general form of the Spearman-Brown formula provides a means of estimating the reliability of a lengthened test.

$$r_{nn} = \frac{nr_1r}{1+(n-1)r_1I}$$

In this formula r_{nn} is the reliability coefficient of the lengthened test, and n is the number of times the length of the test has been increased. Solving the equation for n, we have

$$n = \frac{r_{nn}(1-r_1I)}{r_1I(1-r_{nn})}$$

when written in this form, the number of times the length of the test must be increased to secure a desired coefficient of reliability (r_{nn}) can easily be calculated. On page 202 attention was called to the assumptions on which the derivation of the Spearman-Brown formula is based, and even when these conditions are satisfied the estimated reliability coefficient of a lengthened test should be considered a probable upper limit of the actual reliability.

Since the validity of a test is conditioned by its reliability, the validity will be increased by lengthening the test. The formula is

$$r_{nc} = \frac{nr_{1c}}{\sqrt{n+n(n-1)r_{1I}}}$$

in which r_{nc} is the coefficient of validity of the lengthened test. It should be noted, howcver, that sinbe

$$r_{1c} = r_{z_\infty c_\infty} \sqrt{r_{1I}} \sqrt{r_{cc}}$$

the upper limit of r_{nc} is $r_{z_\infty c_\infty} \sqrt{r_{cc}}$. Hence, if $r_{z_\infty c_\infty}$ does not approach 1.00, it will not be possible to make the test highly valid by lengthening it.

The reliability and validity of a test are affected by the difficulty of the test items, administration time, type of test exercises, method of scoring, directions for doing the exerciscr. and possibly by other factors. Hence, in revising a test to increase its reliability and validity, a testmaker should investigate the possibility of effecting improvement in ways in addition to increasing its length.

12

Development of the Induction Sequence

The survey-action research—pilot project—evalution study of the induction process undertaken in England and Wales by University of Bristol School of Education with the support of Department of Education and Science funds and collaboration from a number of employing authorities and colleges, constitutes something of a model of the relationship between research and reform in teacher education (Bolam and J. K. Taylor, 1972).

As long ago as 1944, the McNair Report on teacher training had identified the importance of the first year of teaching for the development of an individual's career, and this was echoed in other consultative committee reports during the early 1960s. At the same time, it became clear that the then shortage of teachers was being made worse by heavy rates of wastage during the first year after certification.

Thus in 1966 the Department of Education and Science made funds available for a National Survey of some three thousand probationary (i. e. first year) teahers, their head teachers and employing authorities. This phase of the work threw up a great deal of information that was influential in shaping policy on the probationary year. For example, it appeared that whilst only a very small percentage of first-year teachers judged their initial training to have been seriously inadequate, and three-quarters were reasonably satisfied, most were able to identify particular deficiencies, not least in a lack of time and attention devoted to topics they judged of importance to their future career. Attitudes towards training are shown in the table overleaf :

But the survey also exposed many weaknesses in the induction process. Many beginning teachers were not given information of a kind that would facilitate their adjustment to the classroom. For example, over a quarter obtained knowledge of the syllabus or schemes of work to would be expected to teach only within a week of starting work, and 13 per cent of the sample obtained information on these points only on the day that they began teaching! In the words of those who undertook the survey :

> '. . . by the time they had begun teaching, only about one in three probationers had previously met their pupils, only half had met their predecessor and even in primary schools one in five had not seen their probable classroom; yet one would have supposed that these three objectives were very important to some one planning his next years work' (Bolam and J. K. Taylor, 1972, p. 6).

A striking finding from the survey was a comparison between the claim made by head teachers that there existed a member of staff with specific responsibility for the probationary work of beginning teachers, and probationers' own awareness of this fact. In primary schools, 38 per cent of the heads claimed the existence of such a person, but only 19 per cent of the probationers in these schools knew about his existence. The gap in secondary schools was even larger—73 per cent and 26 per cent, respectively. Although the inspectors and advisers employed by the local authority are in many cases expected to make systematic visits to teachers during their first year of service, with particular reference to the provision of an assessment on which the decision about the successful conclusion or the extension of probation may be made, a third of all primary probationers, and 44 per cent of those in secondary schools, had near the end of their first year never been visited in their school by an LEA inspector or adviser.

Alongside the survey work undertaken in Bristol after 1966, a series of experimental guidance programmes was designed, comprising four stages—an induction-day conference early in the autumn term, three or four general discussion meetings later in that first term, certain specific optional courses related to the probationers' needs and interests, with up to eight meetings during the spring and summer terms, and a final over-view conference on a day in the summer term. The response of the probationers to this provision, and the views of the tutors responsible for each stage, were obtained by questionnaire and interview.

The Committee on teacher education under the Chairmanship of Lord James that reported in 1970 (DES, 1970c) was aware of the Bristol research and gave careful attention to future arrangements for induction programmes. By the time the White Paper on policy in this field was published in 1972 (DES, 1972) more findings of the Bristol work had been published (J. K. Taylor and Dale, 1971; Bolam and J. K. Taylor, 1972). Reports and statements had also been issued by several of the teachers' organizations, and from conferences and meetings called to discuss improvements in the induction process.

The White Paper provided for probationary teachers to have a lightened timetable, and to be released for not less than one-fifth of their time for in-service training. It took up and encouraged the recommendations of the James Report concerning the training and designation of 'professional tutors' and the establishment of professional centres, 'based principally on existing training institutions and teachers' centres' (DES, 1972). The White Paper also proposed that pilot schemes for a new style induction process should begin in 1972—73, with a view to the training of professional tutors starting a year later, and a national scheme being introduced during the school year 1975-76.

In the event, economic and other factors conspired to delay the programme of implementing a new induction process, and to reduce the number and scale of the pilot schemes. Only two—in the urban setting of Liverpool, and the more rural environment of Northumberland—were established, and with financial support from the Department of Education and Science got underway in 1974. Arrangements were made for the two 'official' projects and a number of other efforts that were being made by employing authorities on their own initiative, and without additional central government finance, to be evaluated by a team based on the University of Bristol of Education, and including members who had been involved in the earlier survey and experimental scheme.

Once again, extensive data were provided on the response of probationers teachers, heads and employing authority advisers, inspectors and officials.

> 'The basic general criterion adopted to assess the schemes has been that of informed professional judgment: the views of those involved have been obtained through questionnaires, interviews, case studies and observaticn. In this way the evaluators hove gained a reasonably comprehensive and reliable picture of the range of opinions on the scheme held by probationers, teacher tutors, experienced teachers, heads, professional centre staff, advisers and administrators. The evaluators also adopted a common policy of concentrating on the practical issues and problems of the schemes at the level of the LEA, the external course centre and the school' (Bolam and Baker, 1976).

The pilot projects, both official and unofficial, have made it possible to identify a number of problems that have to be faced by those responsible for the implementation of induction schemes. Some of these are of a very practical kind. For example, can the authority afford to find the money necessary to release teachers for a full day each week, and to train and provide time for the teacher-tutors to help the probationers assigned to them? In some cases, existing staff were invited to apply for the teacher-tutor post that had been established in their school.

These carried additional allowances, and small sums (£100+£20 per probationer up to a maximum of £200 per five probationers) were paid to heads or deputy heads with teacher-tutor responsibilities. In the two major projects, it has been calculated that the cost of releasing probationers and tutors was approximately £1,000 per annum per probationer (Bolam and Baker, 1976). The advantages and disadvantages of school-based as distinct from centre-based programmes were considered' as was the provision of guidelines and resource materials for tutors.

At another level, the surveys made available the results of informed professional judgment on the usefulness of the schemes. In the words of the evaluators:

> 'The positive effects of these two schemes include the following: a majority of Northumberland headteachers thought that the probationers' teaching performance had been improved by the scheme; Liverpool advisers said they could identify and help probationers "at risk" more quickly than hitherto; Northumberland heads said that the external courses helped to improve their probationers' teaching performance while, in Liverpool, there, is evidence to suggest that absenteeism amongst probationers has been reduced by the scheme: in both authorities heads considered that the scheme had assisted the schools by easing the probationers' entry into the profession and there is evidence that many probationers are much better informed about professional resources in the area. Finally, the organisers and evaluators of both schemes have remarked upon some unanticipated outcomes: that there has been an "opening-up" of schools, centres and colleges because of the interchange which the scheme has encouraged; that teacher tutors have themselves experienced some significant pro-

fessional development; and that many schools have been stimulated to look afresh at their overall policies.'

At a third level, with more theoretical implications but still of real practical importance as far as the success of induction schemes is concerned, the work done since 1966 has encouraged a debate about, and provided data upon, the role of the teacher-tutor advocated by the James Report and the White Paper. It was not long after the publication of these documents that educationists recognized some of the potential role conflicts that might be involved in introducing teacher-tutor posts. The James Report had been far from explicit about such conflicts, although clear as to the need for designated teacher-tutors :

'Each school must have a member of staff nominated as a professional tutor. . . he would be the link between the school and all other agencies engaged in that work; he would have general oversight of all the practical experience of professional work that new teachers undergo in the first year of their appointment; he would assist his colleagues in the choice and pursuit of third cycle courses. . .in a small school. . .the head himself or his deputy might be designated as the professional tutor. In large schools, one member of staff might spend the greater part of his time discharging the responsibilities here outlined and he should of course be recognized and paid as a major head of department' (DES, 1972, p. 37).

But such a role definition was by no means unambiguous (Buckley, 1972; Maw, 1973; Bolam, 1975 b.) Should the teacher tutor adopt a primarily confidential counselling role, and take little or no part in the final assessment of the probation? What should be the relationship between the teacher-tutor, the head and the local authority adviser? Should the role be limited to the provision of advice and guidance to probationers, or did it extend, as recommended by the James Committee, to the coordination of all the in-service training and education activities of members of staff? Bolam 1975 b) suggests that the two major components in the teacher-tutor role can be identified at the opposite ends of a continuum

PASTORAL←——————→TRAINING

It appears that a large number of tutors identified, their role mainly in pastoral terms, and did not think it proper to intervene in the classroom, even to the extent of observing probationary teachers at work. This was felt by both ptobationers and tutors as smacking too much of the style of initial training that had been terminated by formal certification. In the eyes of many members of the profession, the kind of help that needs to be provided for beginning teachers requires no special skills on the part of experienced colleagues. (This point had been made explicitly in statements issued by some of the teachers' organizations at the time of the White Paper.) Thus few tutors saw it as their task to use techniques such as micro-teaching and interaction analysis which might help the probationer to appreciate more fully the nature and consequences of his or her work in the classroom.

It seems clear that the debate on the nature of the teacher-tutor's role will continue as more local authorities institutionalize formal arrangements for the induction year. Some of the 'unofficial' pilot schemes that were taken into account the recent national evaluation had sought to give their teacher tutor the wider responsibility for school practice arrangements for students induction programmes and in-service coordination for the schools as a whole, although it rather looks at the moment as if most authorities are likely to confine the work of the specially designated teacher tutors to the first and second of these tasks, provisions will need to be made for the more systematic training of teacher-tutors, and the provision of ongoing support for them as they tacle the problem of students and young teachers. Experiment is likely to continue in a search for an optimal pattern of induction-year experiences, and papers and conference reports will no doubt steadily accumulate as the range and scale of this activity increases.

Among the other theoretical issues to which the work under review is relevant are questions about the conditions that inhibit and support the institutionalization of innovations, the problems of assessment, both in terms of role perception and performance and the legitimization of criteria, and the models of supervision relevant to the performance of the teacher tutor role. Bolam (1975b) has suggested that a usefull framework of practice and concepts is provided by the idea of 'clinical supervision', with its stress on the ability of the school-based teacher-tutor to provide individualized help in the context of an intimate knowledge of a specific classroom and school context (Goldhammer, 1969).

This UK work has received particular attention this chapter not only because of its intrinsic importances, but because of its illustrative character in terms of current, trends in teacher education research. This was not simply an acadmic exercise, planned by college or university staff and carried on for reasons of 'curiosity,' although, as we have seen, it has undoubtedly provided evidence relevant to the discussion of theoretical issues. The work was conceived from the start in relation to a problem of practice, which it was in the interest of central government, employing authorities and teachers themselves to solve. If the principal justification for such work was the improvement in the quality of teacher education and teacher performance — and also the removal of a certain amount of human misery, in so far as this was experienced by beginning teachers in regimes where no special provision for their needs existed — it obtained a major impetus from the economic and logistical problems of teacher wastage during the mid-Sixties.

Taken up in the official reports, the institutionalization of a national scheme was hit by economic difficulties. But by that time, with the arrival of a teacher surplus in some areas which reduced the importance of wastage as a problem, the educational professional justification for action were again paramount, and local authorities strove to find ways in which these newly identified needs could be met within the financial constraints to which their budgets were subject.

There seems little doubt there is sufficient steam behind the concern for an improved induction process, and sufficient public interest has been aroused, to ensure that despite the ending of the overall teacher shortage, and the absence of resources originally seen as necessary to the implementation of a scheme, something will in fact be done by most employing authorities and in most schools. There will, no doubt, for some years be some authorities which do little more than before all this started.

But the original surveys, action research, the pilot projects and evaluation and the debate and argument generated; have all had, and will continue to have, their effects on teachers and the schools. At the same time, we may expect that university and college researchers will take up some of the problems already indentified in the pilot stages, and others which will become apparent as induction schemes become more widespread. Theses will be written, conference and meetings organized, and lecture and essay topics included in courses for the advanced diploma and master's degree in education. In all these ways, the research that started in the mid-Sixties will have its impact upon practice. Links will be forged between the latest work and earlier studies of 'reality shock' and the entry into teaching (Becker, 1952; Wagenschein, 1950; Whiteside, Bernbaun and Nobel, 1969), Examples of such related work are already available from London and from Leeds.

A study of probationary teachers in London was undertaken in 1974 by Morton and Mathieson. All probationary teachers who began work in London in September 1973 were followed up by postal questionnaire, an 81 per cent response rate being obtained. It is interesting to note that over one-fifth of all the respondents were twenty-five years or older at the point of beginning teaching, and in many cases had experience of employment in other walks of life before training, or between certification and taking up first appointment. Probationers were asked about the training they had received in relation to specific teaching skills, such as they might be called upon to employ in their first post. Eleven per cent of the respondents thought that more school practice was needed 13 per cent wanted more instruction in professional skills, 15 per cent were critical in some way of their postgraduate courses, and small numbers of other respondents identified more help as being needed with discipline problems, more opportunity required to learn from experience teachers and more instruction needed on organization in schools.

The authority followed up these teachers after they had been working for two terms in London schools. A particularly revealing result of the survey, in relation to the plan being made for the introduction of systematic induction schemes, was that 80 per cent of the respondents said they preferred another teacher as their teacher tutor, only 8 percent preferring e. g. a full-time tutor/counsellor or a college of education lecturer. (This may, however, have been due to the item wording, in which the pharse 'not currently teaching' had been employed to categorize support other than from colleagues.) Nonetheless, the overwhelming majority from all schools, rejected support from anyone not currently teaching in school' (p. 5).

These findings can be compared to those of the Northumberland Pilot Scheme, McCabe, 1975). Probationers identified their main areas of concern as dealing with groups of wide ability range, being aware of children's previous learning, and lack of specific techniques. (The responses of teacher in first schools, middle schools and high schools differ to some extent but these three topics had a high ranking for all groups.)

A research team at the University of Leeds undertook in 1970-71 a survey of the opinions about teacher education of some 4,240 teachers (2,560 primary, 1,680 secondary) (University of Leeds Institute of Education, 1974).

This was before much of the recent publicity about the importance of the induction phase, but showed that many teachers were no happy about the amount of supervision and guidance that was being given to teachers in their first year of service. For example, only 39.2 per cent of secondary and 49 per cent of primary teachers thought the amount of supervision and guidance was 'sufficient,' 60.5 and 50.4 per cent respectively, thought it was 'insufficient', and only a negligible number (5 teachers among the secondary sample of 1,402 and 12 among the primary sample of 1,948) thought it was 'too much'.

There was some different between primary and secondary teacher' views about who should exercise responsibility for such supervision and guidance of probationers. About half the primary teachers thought it should be the school alone, rather than school and inspectorate, or scoool and a local college, or a combination of these, whilst nearly two-thirds of secondary teachers opted for supervision being given by the school alone and only a small proportion wanted to see any involvement by the local college of educational responsible for the initial training of teachers.

The views of probationary teachers and those with between ten and fifteen years' experience on the balance between theory and practice in college courses did not differ significantly. Between three-quarters and nine-tenths of probationary and experienced primary and secondary teachers thought that the course gave 'too much emphasis to theory' Again, only a negligible number thought that theembasis was too much on practice, and remainder were satisfied-with the balance achieved. Probationary and experienced teahers agreed that insufficient attention was given in the course to the teaching of reading and writing — again, the proportions of probationers and experienced teacher with such views varied between three-quaters and nine-tenths of the samples — but only about half the teachers surveyed througt that insufficient attention was given to the teaching of mathematics.

Again, the pattern of agreement between probationers and experienced teachers continued on the balance between the content of main subjects and the method of teaching in college courses for those intending to teach 13- to 18- year-olds. A fifth of the probationers; and rather fewer of the experienced teacher thought that the balance between content and method was 'effective', two-thirds of the probationers and three quarters of the experienced teachers thought there was 'an emphasis on content at the expence of method', and only 12 per cent of probationers and 11 per cent of their experienced colleagues felt that the emphasis was the other way round, on method at the expense of content. Two-thirds of the secondary school teachers in the sample thought that the most effective method of training students of this age group was to ensure that the study of teaching was carried out within the context of the main subject, rather than the main subject and the study of teaching forming separate courses.

13

In-Service Education and Curriculum Development

The close relationship between curriculum development and in-service training is brought out in the report of a group of teachers, researchers and expects on educational administration in West Germany, which in 1973 recommended the establishment of a network of Regional Educational Centres (REC) throughout the Federal Republic, in which there would be explicit interrelation of curriculum development, in-service teacher training and advisory and guidance services (Herz, 1973). The in-service teacher training element of the proposal would be 'project based' and would involve :

Preparatory, orientation and intensive courses providing :

—specialized information;

—introduction to the methodology of curriculum development :

—orientation in methods of scientific inquiry and social sciences.

Collaborative development work.

Group meetings, simulation exercises, audiovisual feedback :

—study of teacher behaviour;

—widening of the behavioural repertoire within the framework of curricular concepts.

Discussion forums, information on the dissemination of developed curricula (including teachers and school administrators).

The stress in the report on school and project-based work, with a high measure of teacher involvement, reflects the conviction of many people in western European countries that the planned 'downward' sequence of research followed by development followed by dissemination (which in curriculum terms has sometimes been called the 'Rational Curriculum Planning' model) has not been successful. In the view of the authors of the German report :

> 'Project-based curriculum reform enables the development of modular curricula, without having to forego academic standards and be forced into do it yourself amatecurism; active participation of teachers, not just reducing participation to formally conferring the right to have a voice in decisions; the in-service training of teachers involving active participation in the formulating and solving of curriculum problems instead of being limited to the abstract ritual of lectures and conferences.'

It may be pertinent at this point to add a comment or two about the curriculum development movement in some of the countries with which we are concerned. There are now curriculum development agencies at state, regional and national level in many countries, the roles of which inevitably differ according to the character of the educational structures that they serve. In a country where it is possible to buy a copy of the curriculum of the primary school from a book shop, the function of such an agency is likely to be very different from where the curriculum serves merely as a highly generalized description of what goes on in the average classroom and the average school.

These differences aside, it is probably true to say the influences that have brought about the creation of explicit curriculum development processes in many countries are broadly similar. At the beginning of the Sixties, educationists, both inside and outside government, were becoming conscious of the slow pace at which curriculum change was going on, and what they saw as the relative failure of the schools to respond to changes in the world outside. There was already a good deal of experience of self-conscious curriculum development activity accumulating in the US, and the Nuffield Foundation and some other independent bodies were beginning to finance projects in the UK.

In England where feelings about teacher and school autonomy in curriculum matters are strong (often invoking a 'tradition' which White (1973) has shown is of somewhat lesser antiquity than many of its proponents believe), the announcement that a Curriculum Study Group had been set up within the then Ministry of Education provoked an outcry from teachers and stimulated the setting up of an official committee which recommended the establishment of the teacher-controlled Schools Council. Yet despite the fact that the main committees of the Council have, through the National Teachers' Associations, strong teacher involvement, the Council has still been criticized on the grounds that it embodies a 'centre-periphery model' of curriculum change which is no longer viable.

> 'The model is too slow to respond to change, too centripetal and too dependent on central direction to provide the dynamism for self-transforming change at the periphery. Concentration at the centre makes the Council remote and monolithic. To many teachers the Council comes to define what is regarded as genuine innovation by those "up there" inauthority rather than to promote and facilitate development at a local level. What is needed are a substantial number of regional centres of curriculum renewal amply funded, embedded in the problems of their areas, drawing on local pools of talent, staffed by teams of change agents (who can move

into schools on request) and linked to other regional centres through an information and resource network. The Council should devolve most of its responsibility for curriculum renewal to these regional centres and see itself as a manager of the network and as a "think tank" challenging curricular assumptions, probing fundamentals and throwing up new ideas for regional centres to consider. This would involve considerable restructuring and reappraisal of the present organization but would serve the interests of educational reform. The Council would then challenge conventional curriculum wisdom instead of largely reflecting it' (Richards 1974).

It is not easy to assess the validity of these criticisms. For the most part, critics have been singularly unforthcoming when asked to propose alternative approaches. Nor is it easy to see how, with its restricted funds, its dependence on a broad basis of political and professional support, and the particular traditions of the United Kingdom in curriculum change, many of the Council's procedures could have been planned otherwise. What is important now is to ensure that the sophistication about the identification of priorities, project planning and design, the production of materials, and implementation and dissemination strategies, that are the result of a growing number of people examining problems of curriculum ch nge, is properly reflected in processes of institutional renewal.

The Schools Council came in for a good deal of criticism in the course of the 'Great Debate' on education sparked off by a speech by the Prime Minister at Ruskin College, Oxford in October 1976. In a discussion document published after this debate, the Secretary of State for Education and Science committed herself to a curriculum review in each local education authority area, in which the Schools Council would be 'invited to play a part'. Although a major restructuring of the Council's committees was under way by the end of 1977, its overall future does not seem seriously at risk.

To the extent that the work of some curriculum development agencies has been based on the 'Rational Curriculum Planning' model referred to earlier in this chapter, it is out of tune with the emphases of some in-service trainingefforts which are focused on changing the curricular consciousness of the teacher, rather than providing him with materials for use. Inglis (1975, p. 54) has criticized what he calls the 'flowchart' model of curriculum change :

> 'It does not follow that the flow-chart fits all, or indeed any of the non-repeatable situations which compose most of our lives. But it is a characteristic of this thought-form that it predicates all human actions as of this type. It derives from modern theories of organization which define efficiency as obtainable by dividing tasks into units—goals, aims, objectives—and arranging these in regular taxonomies. In this way the sorting and control of input, the process of transformation, and the quantification of output can allegedly be scrutinized and regulated. . . .

Curriculum development, as has repeatedly been pointed out, can ultimately occur only in one place—the classroom. Thus we are today seeing more emphasis placed on the part that the individual teacher plays in bringing about curriculum change, and how he might better be prepared for this task. And as was noted in an earlier chapter, this is coming to be true not only for those systems that for some time have left curriculur decisions to individual teachers, but to a growing extent for the centralized systems in which the content of what is to be taught is formally set out in requlations or guidelines.

Ultimately, there will be no substitute for quality. If any one thing is needed to ensure that the curriculum development efforts of a particular country or state or region are successful, it is the ability to attract into the business those men and women who cannot simply devise new 'strategies' and implement particular 'models' of curriculum renewal, but who have a love for their subjects, a respect for the bounded nature of our knowledge and an openness to new structures and forms of organization. We need those who will not be satisfied with the shoddy and the second-rate, who will bring to the whole business an analytical capability, an ability to perceive relationships obviour enough to the rest of us once pointed out, and that passion to teach without which all designs and strategies and organizations are empty.

14

Problems and Trends in Continuing Education

The limitations of continuing education

In the chours of support for improved in-service education and training for teachers that has characterized educational discussion in most developed countries in recent years there has been little room for the mention of doubts and possible drawbacks. Yet it cannot be assumed that this particular area of activity is free of the problems that accompany most large-scale efforts at reform. It has been a familiar experience for a new kind of provision to receive almost universal backing up to the point when questions begin to be asked about its effectiveness in relation to the growing burden of expenditure that it entails. There has been little research undertaken on the effectiveness of in-service education. Part of the trouble with research on effectiveness is that there is very little agreement about what constitutes an effective teaching performance. (See Biddle and Ellena, 1964 and Travers, 1974 for summaries of literally thousands of relevant studies.) It has to be recognized that we simply do not know how a teacher's classroom performance alters over time, or the extent to which it is affected by social and educational context. It is too easy to assume that in-service education is a cumulative process, that each new exposure to ideas and technique can build upon existing experience. But it may well be that the improvement of effectiveness includes a good deal of unlearning as well as new learning, and that as people get older and more established, bad habits become increasingly difficult to cradicate. If this is so, then the relative costs of in-service education are likely to be high. These are not merely theoretical questions. Decisions have to be made about the distribution of resources in short supply. Should priority be given to those teachers who have been longest away from training, or to those relatively more recently qualified? As soon as we make such decisions we have to make assumptions of a kind on which research is potentially capable of throwing valuable light. Neither existing evidence, nor any that is likely to result from work that we can now commission, will provide us with a conclusive basis for decision, but it may help to make such decisions more rational.

Another potential weakness of extended in-service provision is that it will undermine rather than enhance the teacher's sense of mastery and professional self-confidence. The phenomenologists have made clear just how complex and multiform are the assumptions on which rests the common sense, taken-for-granted reality of our everyday world (Schutz, 1962, 1966; Garfinkel, 1967; Douglas, 1971). The explosion of knowledge of the past twenty-five years represents a threat as well as a set of new opportunities. Whether parent or teacher or head or administrator or educational specialist, we are increasingly conscious of the existenee of an enormous volume of knowiedge relevant to our tasks to which for reasons of time or space or language we do not have access, and a somewhat smaller but still considerable body of knowledge which we do possess but which we are not clever or skilful enough to use. A visit to the new accessions section of a library, or attendance at a course, or listening to a lecture from someone who can spend his time reading, talking and thinking about practice rather than practising, is seldom a comfortable experience. Teachers react in different ways. There is a great deal of self-defensive talk about theorists, and the airy stratospheric wooliness of those who have escaped from the classroom. Less evident, but no less real, there is a certain sense of guilt and inadequacy. Some learn to handle the problem of information overload by specialization and the use of various selective filters; some dency the relevance and usefulness of what they hear; some simply stop listening. Defensiveness, cynicism, guilt, over-specialization, denial and the stopping of ears are no basis for the success of an in-service programme. Yet there are among reactions that may follow if we fail to take account of the danger of creating unreal expectations. The problem is not restricted to education. In medicine, in transportation, in urban planning, in social welfare and in much else besides, the gaps between the technically possible and the actual are widening. Changing attitudes towards research support, postgraduate study, and the role of the university in society reflect the consequent tensions. Each new effort at dissemination by bodies set up to stimulate and promote innovation and as a means of making new knowledge available for curriculum development adds to the pressure.

That these risks exist is no argument for not making greater in-service efforts. It is an argument for ensuring that these efforts are built upon an appropriate initial personal and professional education, that they are organized in such a way as to strengthen rather than undermine the teacher's professional identity and to enhance rather than diminish his chances of genuine job satisfaction. And it is no good providing teachers with the knowledge and skills for more effective action if we do not at the same give the conditions and the equipment that will enable this action to be effective. Decisions to give priority to in-service provision above the lengthening of the period of initial training (e.g. in Belgium) or above the further improvement of the pupil/teacher ratio (e.g. in the United Kingdom) imply a judgment about the relative gains from in-service education as compared with other educational reforms. There is indeed some evidence to suggest that class size correlates poorly with educational outcome, and that marginal improvements in pupil/teacher ratios do not in themselves do much to produce better results.

This finding conflicts with common sense and with the judg ment of many teachers, but it is difficult to disagree with Pidgeon (1974) who, after carefully reviewing a wide range of studies, states :

'...the traditional methods by which a teacher passively imparts knowledge to whole classes are likely to be equally effective over a fairly wide range of class size. Many teachers with large classes tend to restrict their curriculum, often to the limited group of subjects more amenable to measurement in research studies, while many others with small classes fail to adapt themselves to the advantages offered and continue with mass methods of instruction...'

As Pidgeon suggests, part of the difficulty in evaluating the results of many of the studies in this field is that only a very limited range of criteria is employed. One study that went beyond the customary tests of performance in basic skills was carried out in 1971 by the Institute of Administrative Research at Teachers College, Columbia. Four criteria of quality—individualization, interpersonal regard, group activity and creativity—were applied to twenty thousand classrooms. A strong relationship between scores on these criteria and class size emerged, and it appeared that the critical break points at which changes in teaching methods took place were when the class dropped below twenty-five pupils, again when it fell below fifteen, and finally when the group under instruction comprised only five members.

It seems clear that the crucial factors are not class size as such, but the mode of teaching employed and the quality of that teaching. Better in-service provision may help teachers to acquire some of the compentencies necessary to adapt their teaching strategies to groups of various size, but unless careful consideration is given to the composition of the total resource 'mix', such enhanced competencies are unlikely to result in improved educational outcomes.

A further potential area of difficulty about in-service expansion is the balance that will be held between courses and activities of different kinds, particularly longer award-bearing programmes and shorter more intensive courses relating to more specific classroom and school problems. There has been anxiety in more than one country employing authorities might place too great a stress upon short courses, which they can readily provide from their own resources, using the services of advisory, inspectorial and other centrally employed staff. An appropriate balance needs to be held between the staff development functions of in-service provision, which are rooted in the needs of institutions and of systems rather than of individuals, and further professional study, which is mainly directed to the career interests of individual teachers.

The distinction is not sharp, since many employer-provided courses are of value in career terms, and large numbers of teachers voluntarily elect to pursue courses more or less directly related to the improvement of performance in their existing posts. But it can be an important distinction, especially when resources are tight and decisions have to be made on applications for secondment to award-bearing courses that will equip the teacher for new levels and types of work. At present only small numbers of teachers are released to study for higher and research-based awards. In the most recent year for which we have figures, only a few hundred master's degrees and a handful of doctorates were awarded in the UK in Education and subject combinations including Education. In contrast, by the end of the Sixties, universities and colleges in the United States, were annually awarding somc 45,000 masters and 3,000 doctors degrees in Education, more than in any other single subject (Taylor et al., 1974). Whatever we may think about the usefulness of some of the existing study programmes for individual teachers and for the educational system as a whole, the small number of advanced awards in the UK seems quite inadequate in relation to a teaching force that will soon be getting on for half a million strong. There is still plenty of room for increasing the number of advanced study opportunities in such fields as, for example, educational administration and special education, where there is currently a great need for more people with high-level skills and knowledge. In most European countries, it will be a long time yet before fears of credentialism, when the national equivalent of the US master's degree becomes a de facto prerequisite for a headship and a PhD for an administrative post, need to be reckoned with.

But it remains important that in-service experience should not be simply a matter of attendance at full-time or part-time courses. As is argued in the final section of this chapter, such experience should be reconceptualized as taking in all the means whereby the teacher can acquire new knowledge and understanding and a higher level of competency. Conferences, workshops, study groups, local, regional and national television and sound broadcasting, travel attachments to industrial and commercial undertakings, sabbatical fellowships in universities and colleges, can all usefully feature in a comprehensive in-service strategy. And in all this, the value of printed materials as a source of information and ideas must not be forgotten. This is not simply a matter of the availability of good libraries and resource centres open to teachers in an area but also of ensuring that in their initial training teachers learn to use and value the literature of their trade.

Then there is also the question of the control of in-service education. There appears to be a general trend for national, regional, and local employing authorities to assume more responsibility for the promotion, organization and financing of in-service education than such bodies have for the initial education of the teacher. There is still a good deal of pluralism in the arrangements in many countries, but this sometimes conceals a subtle yet important conflict about who should control in-service provision. One of the ways in which this has shown itself has been in a series of disputes (e.g. in France, in the United Kingdom) about the part that the universities should play. As a body of people concerned to maintain the highest academic and professional standards, and with a special critical function in society, it would seem proper that universities should have a close organic association with the institutions and the processes by means of which teachers are trained and retrained. Not, of course, a monopoly of authority and influenence in these fields. National, regional and local authorities must quite properly exercise the responsibilities they have for the efficient education of the children in their school. The teachers' associations also have a part to play. What has to be secured is an appropriate balance between all the interests concerned. It is sometimes argued that there are no real differences between them. Surety every elected representative and every administrator, every teacher and every official of a teachers' organization, every university man, like every parent, has a common interest in securing an improvement in the quality of education in our schools ? This is only true in the same sense that all are presumably against sin. In practice, the imperatives of various roles differ, sometimes quite sharply.

The national or local politician, the teachers' association official, the professor, the civil servant, all march to a different drummer. One of our greatest cultural achievements is in creating working systems within eaeh country by means of which such differing imperatives can be reconciled. It is into the creation and maintenance of such systems that so much human effort has to be directed, for they are often tenuous creations, difficult to establish, hard to keep going in working order. Such balances are seldom static, and from time to time reflect the varying fortunes and success of the different interests concerned. Some decisions may reflect the predominance, at a particular time, of financial or administrative considerations. Others will be most influenced by academic or professional factors. On any one issue the outcome will be affected by circumstance, by the presence or absence of particular individuals, by the climate of the moment. What is important is that no one interest group, however confident in the superiority of its judgment, should have a consistent and unchallengeable monopoly of power or influence.

It is possible to argue that in teacher education the present trend is to place too much potential power in the hands of central and local employing authorities, and to create an imbalance that could have serious long-term consequences for the orderly development of institutions and for the freedom of the individuals who work in them. This is not to suggest that central and local government will exercise their responsibilities in an unintelligent or arbitrary manner. Almost without exception, officials have the interests of the schools and teachers and pupils very much in the forefront of their attention, and are professionals in the best sense of that term. But they are the servants of politically-controlled bodies, which recent events in some countries have tended to make more, rather than less, political. Nor is this to argue that education should in some mysterious way be 'above politics' whatever that may mean. Politics, like education, is about how we should live. But educational decisions need to be made on the basis of considerations wider than those of party alone.

The reform of teacher education and training should not tip the balance of power too far in the direction of employing authorities. None of us is right all the time, and the best decisions are more likely to be the product of the adjustment of differences than of the exercise of power by one body, however democratically it may have been elected. Universities and colleges, whieh share aeademic imperatives that are different from those of gome of the other interested parties—but no less important for that—must continue to take a full part in education and training of teachers. Quite apart from the effects on the status of the profession and of the possibility of innovation in teaching, it would be a mistake for responsibility teacher education to become solely the responsibility of institutions under direct political control.

A model for in-service education

It seems that if full advantage is to be taken of the advanced study opportunities for teachers now being developed in most European countries we need nothing less than a complete reconceptualization of what is entailed by the term 'in-service training'. We must avoid any impression that the expansion of in-service provision is simply seen in terms of 'more of the same'. This is not to say that courses and conferences will diminish in importance. The Bristol project on experimental induction courses (Bolam and J. K. Taylor, 1972) showed that 95 per cent of the tutors involved used lectures, against only 13 per cent using films and 21 per cent using case studies. Courses and conferences are inadequate as the basis of provision on the scale that is now being contemplated in many countries. Such provision is likely to be better conceived if instead we stress a number of more general processes—communication, participation, professionalism, coherence and continuity.

Courses and conferences should be seen as part—but only part—of a much broader system of communication by means of which all those who are involved in the educational enterprise—teacher, administrators, research workers, curriculum development specialists, teacher trainers—keep in touch with one another and with developments in their respective fields. To rethink the problem in these terms avoids certain possibly dangerous assumptions, such as that all teachers should attend X courses of Y days duration within a given period.

By stressing communication we are forced to think of all the ways in which contact between and within groups of teachers, advisers, administrators, academics, curriculum specialists and so on can be established and maintained. 'Going on a course' is one such way, but it is not the only. one. For certain purposes, the traditional course and conference is a singularly ineffective means of communicating information, skills or even inspiration; a few hours at home with one or two relevant books (subject to the teachers concerned having acquired during their initial trainning habits of solitary, self-directed study) would be far more helpful. It has to be faced that some teachers remain intellectually flexible and alive, open to new knowledge and ideas and experimental in their approaches, without ever going near an in-service course; equally, it can be guessed that the classroom performance of some very regular attenders remains completely unaffected by the experience.

A stress upon communication also requires that we take into account the relationship between ideas and techniques and the organizational meetings in which these are offered. Although programmes based upon principles of group dynamics, and those which attempt to take into account what is now known about processes of educational change, may go some way to meet this particular desiderata, they may also, if they rely too much upon inter-group process, create new problems and difficulties. To accept an idea within a group of like-minded people on a course or in a workshop setting is easier than trying to apply it against the organizational inertia of a particular school. It is in this context that the idea of school-based in-service education becomes particularly attractive.

The media that might be employed for in-service purposes are very varied. First and foremost there is print—books, journals, pamphlets, broadsheets, circulars. There has been an enormous increase in the volume of such print materials in recent years, stimulated and encouraged by cheap reprographic techniques. and a common complaint is the difficulty of 'keeping up with the literature' of one's subject. It is important that initial teacher education and training should teach the proper use of written materials. In a concern for arranging all manner of unstructured group discussions and practical experience as part of induction and in-service programmes, it has to be remembered that the most varied and easily available sources of information and advice are to be found in print.

It behoves us to pay attention to the library provision that induction and in-service work demand, and to the importance of having available in each area a well-equipped library and resource centre that will meet teachers' needs for print materials. Not many large schools and teachers centres at present have the library and information services that ensure that material relevant to a teacher's needs is made available to him in a form which can be readily assimilated and used. It is perhaps not too fanciful to think of computerized records in colleges and professional centres that will help to match the teacher's needs and interests with the identification and location of suitable materials for his use.

Despite all that we know now about the weaknesses of lectures, it seems likely that these will continue to be a staple of in-service provision for a long time to come. Lectures are easy to organize, familiar and relatively inexpensive. The very lack of audience involvement constitutes a protection for those who might otherwise feel that their ignorance of a topic could be exposed or their views required to be justified. But much greater use is being made of seminars, informal discussions, syndicate work, CCTV, micro-teaching, mini-courses, case studies, simulation and other face-to-face group techniques, all of which encourage a higher level of teacher participation.

In addition to stressing the in-service process as one of communication, we have to devise ways in which participation by those for whom the arrangements are intended can be ensured in the planning and provision of programmes. Several countries seem to be making efforts to make such participation a reality, whether through regional planning groups, teacher representation on national and local committees, formal and informal consultations with the teachers' association, or, as in the United Kingdom, the establishment of teachers centres which are intended to be both controlled and managed by teachers themselves.

A professional model of in-service teacher education requires that whatever is offered stresses the personal and professional autonomy of the teacher, and is in accordance with the principles set out in the discussion of the teacher's professional role in Chapter 4.

The other two principles that can be identified as important in relation to future planning are continuity and coherence. In statement after statement from European governments, and on behalf of education organizations within each country, there is reference to the need for pre-service, induction and in-service education and training to be planned as a single whole, with each stage carefully tailored to what has gone before and what will come afterwards. Whilst there is a strong rhetorical element in such statements, they have considerable implications for the future planning of in-service work, and for decisions about what kinds of content should characterize pre-service study and induction programmes. Given the professional mobility of teachers, and the large number of agencies that, despite a tendency towards more central planning and control, are still involved in in-service education and training, there seems little hope that we shall ever see a systematic programme of study, relevant to the needs of each kind of subject and age group teacher, mapped out from the earlist days of pre-service training, through the induction period to the later stages of a teacher's career. However neat and tidy and compelling such systematization may seem on paper, it seldom if ever represents something that can be achieved in reality. Indeed, it is questionable if such tight articulation of the various stages of education and training is really desirable, given that it would require a degree of control over the teacher's professional development as unwelcome in principle as it is unattainable in practice.

To some extent, coherence will be maintained not by administrative means but as a consequence of the individual's continuing and developing concern with the teaching and study of a particular subject, or his or her focus upon a set of classroom problems. From the point of view of the institutions responsible for providing courses and programmes of study, the principles of continuity and coherence raise questions about what needs to be included and what can safely be left out of each stage of education and training. There seems little doubt that enhanced post-experience opportunities give those responsible for determining the content and organization of initial coures a new chance to assess the value of what they doing, and to defer the introduction of those elements which, although important, can now find a place in the teacher's post-qualification studies.

In England and Wales, rethinking is most marked in the professional studies content of teachers' preparation, both in concurent course for the Bachelor of Education degree and the Teacher's Certificate, and the one-year consecutive course of training for graduates. Paul Hirst, who, with Richard Peters and others did much to influence the organization of educational studies in the UK during the 1960s, has recently argued that the one-year certificate course should concentrate fairly closely on providing students with the knowledge, skills and dispositions that they require in their first teaching jobs (Hirst, 1975). Having suggested that the course be concerned mainly with the demands of the student's first appointment, he goes on to suggest that it should concentrate on two particular areas.

> 'First, there are those activities as a teacher that are manifestly designed to promote the pupils' learning, recognising the very wide range of activities that fall into that category. Secondly, there are the teacher's activities which are necessary to bring about and maintain the social conditions in which these specific activities of teaching can be conducted. . . . Without the ability to cope professionally in these two respects, a person can hardly be said to be carrying out the job of teaching at all. For this reason alone, any satisfactory course must recognise these activities as central and regard the rest as secondary.'

On the basis of the preceding discussion, it is possible to identify a number of the ways in which European countries are seeking to extend their provision of in-service education and training for teachers.

1. First, in most countries the responsibility for updating knowleage and skills is still placed in the teacher's own hands. Participation in in-service training is largely voluntary. Compulsory provision does exist in a few places (e. g. some of the Swiss Cantons, Sweden) and is under discussion elsewhere (e. g. Holland, Austria), but there is no indication of any immediate move in the direction of further legislation that

would make attendance compulsory.

2. Whilst the objectives of in-service provision vary somewhat from one country to another, according to both political and educational priorities. (e.g. in some countries emphasis is placed on the needs of handicapped children, in others on the extension of pre-school provision, in some on mathematics and science, in others on the acquisition of language skills), there is general recognition of the need that educational change has created for the acquisition of new types of skill and knowledge appropriate to emerging structures, new forms of school organization, new patterns of relationships between teachers, pupils, parents and the community, and the availability of a wider range of teaching aids and techniques. There seems little doubt that it is the impact of these changes on the schools, and recognition of the re-training that teachers need to cope with them, that has led to particular emphasis in many countries on the extension of in-service training.

3. Enhanced participation in various forms of in-service work is encouraged more by the establishment of new opportunities, e.g. paid educational leave, possibilities of secondment, payment of travelling expenses and living allowances for those attending courses, etc., than through compulsion.

4. Although in many countries the 'opportunities that now exist for teachers to participate in further education and training are much better than they were a decade ago, they are still very limited in relation to the magnitude of the problems that teachers face. It is not possible on the basis of available information to calculate the number of days that a typical primary or secondary school teacher might spend on in-service education in the course of a year, or longer period. Some such calculation have, as we have seen, been made in a few countries, but these are now somewhat dated, and such surveys have been limited in scope and number. Furthermore, hopes that existed a year or two age about a rapid extension of in-service opportunities have been affected by the economic difficulties in which many countries have found themselves as a

result of the oil crisis, price and wage inflation, and recession.

5. It appears that even in countries where decision-making in matters educational is highly certalized, and the initial education and training of teachers is under close governmental control and supervision, a large measure of pluralism exists in respect of continuing teacher education. As we have seen, both governmental and non-governmental agencies, with national, regional and local bases, participate in laying on courses and conferences that teachers can attend in order to bring their knowledge up to date, or to retrain for new jobs within the education service.

The teachers, organizations in some countries play a significant part as providers, as do a variety of voluntary associations set up by teachers to promote work in particular subjects or fields of interest. Such associations exist in relation to a large number of subject fields, in age groups (e.g. kindergarten, primary, etc.) and special educational problems. Managed and run by teachers themselves responsible for broadsheets, bulletins and fully-fledged journals, such voluntary effort has played, and is likely to continue to play, an important part in the refreshment and upgrading of the teacher. Universitics are also active in the field, especially in respect of longer full-time and part-time courses which lead to additional qualifications.

One of the great advantages as far as the teacher in concerned of taking part in a course of conference run by a voluntary association or by a university is that there can be no question of attendance involving any kind of evaluation or assessment on the part of employing authorities. There is little doubt that inspectors and advisers do in nearly all countries use the opportunity that course and conference attendance provides to observe teachers outside the classroom setting, to assess their response, knowiedge and skills, and to identify those men and women who might later come to assume more senior and responsible roles either in their own schools or elsewhere.

This informal process of assessment and evaluation, either alongside a more formal set of grading procedures, or within the context of the unsystematic (but arguably no less effective) approaches characteristic of certain countries (e.g. the United Kingdom), would seem to serve an important purpose for the adaptation of a teaching force to new needs.

But important as it may be, the fact or the suspicion that some such grading is going on can affect the teacher's desire to take part in an in-service event, and in some circumstances, vitiate the value that it might otherwise have for him. This is particularly true in the case of young teachers, who are less likely to talk about the problems and difficulties they are encountering if they feel that the information so given might be used aginst them. Hence the importance of a voluntary, neutral base for in-service participation such as is provided by the university, by the voluntary association, by the teachers' union and by other bodies not directly linked to the employing authorities. Whilst the possible extension of in-service opportunities in Europe during the next few years may place a greater emphasis on the provision made by governments and employers of teachers, it seems unlikely that this trend will do anything to reduce the value attached to the contribution made by non-governmental organizations, or the desire of teachers to avail themselves of such opportunities.

There is a trend in a number of countries to associate courses and conferences mounted as part of in-service training efforts with the other activities of governments and school systems in the field of educational development and innovation. In-service training is seen as one aspect of a wider process of school and curricular reform. Sometimes, funding agencies are willing to make resources avilable in connection with curriculum research and development projects to ensure that materials and ideas reach those in classrooms and administrative offices most able to use them. This can sometimes add six months or a year or more to the life of a project. Systematic attempts to reform curricula or organization on a national or regional scale are closely associated with appropriate in-service training (e. g.) in Spain and Scandinavia). As has been argued elsewhere in this chapter, in service education in increasingly seen as part, but only part, of the whole system of communication whereby the ideas and techniques developed in universities, research projects, and by groups of teachers themselves, can be diffused and disseminted among those members of the teaching force for whom they are most likely to be useful.

7. It is increasingly recognized that the first year of teaching poses particular problems, for which distinctive solutions are required. Studies of the 'induction year' suggest that special forms of professional and personal counselling are required at this time if a substantial number of young people are not to be lost to teaching due to dissatisfaction, inability to cope with problems, and a pervasive sense of failure. Hence special provision is being made by way of the appointment and training of professional tutors, arrangements for lighter teaching loads, and systematic evaluation and follow-up of the first year (s) of service.

These few points by no means constitute an exhaustive description of the trends that characterize the development of in-service educational and training for teachers in European countries at the present time. Nor are they intended to suggest that there is sufficient uniformity in what is happening in various place to enable the very important differences in objectives, organization and the educational, social and cultural context to be ignored or discounted. Despite all the differences, however, there are important sings of convergence, as might be expected in countries that, at least in comparison wite the developing world, enjoy fairly similar standards of living, and, for the most part, are multi-party states with more or less clear separation of legislature, executive and judiciary.

Concluding Remarks

Whether the volume and quality of research in teacher education increase during the next decade, and are applied to the improvement of courses and programmes, depends upon the balance achieved between several competing pressure.

On the one hand there are signs of a falling of official and professional concern with educational research. Support for such work has been hit by the effects of inflation and public expenditure cuts on research budgets, disenchantment following the inflated claims and expectations of the Sixties, and continued weaknesses in the institutional and dissemination structures by means of which the findings of research are related to practice. The size of the teacher education enterprises is falling as the demand for teachers follows a continuing decline in birth rates, and the relatively poorer opportunities that will exist for employment and promotion in the education professions are unlikely to increase the attractiveness of such work for the able and the scientifically committed. Shifts in the balance of power within teacher education have not been favourable to the position of those individuals and institutions most likely to be concerned with the advancement of fundamental knowledge.

Yes on the other side there are several reasons why inquiries on how teachers are educated and trained, and efforts to apply the outcomes of research on the teaching and learning process and in the social science to the improvement of teacher education, will remain important and deserving of support.

In the first place, the focus of attention in teacher educations will no longer be so exclusively on initial preparation. Annual addition to the already large pool of qualified teachers will be small. If current population trends continue, a substantial proportion of each year's resignations and retirements can be matched by drawing from this pool (to such an extent, in fact, that in more than one country it has been suggested that initial teacher education could be closed down altogether for several years, without detriment to teacher supply and with considerable benefit for the employment prospects of already qualified staff). In England and Wales, it is likely that about half the 'new' teachers recuired will be 'returners' rather than new entrants. A proportion of this intake will have been away from the classroom for a considerable period, and will need some kind of tetrainning. The age distribution of the existing teaching force will be changing. Lower mobility, a more stable pattern of staffing and greater maturity all have their advantages. But there are drawbacks as well. Opportunities for promotion will diminish, as will the number of alternative Jobs in the education professions beyond the school — such as in teacher training. If redundancies are to be avoided, a proportion of teachers will have to be prepared to work with age groups other than those with which they are familiar and for which they were originally trained.

All this makes post-experience education and training much more important than before. Despite economic difficulties, governments remain committed to the expansion of in-service and teacher development activities. But so far very little research has been devoted to the post-experience stages of teacher education and training. The existing literature on the acquisition of new skills by experienced adults has not been brought to bear on the problems of in-service provisions. We do not know what are likely to be the most effective kinds of provision for improving classroom practice and student learning. With significant exceptions, experienced staff have few opportunities to engage in the self-monitoring processes — micro-teaching, simulation and other procedures discussed in Chapter 8 — now available for pre-service trainees. The information needs of practising teachers have received comparatively little attention. As was seen in Chapter 9, in-service training remains voluntary in most countries, and is provided by a number of different agencies. We do not know very much about the characteristics of those teachers who take advantage of such training and those who do not. Whether the lack of articulation between the efforts of a large number of different providing bodies is beneficial for the profession and the schools is also unknown. In all these areas, there is research to be done. Some of the it will be new work. Some of the needed information can be drawn from other fields of inquiry.

A second major concern of education authorities at the present time is the equality of education being provided in the schools. Variants of the 'back to the basics' movement can be found in nearly every developed Western country. Evidence concerning changes in standards of achievement in literacy and numberacy is sparse and generally rather shaky. But whether things are better or worse, there is widespread agreement that they are not 'yet good enough. In looking for explanations, attention has been focused on the efforts made to recruit as many teachers as possible during the years of shortage. It is argued that there are too many men and wowen now in front of classes who really should not be there, and who at other times would either not have been admitted to training or who would not have achieved certification. Despite the political and legal difficulties involved, there is talk about the possibility of indentifying such teachers and encouraging them to seck employment elsewhere. There is stress on the need for greater accountability, at all levels, and for stricter monitoring of pupil progress and school achievement. In much of this there is a seeming inconsistency with 'progressive' ideas that have permeated educational discourse for the past four decades', and which have generally disfavoured the assesment and grading practices that are explict or implicit in the new stress on monitoring and accountability. Yet it is by no means the case today that such stress is the prerogative of conservative and elitist educator. The old categorizations of formal and progressive, child-centred and subject-centred, discipline-based or 'intergrated', no longer serve to order the range of ideas and attitudes that circulale in research team, lecture room or school.

If this argument is accepted, if follows that much of the research that, directly or indirectly, was either predicated upon or served to reinforce these categorizations is now of somewhat doubtful relevance as a guide to action. The development of assesment techniques and forms of supervision that satisfy the contemporary press for accountability, yet respect what we have learned over recent decades about how groups and individuals respond to change and modify their practices, poses important problems for teacher education, on which research is now urgently needed.

A third consideration that emphasizes the importance of continued investment in teacher education research arises from the great variety of method and techniques now available for inclusion in pre-service and post-experience programmes. These are much more numberous than a decade ago, and some involve expensive capital provision. Developments in electronics and computer technology have considerable long-term implications for how teachers are educated and trained. With the aid of cheap hand-held calculators, individual students can cope with data of a kind that would once have made forbiding demands on time and enthusiasm. With the help of computer-based retrieval systems, policy makers, researchers and practitioners can have access to findings that would once have taken months if not years to assemble. Sophisticated apparatus is available to monitor stress and to plot the physiological concomitants of different kind of learning and teaching. All this demands systematic research-based evaluation if money and time are not to be wasted.

Fourth, there is need to rekon with the changes in the curriculum and organization of teacher education that have been taking place in several countries as a consequence both of the changing takes of teachers and of new patterns of relationship between teacher education and other kinds of post-secondary provision. The regime, style and context of teacher training carried out in a university or other multi-faculty institution are in many cases very different from those found in single-purpose colleges.

The existing balance between concurrent and consective forms of initial training is in many places changing, especially where efforts are being made to reduce the hitherto sharp distinctions between preparation for primary and for secondary teaching. The timing and sequence of practice teaching are particularly affected by such changes. There has been little really systematic study and evaluation of the gains from one pattern of organization as against another. Nor has enough thought been given to the significance for the content of initial training of the extension of post-experience study opportunities. What should go into the initial years of training and what can safely, and beneficially, be left until later ?

These are only a few of the areas of reform in teacher education in relation to which more research and inquiry are needed. A high proportion of the research data already available comes from the United States and does not translate readily to European conditions. There are too few major centres in Europe where teacher education research is a major concern. Researchers are scattered, the work done is often a spin-off from studies that have other foci, and its implications for the courses and programmes followed in teacher-preparing institutions are poorty worked out. As we have seen in the earlier chapters of this book, many factors enter into the impulse to reform teacher education, arising from population changes economic conditions, social policy imperatives, political adjustments, school reorganization and curriculum development. Research-based knowledge is seldom in itself the chief influence on the speed and direction of particular changes. Yet such knowledge plays an important part as stimulant, in calling for answers to questions that might otherwise not have been asked; as context, in providing the language, the concepts and the styles of throught within which a reform is pursued, and, especially in the form of systematic evaluation, as corrective to exaggerated claims and a brake upon precipiate action. Research is not going to produce major 'discoveries' which provide a more or less permanent solution to the problems that face educators of teachers; the rise and decline of Performance Based Teacher Education in the United States shows, if demonstration is required, that such hopes are illusory. But if the quality and quantity of student learning are to increase, if schools are to be happier places, if teachers are to enjoy and obtain greater satisfaction from their work, then teacher education has to be improved, and an indispensable element. in that process of improvement is the existence of an active body of interested research workers, with sufficient resources and facilities to ensure that their work can be fruitful of new and usefull knowledge, linked to the wider community of educational and social science researchers on the one side, attuned to and understanding of the problems of teachers and schools on the other. Activities sponsored by inter-governmental bodies such as the Council of Europe have done much to identify the strengths and weaknesses of particular areas of educational research, and to suggest ways in which improvement might be secured. The commissioning by the Council of this study may be seen as a modest contribution to this process.

Bibliography

Ackerman, J.M. (1972) Operant Conditioning Techniques for the Classroom Teacher. Glenview, Illinois: Scott Foresman & Co.

Althusser, L. (1969) For Marx. London: Penguin.

Applebee, A.N. (1976) 'Micro-Teaching, Component Skills and the Training of Teachers: An Evaluation of a Research and Development project,' British Journal of Educational Technology, 7, 2, May.

Aquino, J. (1976) Performance Based Teacher Education: A Source Book. Washington, D.C.: American Association of Colleges for Teacher Education (PBTE Series No. 21).

Argyris, C. (1971) Review of B/F. Skinner, 'Beyond Freedom and Dignity,' Harvard Educational Review, 41, 4.

Association D'etude Pour L'Expression De La Recherche Scientifique (1969) Pour une Ecole Nouvelle: Formation des Maftres et Recherche en Education. Paris: Dunod.

Association of Institute and School of Education In-Service Tutors (1973) The Universities and the In-Service Education of Teachers. London: The Association (mimeo).

Atkin, J.M. and Raths, J.J. (1974) 'Changing Patterns of Teacher Education' in OECD New Patterns of Teacher Education and Tasks. Country Experience: United States. Paris: The Organisation.

Baker, H.P. (1970) Film and Video Tape Feedback: A Review of the Literature. Austin, Texas: Research and Development Center for Teacher Education.

Bandura, A. (1969) Principles of Behavior Modification. New York: Holt, Rinehart & Winston.

Bandura, A. (Ed.) (1971) Psychological Modelling. Chicago: Aldine.

Barnard, H. (Ed.)(1863) German Educational Reformers. Hertford, Connecticut: Brown & Gross.

Barnett, D.C. (1975) 'The Emergence of New Concepts for Teacher Education Field Experience', Interchang, 6, 1.

Bartholomew, J. (1975) 'Theory and Practice: An as yet Unaddressed Issue ? 'Education for Teaching, 97.

Becker, H.S. (1952) 'Social Class Variations in Teacher—Pupil Relationship', Journal of Educational Sociology, 25.

Becker, H.S., Geer, B. and Hughes, E. (1968) Making the Grade. New York: Wiley.

Belbenoit, G. (1974) 'Teachers as Innovators: The Teacher's Role in Curriculum Development. A French View'. Paris: OECD, DAS/EID/74.81 (mimeo).

Bell., J. (1966) 'Learning Their Job in a Comprehensive', Times Educational Supplement, October 14.

Bellack, A.A. (Ed.) (1966) The Language of the Classroom. New York: Teachers College.

Bennett, N. (1976) Teaching Styles and Pupil Progress. London: Open Books.

Bensman, J. and Lilienfeld, R. (1973) Craft and Consciousness. New York: Wiley.

Berger, P., Berger, B. and Kellner, H. (1974) The Homeless Mind. London: Penguin.

Bernstein, B.B. (1970) 'Education Cannot Compensate for Society', New Society, 26 February; quoted Silver, 1971, p. xxiv.

Bernstein, B.B. (1971) 'On the Classification and Framing of Educational Knowledge'. In: Young, M.F.D., Knowledge and Control. London: Collier Macmillan.

Biddle, B.J. and Ellena, W.T. (Eds.) (1964) Contemporary Research on Teacher Effectiveness. New York : Holt, Rinchart & Winston.

Biddle, B.J. and Dankin, M.J. (1974) The Study of Teaching. New York: Holt, Rinehart & Winston.

Black, M. (1967) 'Rules and Routines'. In: Peters, R.S. (Ed), The Concept of Education. London: Routledge & Kegan Paul.

Blau, B.M. (1964) Social Behavior as Exchange. New York: Wiley.

Bolam, R. (1972) 'Guidance for Probationary Teachers', Trends in Education, 21.

Bolam, R and Taylor, J.K. (1972) The Induction and Guidance of Beginning Teachers, Paper presented to Section L of the Annual Meeting of the British Association for the Advancement of Science, Leicester (mimeo).

Bolam, R. (1975a) 'The Teacher Induction Pilot Schemes Project', London Educational Review, 4, 1.

Bolam, R. (1975b) Supervisory Role of the Teacher-Tutor—a Complex Innovation. Paper presented to the British Educational Research Association Annual Conference, Stirling (mimeo).

Bolam, R. and Baker, K. (1976) 'The National Evaluators Repert. The Official and Unofficial Schemes', Reports on Education, No. 84, March, London, Department of Education and Science.

Council of Europe (1975f) Committee for General and Technical Education: Continued Training of Teachers in General and Teachnical Education. Inventory of Current Organisation in CCC Member States: Belgium. Strasbourg: The Council DECS/EGT (75) 73 (mimeo).

Council of Europe (1975g) Committee for General and Technical Education: Continued Training of Teachers in General and Technical Education. Inventory of Current Organisation in CCC Member States: Switzerland. Strasbourg: The Council DECS/ECT (75) 74 (mimeo).

Council of Europe (1975h) Committee for General and Technical Education: Continued Training of Teachers in General and Technical Education. Inventory of Current Organisation in CCC Member States: Germany. Strasbourg: The Council DECS/EGT (75) 95 (mimeo).

Council of Europe (1975i) Committee for General and Technical Education: Continued Training of Teachers in General and Technical Education. Inventory of Current Organisation in CCC Member States: Iceland. Strasbourg: The Council DECS/EGT (75) 97 (mimeo).

Council of Europe (1975j) Committee for General and Techical Education: Continued Training of Teachers in General and Technical Education. Inventory of Current Organisation in CCC Member States: Netherlands. Strasbourg: The Council DECS/EGT (75) 102 (mimeo).

Duckenfield, M. (1976d) 'Unified Teacher Training Courses Proposed', Times Higher Education Supplement, December 3.

Duckenfield, M. (1977a) 'Back to Basics Boost,' Times Educational Supplement, March 11.

Duckenfield, M. (1977b) 'Quota System will Stabilize Admissions', Times Higher Education Supplement, March 25.

Dumuile, B. (1907) 'The French Training College System' in Board of Education Special Reports on Educational Subjects XVIII. London: HMSO.

Dungworth, D. (1975a) 'Young Voters Make Sharp Swing to the Right', Times Educational Supplement, January 31.

Dungworth, D. (1975b) 'Swingeing Cuts Hit Class Timetables,' Times Educational Supplement, October 17.

Dungworth, D. 1975c) 'Threat to Impose Limits on Sixth Form

Numbers', Times Educational Supplement, November 7.

Dungworth, D. (1975d) 'Moves to Ban "Extremists", 'Times Educational Supplement, November 14.

Dungworth, D. (1976a) 'Compromise Law Heralds Modest University Shake-Up', Times Educational Supplement, January 16.

Dungworth, D. (1976b) 'Pre-School Places and Staff Continue to Rise Sharphly', Times Educational Supplement, February 13.

Dungworth, D. (1976c) 'Bonn Fails to Agree on How to Restrict jobs for "Extremists", Times Educational Supplement, March 19.

Dungworth, D. (1976d) 'Cuts Hit University Research', Times Higher Education Supplement, April 9.

Durkheim, E. (1956) Education and Sociology. Glencoe, Illinois: The Free Press.

Durkheim, E. and Mauss, M. (1963) Primitive Classification. London: Cohen and West.

Eason, T.W. (1970) Colleges of Education: Academic or Practical ? Slough: NFER.

Easton, D. (1965) A Systems Analysis of Political Life. Chicago: John Wiley.

Eklund, H. (1971) Enkat rorande informationen om Lgr 69. En undersokning av attityder till ett centralt utarbetat fortbildningsmaterial, Lararhogskolan i Linkoping, Institutionen fot Pedagogik: Rapport.

Eklund, H. (1974) 'In-Service Teacher Training: Some Socio-educational Aspects', Department of Education.

Linkoping School of Education, Preliminary Reports.

Elam, S. (2971) Performance-Based Teacher Education : What is the State of thc Art ? Washington, D.C.: American Association of Colleges for Teacher Education (PBTE Series No. 1).

Elliott, J. and Adelman, C. (1975) 'Teachers' Accounts and the Objectivity of Classroom Research', London Educational Review, 4, 2/3.

Elliott. J. and Labbett, B. (1975) 'Teaching, Research and Teacher Education', Education for Teaching, 96, Spring.

Elvin, H.I. (1964) 'Education and our Social Thinking', Educational Review, 17, 1, November.

Erickson, D.A., (1963) 'Dimensions of Administrative Performance that Hemphill Missed', School Review, 72, 4.

Esland, G.M. (1971) 'Teaching and Learning as the Organisation of Knowledge'. In Young, M.F.D. (Ed.), Knowledge and Control. London: Collier Macmillan.

Eudised (1975) R and D Information, Experimental Issue: Denmark and Norway. Strasbourg: Documenration Centre for Education in Europe.

Farr, W. (1975) 'Nurseries Get Extra Boost', Times Educational Supplement, December 26.

Farr, W. (1976) 'Reforms Stress Needs of Individual', Times Educational Supplement, March 26.

Ferry, G. and Blouet, C. (1967) 'Les Relations entre les Membres du Premier Cycle dans un Lyceø de la Region Parisienne' in Association d'Etude your l'Expansion de la Recherch Scientifique—Les Enseignements du Second Degre: Leur Situation dans l'Etablissement Scolaire, Paris: Dunod.

Fuller, F.F. and Manning, B.A. (1973) 'Self-Confrontation Reviewed', Review of Educational Research, 43, 4.

Gage, N.L. (1972) Teacher Effectiveness and Teacher Education. Palo Alto, California: Pacific Books.

Gagne, R.M. and Briggs. L.J. (1974) Principles of Instructional Design. New York: Holt, Rinchart & Winston.

Garfinkel, H. (1967) Studies in Ethnomethodology, Englewood Cliffs, New Jersey: Prentico Hall.

Geissler, G. (1973) 'Eingliederung der Leherbidung in die Universitat (Das Hamburger Beispiel)'. Weinheim: Beltz.

Gellner, E. (1965) Thought and Change. London: Weidenfeld and Nicolson.

Gellner, E. (1974) Legitimation of Belief. Cambridge: Cambridge University Press.

George, L. (1976) 'Primary Figures Fall Sharply', Times Educational Supplement, December 17.

George, L. (1977a) 'Admission by Weighted Lottery to be Retained Until 1980', Times Higher Education Supplement, January 21.

George, L. (1977b) 'When a Degree is a Handicap', Times High Education Supplement, March 25.

George, (1977c) 'More Courses Faced with Increased Quotas', Times Higher Education Supplement, April 8.

Hakansson, B. and Wikander. K.G. (1974) The Teaching Practice Term in the Training of Class Teachers.

Malmo: University of Malmo School of Education (mimeo).

Hallenstein. D. (1975) 'Job Shortage Boosts Numbers', Times Educational Supplement, November 28.

Hargreaves, D.H. (1967) Social Relations in a Secondary School. London: Routledge & Kegan Paul.

Hargreaves, D.H.; Hestor, S.K. and Mellor, F.J. (1976) Deviance in Classrooms. London: Routledge & Kegan Paul.

Haring, N.G. and Phillips, E.L., (1972) Analysis and Modification of Classroom Behavior, Englewood Cliffs, New Jersey: Prentice Hall.

Harre, R. and Secord, P.F. (1972) The Explanation of Social Behaviour, Oxford: Basil Blackwell.

Harre, R. (1975) 'The Origins of Social Competence in a Pluralist Society', Oxford Review of Education, 1,2.

Havelock, R.G. (1973) Planning for Innovation though Dissemination and Utitization of Knowledge. Ann Arbor, California: Center for Research on Utilization of Scientific Knowledge.

Heater, D.B. (1969) The Teaching of Politics. London: Methuen.

Hencke, E. (1975) 'Teacher Supply : A Case of Manpower Planning', Higher Education Review, 8, 1, Autumn.

Herz, O. (1973) 'Curriculum Development at the Regional Level through Regional Education Centres' International Review of Education, XIX.

Hilsum, S. and Cane, B.S. (1970) The Teacher's Day. Slough: NFER.

Hirsch, F. (1976) Social Limits to Growth. London: Routledge & Kegan Paul.

Hirst, P.H. (1974) Knowledge and the Curriculum, London: Routledge & Kegan Paul.

Hirst, P.H. (1975) 'The PGCE Course: its Nature and their Objectives'. Papers for the Conference on the PGCE, December 1975, London, Universities Council for the Education of Teachers.

Hoffman, J. (1975) Marxism and the Theory of Praxis. London: Lawrence and Wishart.

Homans, G. (1950) The Human Group, London; Routledge & Kegan Paul.

Horvat, J.J., Bridges, E.M. and Stroufe, G.E. (1965) Case Studies and Educational Administration: An Information Storage and Retrieval System. Columbus, Ohio: Universities Council for Educational Administration.

Houston, W.R. (Ed.) (1974) Exploring Competency Based Education. Berkeley, California: McCutchan.

Howey, K. (1975) Promising Practices in the Training and Renewal of Teacher Educators. Washington, D.C.: ERIC Clearinghouse on Teacher Education (SP 008 800).

Inglis, F. (1975) Ideology and the Imagination. Cambridge: University Press.

Institute for Educational Research, University of Jyvaskyla (1975) 'The Reform of Teacher Education in Finland', KTL Newsletter, 1.

Jackson, P.W. and Belford, E. (1965) 'Educational Objectives and the Joys of Teaching', School Review, 73.

Jackson, R. (1974) 'The Democratisation of Curriculum Control in Four Countries', Journal of the Institutes of Education of the Universities of Newcastle upon Tyne and Durham, 25.

Jamieson, G. H, (1973) 'Simulation: Some Implications of Skill Theory', Programmed Learning and Instructional Technology, 10, 4, July.

Jamison, D. et al. (1974) 'The Effectiveness of Alternative Instructional Media: A Survey', Review of Educational Research, 44, 1, Winter.

Janne, H. (1974) 'For a Community Policy in Education', Western European Education, VI, 1, Spring.

Jansen, M., Jenson, P.E. and Mylov, P. (1972) 'Teacher Characteristics and Other Factors Affecting Classroom Interaction and Teaching Behaviour', International Review of Education, 18.

Jansen, M., Hansen, M. and Leerkov, A. (1975) 'The Specialists, the Consultant and the Form Master', Eudised R and D Documentation. Denmark and Norway. Strasbourg: Documentation Centre for Education in Europe.

Joyce, B.R. and Weil, M. (1973) 'The Teacher Innovator: Models of Teaching as the Core of Teacher Education', Interchange, 4, 2/3.

Keddie, N. (1971) 'Classroom Knowledge'. In: Young, M.F.D. (Ed.), Knowledge and Control. London: Collier Macmillan.

Keller, F.S. (1968) 'Goodbye, Teacher...', Journal of Applied Behavioural Analysis, 1.

Keller, F.S. (1974) 'PSI and Reinforcement Theory'. In Keller, F.S. and Sherman, J.G., 1974.

Keller, F.S. and Sherman, J.G. (1974) The Keller Plan Handbook. London: W.A. Benjamin.

King, E.J., Moor, C.H. and Mundy, J.A. (1974) Post-Compulsory Education: A New Analysis in Western Europe. London: Sage Publications.

Klason, L.E. (1971) Insyn i skolan: Lararnas bedo mning arbetssituationen och deras syn pa graden av maiuppfyllelse i grundskolan. Stockholm: Sveriges Lararforbund.

Klingler, J. et al. (1975) 'Research into the Role of the Teacher' Eudised R and D Information, Experimental Issue : Austria and Germany. Strasbourg: Documentation Centre for Education in Europe.

Kloss, G. (1975) 'Teacher Training Cutbacks as Economy Falters', Times Higher Education Supplement, January 31.

Kloss, G. (1976a) 'West Germans Look Ahead to Shrinking Staff Requirement', Times Higher Education Supplement, February 20.

Kloss, G. (1976b) 'Sharp Drop in Popularity of Teaching', Times Higher Education Supplement, December 10.

Kloss, G. (1977a) '"Extremists" Decree Entering Sixth Year', Times Higher Education Supplement, February 18.

Kloss, G. (1977b) "Waiting Time" Grows as 50,000 University Applicants are Turned Away in Germany', Times Higher Education Supplement, February 25.

Leach, E. (1970) 'Braintwister'. In: Hayes, E.N. and Hayes, T. (Eds,), Claud Levi-Strauss: The Anthropologist as Hero, Cambridge, Massachusetts: MIT Press.

Learning Systems Institute, Michigan State University (1966) Variable Interval Sequence Action Camera. Papers of the Institute, No. 40; Selective Observations Simulator, Papers of the Institute, No. 41.

Leavis, F.D. (1975) The Living Principle: English as a Discipline of Thought. London: Chatto and Windus.

Leonard, W.P. (1971) 'Objective Performance Data', Audio-Visual Instruction, 16.

Lewis, D. (1969) 'New Urban Structures' in Naier, A. and Rescher, N. (Eds.), Values and the Future, New York: Fee Press.

Mccable, C. (1975) Evaluation Report No. 7. Newcastle upon Tyne : University of Newcastle upon Tyne School of Education.

Mccormick, J. (1972) 'Simulation and Gaming in Teaching Method', Programmed Learning and Educational Technology, 9.

Mcleish, J. (1969) Teachers' Attitudes: A Study of National and Other Differences. Cambridge: Institute of Education.

Mcleish, J. (1970) 'Systems, Models, Simulations and Games in Education'. In: Armstrong, R.H.R. and Taylor, J.L, (Eds.), Instructional Simulation Systems in Higher Education. Cambridge: Institute of Education.

Mcphail, P., et al. (1972) Moral Education in the Secondary School. London: Longmans.

Mannheim, K. (1936) Ideology and Utopia. London: Routledge.

Marklund, S. and Gran, B. (1974) Research and Innovation in Swedish Teacher Training. Stockholm: National Board of Education (mimeo).

Martin, A. (1975) The Last Generation. Melbourne: Fontana.

Martin, N., Burgess, T. and Spencer, M. (1976) 'School Partnerships as the Base of Theory as well as Practice', British Journal of Teacher Education, 2, 1, January.

Mathieson, E. and Mico, E. (1974) In-Service: Evaluation of Six Week or Longer Courses 1972-73. London, ILEA Research and Statistics Group (mimeo).

Matthews, G. (1975) 'The Keller Plan', Trends in Education.

Maw. J. (1973) 'Early History of Research on Teacher Behaviour,' International Review of Education, 18, 4.

Meigham, R. (1974) 'Children's Judgements of the Teaching Performance of Student Teachers', Educational Review, November.

Naeslund, J. (1969) 'Attitudes of Students Towards Closed Circuit Television in Teacher Training', Research Bulletin 13, Stockholm, School of Education.

Nash, P. (1973) A Humanistic Approach to Performance-Based Teacher Education. Washington, D.C.: American Association of Colleges for Teacher Education (PBTF Series No. 10).

National Board of Education (1969) 'Qualitative Evaluation of Teacher Training' (the KUL Project), School Research News-Letter, 6.

Oakeshott, M. (1967) 'Learning and Teaching'. In: Peters, R.S. (Ed.), The Concept of Education. London: Routledge & Kegan Paul.

OECD/DIL (1969) Study on Teachers: France—Ireland. Paris: OECD.

OECD (1974a) Conference on Teacher Policies: Country Reports—Austria, DAS/EID/74.55 (mimeo). Paris: The Organisation.

OECD (1974b) Conferenee on Teacher Policies: Country Reports—Austria. DAS/EID/74.55/02 (mimeo). Paris: The Organisation.

OECD (1974c) Conference on Teacher Policies: Country Reports—Finland, DAS/EID/74.55/22 (mimeo). Paris: The Organisation.

OECD (1974d) Conference on Teacher Policies: New Patterns of Teacher Education and Tasks. Country Reports—Turkey, DAS/EID/74,55 (mimeo). Paris: The Organisation.

OECD (1974e) Conference on Teacher Policies: New Patterns of Teacher Education and Tasks. Country Reports: Denmark, DAS/EID/74.55/05 (mimeo) Paris: The Organisation.

Pandit, B.B. (1975) 'Linguistics and Sociology'. In: Bartsch, R. and Venneman, T. (Eds.) Linguistics and Neighbouring Disciplines. Amsterdam: North Holland Publishing Co.

Peck, R.F. and Tucker, J.A. (1973) 'Research on Teacher Education'. In Travers, R.M.W. (Ed.), Second Handbook of Research on Teaching. Chicago: Rand McNally.

Perlberg, A. (1972) 'Micro Teaching', International Review of Education, XVIII.

Perrott. E. et al., (1975) 'Changes in Teaching Behaviour after Completing a Self-Instructional Micro Teaching Course', Programmed Learning and Instructional Technology, 12, 6.

Pirages, D.C. (1973) 'Behavioural Technology and Institutional Transformation'. In: Wheeler, H., 1973.

Platt, J.R. (1973) 'The Skinnerian Revolution'. In: Wheeler, H., 1973.

Poinssac, J. (1974) 'Experiment of the College of Secondary Education at Marly-le-Roi and its Implications for Teacher Tasks'. In: OECD, New Patterns of Teacher Education and Tasks: Country Experience—Belgium, France, United Kingdom. Paris; The Organisation.

Polanyi, M. (1958) Personal Knowledge. Chicago: University of Chicago Press.

Richards, C.. (1974) "The Schools Council — A Critical Examination,' Universities Quarterly Summer.

Richards, I. A. (1938) Interpretation in Teaching. London: Routledge.

Rodhe, B. et al., (1974) 'New Patterns of Teacher Tasks in Sweden: A Report on Experience in the Malmo Region.' In: Oecd, New patterns of Teacher Education and Tasks; Country Experience — Sweden. Paris: The Organisation.

Rossner, B. and Kay, P. M. (1974) 'Will the Promise of C/PBTE be Fulfilled?, Phi Delta Kappan, January.

Runciman, W. G. (1976) 'Conventions and Contradictions' Times Literary Supplement, January 16.

Rutherford, R. B. (1973) "The Effects of a Model Videotape and Feedback Videotapes on the Teaching Styles of Teachers in Training", Journal of Experimental Education, 42, 1

Shelling, T. C. (1960) The Strategy of Conflict. Cambridge, Massachusetts: Harvard University Press.

Schild, E. O. (1966) 'The Shapping of Strategies,' American Behavioral Scientist, 10, 3.

Schools Council, (1968) Young School Leavers. London: HMSO.

Schutz, a (1962, 1966) Collected Papers. The Hague : Nijhoff.

Searle, C. (1975) Classrooms of Resistance. London : Writers and Readers Publishing Cooperative.

Seeman, H. R. (1964) Die Schulpraxis in der Lehrerbildung. Weinheim. Verlag Julius Beltz.

Seldin, P. (1975) How Colleges Evaluate Professors: Current Policies and Practice in Evaluating Classroom Teaching Performance in Liberal Arts Colleges. New York : Blythe-Pennington.

Selmes, C. (1974) 'The Use of Simulation Material in the Teaching of Psychology to Student Teachers,' Psychology Teaching, 2, 1, May.

Sharp, R. and Green, A. (1975) Education and Social Control, London: Routledge & Kegan Paul.

Shipman, M.D. (1969) Participation and Staff/Student Relations: A Seven-Year Study of Social Changes in . Expanding College of Education. London : SHHE.

Tansey, P. J. (1969a) 'Simulation in Teacher Education', for Teaching, 79.

Tansey, P. J. (1969b) 'Teacher Training in England : A Suggestion for Integration,' Educational Sciences, 3, October.

Taylor, J. K. and Dale, I. R. (1971) A Survey of Teachers in Their first Year of Service. Bristol: University of Bristol School of Education.

Taylor, W. (1969a) 'Educational Goals and Outcomes in England.' In Bressler, M. and Tumin M. M. (Eds), Evaluation of the Effectiveness of Educational Systems. Washington, D. C. : U. S. Department Health, Education and Welfare, Bureau of Research.

Taylor, w. (1969a) 'Recent Researh on the Education of Teachers; An Overview.' In: Taylor, W. (Ed.) Towards a Policy for the Education of Teachers. London: Butterworth.

Taylor, W. (1969b) 'Recent Research on the Education of Teachers : An Overview'. In Taylor, W. (Ed.) Towards a Policy for the Education of Teachers. London : Butterworth.

Taylor, W. (1969c) Society and the Education of Teachers. London: Butterworth.

Taylor, w. (1969d) 'Issues and Problems in Training the School Administrator'. In: Baron, G. and Taylor, W. (Eds.)

Educational Administration and the Social Sciences. London : Athlone Press.

Taylor, W. (1970b) 'In-Service Training' In: Taylor, G. (Ed.) The Teacher as Manager. London : Councils and Education Press.

Taylor, W. (1970b) Policy and Planning for Post-Sccondary Education : A European Overview, Strasbourg. Council of Europe.

Taylor, W. (1971) 'Retrospect and Prospect in Educational Research', Educational Research, 15, 1.

Taylor, W. (1972a) Heading for Change, London : Routledge & Kegan Paul.

Taylor, W. (1972b) Theory into Practice. Cardiff : HTV Publications.

Taylor, W. (Ed.) (1973) Research Perspectives in Education. London : Routledge & Kegan Paul.

Taylor, W. et al. (1974) 'Report of Consultants', Perspectives and Plans for Graduate Studies 2 : Education 1973. Toronto : Advisory Committee on Academic Planning, Ontario Council on Graduate Studies, Council of Ontario Universities.

Taylor, W. (1975a) 'Research and Practice in Educational Administration'. In : Hughes, M.A. (Ed.), Educational Administration : International Perspectives. London : Athlone Press.

Taylor, W. (1975b) 'Teacher Education', Encyclopaedia Britannica.

Taylor, W. (1975c) 'The Universities and In-Service Education', British Journal of In-Service Education, 1, 3, Summer.

Undeutsch, U. (1964) Motive der Arbiturienten fur die Wahl oder Ablehnung de Volksschullehrerberufs Frankfurt : Max Trager Stiftnung.

University of London Institute of Education (1976) PGCE Course Book. London : The Institute.

University of Nottingham school of Education (1975) Children, Schools, Teachers Nottingham : The School.

Utsey, J. et al. (1966) 'Simulation : A Breakthrough in the

Education of Reading Teachers', Phi Delta Kappan, XLVII.

Vaigo, A.C. (1975) 'University Building Comes to a Halt', Times Higher Education Supplement, January 10.

Wagemakers. J. (1974), 'Applicants Who Fail to Gain Admission to University: An Exploratory Study', University of Nijmegen: Higher Education Research Unit, Monograph No. 10.

Wagenschein, M. (1950) Reality Shock: A Study of Beginning Elementary School Teachers. MA Thesis, University of Chicago.

Walford, R. (1972) A Note on the Evaluation of Games and Simulations, Cambridge (mimeo).

Walker, R. and Adelman, C. (1975) A Guide to Classroom Observation. London: Methuen.

Ward. R.A, (1974) 'Minicourses and Their Application to Teacher Education', Journal of Teacher Education XXV, 4.

Ward, T. (1966) The Professional Decision Simulator. East Lansing, Michigan; Learning Systems Institute, Michigan State University.

Webster, J.R. (1975) 'The Implementation of an Integrated Approach to Teacher Training', British Journal of Teacher Education, 1, 2.